N3/3

Accessi...

D0305302

ANSELMENT   822.4
                             78/2360

Farquhar:
and "Th

Book...

2

WITHDRAWN

Farquhar

The Recruiting Officer

and

The Beaux' Stratagem

A CASEBOOK

EDITED BY

RAYMOND A. ANSELMENT

CHESTER COLLEGE

ACC. No. 78/2360 DEPT.

CLASS No. 822. 4 FAR A62

LIBRARY

M

Selection, editorial matter and Introduction
© Raymond A. Anselment 1977

All rights reserved. No part of this publication
may be reproduced or transmitted, in any form
or by any means, without permission.

First published 1977 by
THE MACMILLAN PRESS LTD
London and Basingstoke
Associated companies in New York Dublin
Melbourne Johannesburg and Madras

ISBN 0 333 21145 6 (hard cover)
0 333 21146 4 (paper cover)

Printed in Great Britain by
UNWIN BROTHERS LTD
THE GRESHAM PRESS
OLD WOKING, SURREY

This book is sold subject to the standard conditions
of the Net Book Agreement.

The paperback edition of this book is sold subject to the condition
that it shall not, by way of trade or otherwise, be lent, re-sold,
hired out, or otherwise circulated without the publisher's prior
consent in any form of binding or cover other than that in which
it is published and without a similar condition including this
condition being imposed on the subsequent purchaser.

Shakespeare: *Henry IV Parts I and II*   G. K. HUNTER
Shakespeare: *Henry V*   MICHAEL QUINN
Shakespeare: *Julius Caesar*   PETER URE
Shakespeare: *King Lear*   FRANK KERMODE
Shakespeare: *Macbeth*   JOHN WAIN
Shakespeare: *Measure for Measure*   G. K. STEAD
Shakespeare: *The Merchant of Venice*   JOHN WILDERS
Shakespeare: *Othello*   JOHN WAIN
Shakespeare: *Richard II*   NICHOLAS BROOKE
Shakespeare: *The Tempest*   D. J. PALMER
Shakespeare: *Troilus and Cressida*   PRISCILLA MARTIN
Shakespeare: *Twelfth Night*   D. J. PALMER
Shakespeare: *The Winter's Tale*   KENNETH MUIR
Shelley: *Shorter Poems and Lyrics*   PATRICK SWINDEN
Spenser: *The Faerie Queene*   PETER BAYLEY
Swift: *Gulliver's Travels*   RICHARD GRAVIL
Tennyson: *In Memoriam*   JOHN DIXON HUNT
Webster: *'The White Devil' and 'The Duchess of Malfi'*   R. V. HOLDSWORTH
Virginia Woolf: *To the Lighthouse*   MORRIS BEJA
Wordsworth: *Lyrical Ballads*   ALUN R. JONES AND WILLIAM TYDEMAN
Wordsworth: *The Prelude*   W. J. HARVEY AND RICHARD GRAVIL
Yeats: *Last Poems*   JON STALLWORTHY

The English Novel: Developments in Criticism since Henry James   STEPHEN HAZELL
The Romantic Imagination   JOHN SPENCER HILL

TITLES IN PREPARATION INCLUDE

George Eliot: *'The Mill on the Floss' and 'Silas Marner'*   R. P. DRAPER
T. S. Eliot: *'Prufrock', 'Gerontion', 'Ash Wednesday' and Other Shorter Poems*
   B. C. SOUTHAM
Hardy: *Poems*   JAMES GIBSON AND TREVOR JOHNSON
Jonson: *'Every Man in His Humour' and 'The Alchemist'*   R. V. HOLDSWORTH
Shakespeare: *'Much Ado about Nothing' and 'As You Like It'*   JENNIFER SEARLE
Shakespeare: *The Sonnets*   PETER JONES
Sheridan: *'The Rivals', 'The School for Scandal' and 'The Critic'*   WILLIAM RUDDICK
Thackeray: *Vanity Fair*   ARTHUR POLLARD

CONTENTS

Part Three: *Comment on Production*

ACKNOWLEDGEMENTS

The editor and publishers wish to thank the following who have kindly given permission for the use of copyright material: Ronald Berman, essay 'The Comedy of Reason' in *Texas Studies in Literature and Language*, VII, 2 (Summer 1965), reprinted by permission of the author and University of Texas Press. Bertolt Brecht, extracts from *Collected Plays of Bertolt Brecht*, vol. IX, © 1959 by Suhrkamp Verlag. Translation © 1972 by Ralph Manheim and John Willett, reprinted by permission of Methuen & Co. Ltd. Bonamy Dobrée, extract from *Restoration Comedy, 1660–1720* (1924), reprinted by permission of Oxford University Press. A. J. Farmer, extract from 'George Farquhar' in *Writers and Their Work* series, reprinted by permission of the British Council. William Gaskill, extracts from 'Finding a Style for Farquhar' from an interview by Catherine Itzin and Simon Trussler and published in *Theatre Quarterly*, 11 (1971), reprinted by permission of T.Q. Publications Ltd. Vincent F. Hopper & Gerald B. Lahey, extracts from Introduction to *The Beaux' Stratagem*, reprinted by permission of Barron's Educational Series Inc. Kenneth Muir, extract from *The Comedy of Manners*, reprinted by permission of Hutchinson Publishing Group Ltd. John Palmer, extracts from *The Comedy of Manners* (1913), reprinted by permission of G. Bell & Sons Ltd, Publishers. Alan Roper, essay 'The Beaux' Stratagem: Image and Action' from *Seventeenth-Century Imagery: Essays on Uses of Figurative Language from Donne to Farquhar*, edited by Earl Miner, © 1971 by the Regents of the University of California, reprinted by permission of the University of California Press. Eric Rothstein, extracts from *George Farquhar*, © 1967 by Twayne Publishers Inc., reprinted by permission of Twayne Publishers, a Division of G. K. Hall & Co., Boston. William L. Sharp, extracts from 'Restoration Comedy: An Approach to Modern Production' in *Drama Survey*, VII, reprinted by permission of the author. Albert Wertheim, (1969–9) 'Bertolt Brecht and George Farquhar's *The*

Recruiting Officer' from *Comparative Drama*, VII (1973), reprinted by permission of the Editors of *Comparative Drama*. The publishers have made every effort to trace the copyright-holders but if they have inadvertently overlooked any, they will be pleased to make the necessary arrangement at the first opportunity.

GENERAL EDITOR'S PREFACE

The Casebook series, launched in 1968, has become a well-regarded library of critical studies. The central concern of the series remains the 'single-author' volume, but suggestions from the academic community have led to an extension of the original plan, to include occasional volumes on such general themes as literary 'schools' and genres.

Each volume in the central category deals either with one well-known and influential work by an individual author, or with closely related works by one writer. The main section consists of critical readings, mostly modern, collected from books and journals. A selection of reviews and comments by the author's contemporaries is also included, and sometimes comment from the author himself. The Editor's introduction charts the reputation of the work or works from the first appearance to the present time.

Volumes in the 'general themes' category are variable in structure but follow the basic purpose of the series in presenting an integrated selection of readings, with an Introduction which explores the theme and discusses the literary and critical issues involved.

A single volume can represent no more than a small selection of critical opinions. Some critics are excluded for reasons of space, and it is hoped that readers will pursue the suggestions for further reading in the Select Bibliography. Other contributions are served from their original context, to which some readers may wish to turn. Indeed, if they take a hint from the critics represented here, they certainly will.

A. E. DYSON

For Carol and Jessica

INTRODUCTION

Near the end of a monthly miscellany for May, 1707, a succinct paragraph (reproduced below, Part One) notes 'the Death of Mr. *Farquhar*, whose last two Plays had something in them that was truly *humorous* and *diverting*'. In characterising his achievement in *The Recruiting Officer* and *The Beaux' Stratagem*, the announcement somewhat reservedly notes that although the comedies do not conform to more traditional norms of aesthetic correctness 'such as love to laugh at the *Theatre*, will probably miss him more than they now imagine'. More than a century later, when the last plays of Farquhar had indeed confirmed an enduring popularity among theatregoers, another unsigned appraisal (in *The Athenaeum*, 2 January 1841) more enthusiastically proclaims, 'There is more of genuine vivacity about Farquhar, more the result of genius, than of the wick and oil that saturates the writings of the others, – Congreve especially. One is unwilling to try him by any standard, or to assign the *why* we like him: it is enough to love, for where the heart is, there will the mind be also.' Writers less reluctant to judge have, of course, since sought and applied their own standards. All agree that *The Recruiting Officer* and *The Beaux' Stratagem* are Farquhar's greatest dramatic accomplishments; the nature and the extent of his success, however, remain disputed.

The disagreements stem largely from the comedies' unique appeal. Written for the publicly supported theatres of Queen Anne's reign rather than the somewhat more court-oriented audience of the earlier Restoration playwrights, both plays appear from the outset unconventional, though 'peculiarly happy' in their approach.[1] Figures and events have some counterparts in the English tradition of drama, and Farquhar is commonly compared to other contemporary dramatists, but the comedies' distinctly different country environment offers a new immediacy. As the dedicatory epistle of *The Recruiting Officer* contends, and both popular opinion and later evidence confirm,[2] they portray the humours of a rural society Farquhar had actually encountered during his own brief career as a recruiting officer in Queen Anne's army. Initial reactions to their imaginative transformations on to the London stage further suggest that in the process he fulfilled the belief of his 'Discourse upon Comedy' that success is ultimately judged outside the realm of Aristotle and dramatic theory 'in the Pit, Box, and Galleries'.

Popular approval was immediate and sustained. *The Recruiting Officer* opened on 8 April 1706, to an enthusiastic reception at Drury Lane; and four days later Bernard Lintot issued the first of three quarto editions published that year. Following a successful run in April, and additional performances given in London, Bristol and Bath, *The Recruiting Officer* played a significant role that autumn in the growing controversy between the rival theatres. Christopher Rich chose the play to inaugurate the new season on 24 October, and some of the players who had abandoned his Drury Lane theatre countered with their own performance at the Queen's in the Haymarket the next month. Throughout the continued theatrical competition the rivals often produced *The Recruiting Officer*, several times offering performances on the same night. On 8 March 1707, the opening of *The Beaux' Stratagem* at the Queen's Theatre introduced another extremely popular play which would also figure prominently in the controversy that year. After the next season, when the plays were staged only at Drury Lane, *The Recruiting Officer* and *The Beaux' Stratagem* became part of the repertory of each theatre. A wider reading public was also assured with the publication in 1709 of *The Comedies of Mr. George Farquhar* and in 1711 of the complete works. While both were being reissued in their many editions, distinguished performers like Anne Oldfield and David Garrick supported the individual successes of two comedies which had become among the century's most popular stock plays. They would continue their wide popularity well into the nineteenth century; then a more moderate acceptance would sustain the various editions and the important though less frequent productions such as those by the National Theatre in 1963 and 1970.[3]

Critical reaction to Farquhar's accomplishment, on the other hand, was at first qualified. Apart from Arthur Bedford's intemperate attack on the purportedly immoral and unpatriotic nature of *The Recruiting Officer*, evaluations were favourable though reserved. The announcement of Farquhar's death in *The Muses Mercury*, the first significant judgement, seems to hedge its praise of a playwright who ignored the established conventions; yet the miscellany adds at the same time and again in its September issue that Farquhar's general appeal confirms his 'Genius for Comedy'. Alexander Pope's more famous criticism of the dramatist's 'pert low Dialogue' likewise is not entirely negative. In the context of the poem, Pope cites Farquhar's artistic lapse to illustrate 'how seldom even the best succeed' in meeting the demands of the comic muse. This tendency towards mixed praise becomes most apparent in Theophilus Cibber's *The Lives of the Poets* (1753), a publication that draws its assessment of Farquhar largely from opinions common in the first half of the century. In characterising the wit, imagination and intellect of a playwright who 'used no art' to create natural, diverting characters, Cibber describes a 'sprightly' rather than a great genius. The characters are not complex, the dialogue lacks polish, and the wit is not very substantial; still, Cibber notes, the playwright continues to succeed on the stage.

Subsequent eighteenth-century evaluations become less concerned with aesthetic correctness and more aware of the plays' obvious popular appeal. Oliver Goldsmith, despite token objections to their pert dialogue and unforceful characterisations, recognises that Farquhar's comedies are 'more lively, and, perhaps, more entertaining' than those of either Congreve or Vanbrugh. While he offers no explicit analysis of their continued success, several possibilities emerge in Francis Gentleman's *The Dramatic Censor* (1770). Farquhar, Gentleman observes, 'is not so rich, but more natural than *Congreve*, his plots are not so laboured and correct, yet are full as agreeable; his characters are all well selected from the volume of life, pleasingly grouped, and well disposed of at the catastrophes' (II 468). Central to the 'unforced pleasantry' he finds in all of Farquhar's plays is an emphasis on 'natural'. A possible synonym for Goldsmith's 'lively', the word suggests a vivacity and freedom now favourably opposed to an artifice that seems constraining in its correctness. Similar positive connotation also appears in its other meaning, a fidelity to life;

and by the end of the century a shift in sensibility makes their usage more commonplace. Neither of the other major contemporary dramatists, states Charles Dibdin's *A Complete History of the English Stage* (1800), possesses Farquhar's ability to create original plots and to dramatise 'natural and unaffected' characters that harmoniously encompass a range of human manners: '*Congreve's* nature was fine, elegant, distant, and self important, you admired but had no inclination to approach; *Vanbrugh's* nature, which was gay, thoughtless, extravagant, and unworthy, you laughed at but could not approve; but the nature of *Farquhar* which you saw every day in life, and which rationally made up the most laudable of your relaxations, you naturally felt and cherished.' (IV 292)

Commentary on the two comedies in the early nineteenth century continues to appreciate this dramatic immediacy. Their vivacity, variety and entertaining naturalism appeal widely to an audience less preoccupied with narrowly defined aesthetic rules; and their great popularity establishes Farquhar among the foremost of English dramatists. The 1819 Oxberry editions of *The Recruiting Officer* and *The Beaux' Stratagem* are typical in praising the effortless and lively manner in which characters and episodes assume on the stage the illusion of 'real life' or the 'perfectly natural'. Valued also are the spirit, fancy, and surprise found particularly in the final comedy; but foremost is an interest in their characters. Though part of another era, many of Farquhar's creations hold for the period a timeless appeal: 'it will be long', the introduction to *The Beaux' Stratagem* observes, 'before we find (upon the stage, at least,) any thing more amusing than the unpremeditated gallantry and easy impudence of Archer, the reluctant scruples of Mrs. Sullen, the good-natured susceptibility of Cherry, and the well-meaning, unconscious stupidity of Scrub' (p. ii).

The author of these observations, William Hazlitt, more explicitly indicates in his important *Lectures on the English Comic Writers* (1819) the pleasure these characters engender. When he tells his audience at the Surrey Institution that Farquhar's pleasurable characterisations originate from a 'truth and nature' not present to the same extent in Congreve, Wycherley, or Vanbrugh, it is more apparent that the terms convey a moral evaluation. Hazlitt does appreciate the ease, spontaneity and animation commonly attributed to Farquhar's comedies, but his further emphasis on 'cordial good humour' and 'fine animal spirits' assumes they are good-natured as well as natural. Their comic heroes possess the semblance of truth and nature because, the lecture generalises, their 'natural enthusiasm' creates a pleasant feeling of moral approval. Hazlitt finds them, in short, good-willed and honourable men who seem to reflect their author's own disposition; and he readily admires the pleasant fellowship of their world. Although his admiration does not produce any new or extensive commentary on either *The Recruiting Officer* or *The Beaux' Stratagem*, Hazlitt's lecture expresses a significant change in perspective.

His emphasis, while not entirely original, stresses the plays' moral acceptability. Earlier judgements had occasionally regarded Farquhar as the least morally offensive of the Restoration comic playwrights; now the issue would become increasingly central to his nineteenth-century reputation. Already *The Beaux' Stratagem* had been deplored by Mrs Inchbald as a dangerous threat to easily misled youth; and soon another major collection of drama, Cumberland's *British Theatre* (c. 1829), would also confront the problem in commenting on the play. It concludes, however, that the indelicacies are few and readily omitted; in fact, 'Farquhar, at least improved on the *morals*, if not the wit, of his admired predecessors.'[4] Even more favourable judgement, based essentially on Hazlitt's position, is developed in Leigh Hunt's important 1840 edition, *The Dramatic Works of Wycherley, Congreve, Vanbrugh, and Farquhar*.

Of the four comic dramatists, Hunt considers Farquhar the 'truest dramatic genius'; and he argues more forcefully than any previous writer for the playwright's continued popularity. Central to his evaluation are the animal spirits and good humour Hazlitt had already praised; indeed his specific judgement of *The Recruiting Officer* weighs its spirited good nature against some questionable morals, and his briefer assessment of *The Beaux' Stratagem* stresses a 'bold, healthy, admirable' moral. But it is obvious that Hunt finds the issue of morality troublesome. He cannot agree with Charles Lamb, whose 1823 essay 'On the Artificial Comedy of the Last Century' he reprints, that

Restoration comedy is an entirely unreal 'Utopia of gallantry' indifferent to the values of the real world; but he will not embrace completely the opposite position even though he admires Farquhar's fidelity to life. 'Animal spirits', he contends, 'often say more than they mean'; thus Hunt is forced to ask his audience to make some allowance for the lively wit and passion of unfettered genius. Although he also interestingly asserts that the cruelty of Farquhar's rakes often may be a calculated response to hypocrisy and deceit, his impression of a humane, good-natured playwright would most influence later similar bids for tolerance.

The immediate reaction to Hunt's defence suggests the extremes that increasingly shaped Farquhar's nineteenth-century reputation. The review published in *The Athenaeum* of January 1841 (quoted above) seconds the edition's evaluation of Farquhar's superiority and offers to judge him only with the heart. Another published the same month in the *Edinburgh Review* is less charitable; the reviewer, Thomas Babington Macaulay, prematurely ends his essay without the promised discussion of Farquhar, but his general position implies a judgement. Refusing to accept Hunt's appeal for tolerant understanding, Macaulay insists that any assessment of Restoration comedy must condemn a body of literature which deliberately ridicules traditional values in its celebration of the immoral. The majority of Victorians accepted this general view.

Those who take the position of Hunt and Hazlitt in the remaining decades of the century more noticeably stress Farquhar's uniquencess in moral valuations. Thus the next significant study, Charles Cowden Clarke's essay of January 1872 published in the *Gentleman's Magazine,* lauds a morally desirable concern for others. Silvia is memorable in *The Recruiting Officer*, a play Clarke considers otherwise lively though mediocre, because her motives are 'natural, and lovely too, as indeed are all the *kind* impulses of nature' (VIII 55). Archer, similarly, stands apart from other Restoration stage gallants for his actions betray none of their characteristically 'absorbing indifference to others'. Aesthetic considerations are also less apparent than moral judgements in H. A. Huntington's favourable response to the 1879 production of *The Beaux' Stratagem* at the Imperial Theatre. His *Atlantic Monthly* essay (March 1882), distinguishing its 'comparatively inoffensive' plot and 'decenter' language from the standard Restoration fare, judges Farquhar relatively moral: 'Far less coarse and with a lighter and airier touch than either Vanbrugh or Wycherley, he has none of the devil's wit of Congreve.'[5] This Victorian tendency to make the author and his plays respectable is most apparent in Louise Guiney's long, general piece on Farquhar reprinted in *A Little English Gallery* (1894). Intent upon exempting Farquhar from the charges Macaulay levels in his essay, she finds in his comedies the 'honest mirth' and the kind pensiveness of a 'true humorist'. His major characters, who constantly take the opportunity for honourable actions, become for Mrs Guiney 'worldlings' opposed to 'worldliness'; rogues are innocuously roguish; and even the most selfish are morally sensitive. Seen from her Victorian perspective, the world of Farquhar's comedies is suffused with an admirable tenderness, generosity, and sympathy not found in his contemporaries' 'heartlessness'.

The same view is not held with similar conviction in the remaining nineteenth-century criticism. While Farquhar's editors Charles Ewald (1892) and H. Macaulay Fitzgibbon (1898) defensively invoke his 'cheery humour' and 'kindly heart' or lamely allow 'virtue is not *always* uninteresting in his pages', literary historians are more divided in their judgements. Percy Fitzgerald (1882), who accepts Macaulay's view of 'the revolting indecency of the era', approvingly singles out 'jovial humourous Farquhar' and *The Beaux' Stratagem*, a comedy 'full of the freshest humour'. Edmund Gosse (1888) also acknowledges Farquhar's 'natural cheerfulness' but with greater reservation: 'His flighty beaux and swaggering cavalry officers too frequently forget to counsel or reprove, but Farquhar succeeds in being always wholesome, even when he cannot persuade himself to be decent.' Adolphus Ward (1899) is less sympathetic. Concerned about the vivid though coarse portrait of country life in *The Recruiting Officer* and the challenge to 'the sanctity of the marriage-tie' in *The Beaux' Stratagem*, his brief but assertive survey faults Farquhar on several grounds: 'his dialogue is in general less gay and sparkling, and while his morality is no better than that of the most reckless of his contemporaries, he has a coarseness of fibre which renders him more offensive to a refined ear'.[6]

Ward's characterisation prompted William Archer's vigorous refutation, an essay which despite its biases anticipates in 1905 the modern revaluation. Archer's contention that the plays always avoid a Restoration tendency to revel in the 'merely malodorous' and his emphasis on their humour, humanity and wholesomeness recall an established nineteenth-century impression, but his argument for the final comedies' laudable moral progression is distinctly different. Archer, an admirer of Ibsen and Shaw, highly values in *The Recruiting Officer* and *The Beaux' Stratagem* Farquhar's increasingly 'moral feeling' and 'sober criticism of life'. Although the limits of his introduction prevent any substantial discussion of this high seriousness, he offers as proof Farquhar's sympathetic attitude towards their 'natural, agreeable' heroines and his rational, 'serious discussion of the ethics of divorce'. Besides this new emphasis on the last comedies' serious nature, Archer further distinguishes their aesthetic integrity. In the first substantial consideration of the comedies' dramatic mode, he revalues their unique ease and naturalness. Criticisms of their absence of wit and dialogue thereby become irrelevant because both plays have abandoned the Restoration coterie comedy. Again a bias for realistic drama and a desire to defend Farquhar colour his enthusiastic approval of an 'unforced, buoyant gaiety' naturally suited to the new world of English inns and influence his specific emphasis on the naturalness of characters and action; but the distinctions are important. Both aesthetically and morally Archer directs attention towards the plays themselves and their distinctive complexity.

Modified and refined by Louis A. Strauss in an introduction to a 1914 edition, this approach provides the first significant twentieth-century analysis of the plays. To Strauss, Farquhar is an important dramatist, a 'prophet of a new order', whose promise was fulfilled in the end; and he supports this contention with the first detailed overview of the playwright's development. His thesis appears indebted to Archer: Farquhar 'added nothing new: he had no theory of a regenerated drama. And yet, by virtue of his healthy nature, he responded to the changing ideals of the life about him; and with a touch he re-combined the elements into a new comedy, a comedy as fresh and natural as that just preceding had been artificial.' Strauss shares Archer's enthusiasm for a realistic vein of comedy, and he too lapses into a nineteenth-century appreciation of Farquhar's 'healthy nature', but he is both more moderate and more thorough in his discussion of Farquhar's attempts to find a new mode suited to the changing values. *The Recruiting Officer* and *The Beaux' Stratagem* in his analysis are not as markedly separated from the preceding drama; both plays combine the lightness and wit of the earlier comedy of manners with a thorough understanding of human nature to produce what the essay terms 'comedy of life'. More incisively than any previous commentator, Strauss explores the vividness and the originality of the two comedies' characters; he also proposes a more comprehensive understanding of a dramatic mode that includes but subordinates dialogue and wit to character, plot and situational humour. Although he, too, notes the comedies' underlying sense of kindness and wholesomeness, his readings of their moral tone further reveal his sensitivity to the dramatic experience. His interpretation of a thoughtful though not insistently critical author would be reconsidered by later criticism, but Strauss is decidedly modern in his desire to view troublesome questions like the issue of divorce in the context of the comedies and the period. Despite its vestigial nineteenth-century biases his introduction significantly directs attention toward the plays' characteristic comic vision.

Only one other study written during this time is of any comparable importance. In *The Comedy of Manners* (1913) John Palmer had meanwhile concluded that Farquhar actually destroyed a tradition of comedy. His judgement depends upon the book's assumption that any art imaginatively shapes life; its motivation, Palmer assumes, 'is not the impulse of a moralist to improve the world: it is the impulse of an artist to express it'. Integrity, sincerity and consistency then become more important; and it is on these grounds that Palmer faults Farquhar. Unwilling to grant him the humanity and freshness commonly attributed to the last plays, he charges Farquhar with a confused sense of moral and artistic consistency. The final comedies in this interpretation only seem to instil new life into the theatre; for Palmer the imposition of moralistic sentiments and motivations upon the Restoration comedy of manners results in a disconcertingly bifurcated vision. No room is left in Palmer's heavily slanted disjunctive for any leeway or understanding. Intent upon defending the comedy of manners against its moralist critics, his apology deems sentimental in Farquhar the sensibility others had commonly found wholesome, humane and moral. More fully developed, his criticism would later reoccur in both negative and positive judgements unable to agree entirely with the unified sensibility Strauss perceives.

But for a long time twentieth-century assessments accept Farquhar's transitional nature with little new insight into either *The Recruiting Officer* or *The Beaux' Stratagem*. Ernest Bernbaum's *The Drama of Sensibility* (1915), for example, briefly and dispassionately notes a tentative inclination towards sentimentalism in the relationship between Archer and Mrs Sullen and in the transformations of Aimwell and Dorinda. Bonamy Dobrée's *Restoration Comedy* (1924) concludes at greater length that the comedies avoid sentimentalism in their neo-Elizabethan gusto. Dobrée's impression of an amused though common-sensical playwright has some affinity with Louis Strauss's view; John Palmer's misgivings are adopted in an almost token manner in H. T. E. Perry's *The Comic Spirit in Restoration Drama* (1925). A more reactionary position in Allardyce Nicoll's *A History of Early Eighteenth Century Drama* (1925) revives Adolphus Ward's criticism of Farquhar's indelicate taste and asserts the less fashionable belief that in *The Beaux' Stratagem* comedy of manners replaces realism as Farquhar once again captures the older Restoration spirit. Other literary surveys look forward: Charles Whibley considers the final plays departures from the comedy of manners that anticipate and even influence the development of the English novel, and George Henry Nettleton admires the freedom from cynicism and cruelty in an 'Irish good-humour' that links Farquhar with Goldsmith.[7]

No extensive discussion of the plays was to occur until the post-war period. Then in 1946 Peter Kavanagh published a chapter on Farquhar in *The Irish Theatre* notable mainly for its emphasis on the 'bitter and critical theme' beneath the apparent humour of *The Beaux' Stratagem*. Adding to Archer's older notion of Farquhar's seriousness an explicit comparison with Shaw, Kavanagh asserts that the comedy is really a treatise in favour of divorce, and only those who fail to take into account Farquhar's characteristically Irish blend of jest and earnest will miss its gravity. Willard Connely's 1949 biography of the playwright also considers the question of divorce, particularly in light of the play's indebtedness to Milton's divorce tracts, and it too is not averse to reviving an emphasis on the comedies as expressions of Farquhar's own situation. Heavily dependent upon plot summary rather than analysis, the biography is most interesting in its attempts to locate the plays in the context of Farquhar's life and times.

Despite this new biography and the renewed general interest in Restoration comedy, Farquhar does not immediately benefit from the rethinking apparent in the burgeoning modern scholarship. Frederick Boas provides lengthy summaries of the plays in *An Introduction to Eighteenth-Century Drama* (1953), but no new insights are offered. Instead a chapter on Farquhar in Louis Kronenberger's *The Thread of Laughter* (1952) revives John Palmer's unsympathetic assessment in its criticism of the last plays' uncertain tone. Because Farquhar can neither satisfactorily focus his own considerable talent nor resolve the issues he raises, Kronenberger contends that *The Recruiting Officer* becomes overly involved in plot complications while *The Beaux' Stratagem* blurs its serious note in the spirited gaiety generated from a thin intrigue. Other commentary on the plays – an essay by Fitzroy Pyle and reprintings of Archer, Palmer and Perry – re-establish dated impressions.[8]

Beginning in the sixties criticism has begun to reassess Farquhar's intentions and achievements in *The Recruiting Officer* and *The Beaux' Stratagem*. Although considerable variation still exists in the discussions of their nature and over-all success, the essays reflect the modern tendency towards refined historical and textual analyses. Farquhar is no longer grouped as a matter of course with Etherege, Wycherley or Congreve; and his complex relationship to Restoration comedy is more clearly understood. Liberated from earlier preconceptions and considered on their own terms, the comedies reveal Farquhar's attempts to resolve the distinctive issues and modes of his comic vision. Controversy about tone and intention still preoccupies the criticism, but a recognition of greater subtlety has displaced the older, more one-sided impressions. While judgements of the comedies' effectiveness are still quite markedly divided, here too recent studies understand apparent weaknesses more sensitively.

The most comprehensive consideration of Farquhar's dramatic integrity, Eric Rothstein's *George Farquhar* (1967), illustrates the growing recognition that the comedies' realistic characters, involved plots and moral vision should not be narrowly judged by the standards of Restoration comedy. Accepting the earlier realisation that their nature is attuned to an historical shift towards the natural he explores the dramatic implications of a form of comedy in which a harmonising moral vision supplants in importance the earlier premium on witty individualism. 'Moral' and 'natural', the two focal points of most Farquhar criticism, are thereby given renewed significance in an analysis of his development, 'a return to a system of external norms . . . which joins the moral and the natural through the ideal of law'. Without making their tones too serious, this reading proposes that a 'natural law' based on reason and experience does in fact determine the values and movements of *The Recruiting Officer* and *The Beaux' Stratagem*. The results, in Rothstein's analysis, are thematic and formalistic unities that redeem the comedies from the criticism of inconsistency.

Free from the biases found at times in the earlier use of 'transitional', other studies of *The Beaux' Stratagem* also demonstrate Farquhar's dramatic sophistication. Vincent Hopper and Gerald Lahey, in a modern counterpart to Louis A. Strauss's seminal essay, analyse the 'masterful harmonizing skill' displayed in the final comedy. Their attention to the complexities in character and their sense of Farquhar's delicately poised wit also go beyond Strauss's initial perceptions to a fuller appreciation of the comedy's principal figures and to a reappraisal of its problematic ending. Where Hopper and Lahey view the conclusion as an expedient though not overly serious solution, Ronald Berman emphasises a conscious awareness of limitation that gives new meaning to Palmer's unsympathetic notion of transition. Farquhar, in this interpretation of the comedy, deliberately exploits the tension between equally undeniable realities of love and money that signals the end of an era. A more unified vision that intergrates them is then proposed in Alan Roper's longer essay. Combining some of the older observations with the new understanding of Restoration comedy, Roper develops the 'conspicuous (if at times forcibly imposed) integrity of action, dialogue, and setting' that in *The Beaux' Stratagem* seems closer to Elizabethan than to Restoration drama.

Finally the intensified awareness of both comedies' tonal and thematic complexities is apparent in modern productions, most notably in the National Theatre presentations in 1963 of the *The Recruiting Officer* and in 1970 of *The Beaux' Stratagem*. The proper style found for Farquhar in the first production admittedly owes much to Brecht's *Pauken und Trompeten (Trumpets and Drums)* – a 1955 adaptation discussed in Wertheim's essay; but the long recognised attractiveness of both comedies, as William Gaskill indicates in his discussions of the production, is undeniable. And as William L. Sharp suggests in an alternative approach to production, Farquhar's modernity is still considered by some to be deeply rooted in the spirit of Restoration comedy. The difference in Gaskill's and Sharp's emphases, like the various critical interpretations, ultimately confirms the richness and significance the plays hold for a diverse audience. Though Farquhar's reputation is not now as secure as some of his contemporary playwrights, the following selection of essays suggest that his final two comedies caught and continue to hold the attention of those interested not only in the development of a dramatist or the evolution of English comedy but also in the appreciation of entertaining theatre.

NOTES

1. *The Works of the Late Ingenious Mr. George Farquhar* (Dublin, 1728) A3 r.

2. Eugene Nelson James's *The Development of George Farquhar as a Comic Dramatist* (Mouton, 1972) discusses in detail the common belief that Farquhar's major characters are in part autobiographical. See also Cibber and Hunt below (Part One) and Rothstein (Part Two).

3. The major source for the early history of the plays is Emmett L. Avery's *The London Stage 1660 – 1800* (Carbondale, Ill., 1960) Part 2. Michael Shugrue and A. Norman Jeffares also provide in their editions very useful discussions of the comedies' early and later stage histories.

Both, in addition, indicate significant alterations and omissions made in the second edition of *The Recruiting Officer* to appease readers who might take offence at Farquhar's witty liberties. Succinctly summarised by Jeffares, 'Plume's song and a suggestive speech of Rose's in III i and all of V i are omitted. There is some expansion of II i, and ten lines in French in IV i are suppressed in favour of twenty in English.' (p. 18)

4. *British Theatre* (*c*. 1829) Vol XXI.

5. H. A. Huntington, 'Captain Farquhar', *Atlantic Monthly*, XLIX (March 1882) 399 – 407

6. Charles Ewald, *The Dramatic Works of George Farquhar* (London, 1892) p. xv; H. Macaulay Fitzgibbon, *The Beaux-Stratagem* (London, 1898), p. viii. Percy Fitzgerald, *A New History of the English Stage* (London, 1882) 184; Edmund Gosse, *A History of Eighteenth Century Literature (1660 – 1780)* (London, 1888; 1929) p. 72; Adolphus Ward, *A History of English Dramatic Literature* (London, 1899) vol. III, p. 482.

7. Charles Whibley, 'The Restoration Drama', in *The Cambridge History of English Literature* (1912); George Henry Nettleton, *English Drama of the Restoration and Eighteenth Century (1642 – 1780)* (New York, 1914; 1932).

8. Kaspar Spinner's *George Farquhar als Dramatiker* (Bern, 1956) has not influenced subsequent criticism of Farquhar.

NOTE ON TEXTS

Modern essays which do not cite a special text have been standardised with A. Norman Jeffares's editions in the Fountainwell Drama Texts.

PART ONE

Critical Comment
1706 to 1924

Arthur Bedford (1706)

The *French* being beaten at *Hockstead* and *Ramellies*, the Siege of *Barcelona* being raised in Spain, and our *Generals* gaining the Love of that Nation, by a more prudent Behaviour in a second Expedition, there was no Way to oblige the common Enemy, and prevent our farther Successes, except by hindering the *Raising of Recruits* for the *Army*. Accordingly, there was lately published a *Comedy* call'd *The Recruiting Officer*, to render this Employment as odious as possible. This was acted in *London* by some who stile themselves *Her Majesties Servants*, and also in *Bristol*, whilst others were beating up for *Volunteers*. Here one *Captain* is represented as a notorious Lyar, another as a Drunkard, one intreagues with Women, another is scandalously guilty of *debauching* them; and tho' the *Serjeant* was married to five Women before, yet the *Captain* perswades him to marry another, as a Cloak for such Roguery, to make up his five Wives half a Dozen, and to cheat the *Queen*, by entering a child born the Day before into the Muster-Roll, and after all he stiles these *Debaucheries an Air of Freedom, which People mistake for Lewdness, as they mistake Formality in others for Religion*, and then proceeds in commending his own Practice, and exposing the other. In this *Play* the *Officers* are represented as quarrelsom, but Cowards. The *Serjeant* makes the *Mob* drunk to list them, gives two of them two Broad Pieces of Gold, for Pictures, and finding the Money upon them, pretends that they are listed: At another Time he is ready to swear any thing for the good of the Service; and also persuades Men to list in the Disguise of a *Conjurer*, with most profane Language in Commendation of the *Devil*; and all this is to make good the saying of *Virgil* inserted in the Title Page, *Captiq; dolis, donisq; coacti*. In this Play the *Officers* confess, that they greatly abuse the new listed *Soldiers*; *Debauching* of the Country Wenches is represented as a main Part of the Service; All the private Centinels are guilty of stealing Horses, Sheep and Fowls, and the *Captain* desires, that he may have but one honest Man in the Company for the Novelty's sake. Afther this the *Justices of the Peace* are made the Jest of the *Stage*, for discharging their Duty in listing of Soldiers, and the *Constable* hath a lash into the Bargain, that no one who serves his country on this Occasion, may escape the *Play-house* Censure. Some of their Expressions relating to the *Officers* of the Army will shew us the Temper, Fine Language, and the gratitude of the *Stage*.

Page 55, line 9. Of *Generals*.
You never knew a great General in your Life, that did not love a Whore.

Page 35, line 2. Of *Field-Officers*.
You shall receive your Pay, and do no Duty. [Answer] *Then you must make me a Field-Officer.*

Page 31, line 3. Of all other *Officers*.
The Officers every Year bring over a Cargo of Lace to cheat the Queen of her Duty, and the Subjects of their Honesty.

Page 31, line 16.
The Officers are curs'd, saying, that *they do the Nation more Harm, by Debauching us at Home, than they do good by Defending us abroad.*

Page 38, line 3. Of *Captains*.
A bold Step – [Note: Here are two smutty Entenders in the Characters of a Captain, which must be omitted] *and an impudent air are the principal Ingredients in the Composition of a Captain.*

Page 25, line 36. Of *Serjeants*, spoken by a *Serjeant*.
Cast up the whole Sum, viz. Canting, Lying, Impudence, Pimping, Bullying, Swearing, Whoring, Drinking, and an Halbard, and you will find the Sum Total will amount to a Recruiting Serjeant.

Page 6, line 31, spoken of *Recruiting Officers*, by a *Captain* employed in this Business.
What! No Bastards! and so many Recruiting Officers in Town! I thought 'twas a Maxim among them to leave as many Recruits in the Country as they carried out.

It may be observed, That when the *Souldiers* were guilty of *Immoralities* in Spain, they were caress'd by the Stage, and there crown'd with Success; but now we hear of no such Complaints, they are censur'd and ridicul'd. When they really were debauch'd, they were never thus affronted; but since the Endeavours used to reform the Army, they are thus expos'd. The greater and more signal the Services are, which they do the Nation, the more the *Play-Houses* shew their Resentments; and whilst others justly applaud them for their Merits, the *Poets* and *Actors* are the only Persons who thus lampoon them. What Thanks are due to such Men from the *French* King I shall not determine, but I am sure, that they deserve none from the *English Government*; and if neither Mr. *Dennis* nor this *Author* can render the Stage more useful, we are not, in the least, beholden for their Assistance. I suppose, that both the *Queen, Lords*, and *Commons* have different Sentiments concerning the Merits of the *Officers*; and These who stile themselves in Print, *Her Majesty's Servants*, are the only Men, who publickly undervalue such as hazard their Lives in *Her Majesty's Service*.

SOURCE: *The Evil & Danger of Stage-Plays* (1706)
pp. 149—54.

John Oldmixon (1707)

All that love Comedy will be sorry to hear of the Death of Mr. *Farquhar*, whose two last Plays had something in them that was truly *humorous* and *diverting*. 'Tis true the Criticks will not allow any Part of them to be regular, but Mr. *Farquhar* had a Genius for Comedy, of which one may say, that it was rather above Rules than below them. His *Conduct*, tho not *Artful*, was *surprizing*: His *Characters*, tho not Great, were Just: His Humour, tho *low*, diverting: His *Dialogue*, tho *loose* and *incorrect*, *gay* and *agreeable*; and his *Wit*, tho not *super-abundant, pleasant*. In a word, his Plays have in the *toute ensemble*, as the Painters phrase it, a certain Air of *Novelty* and *Mirth*, which pleas'd the Audience every time they were represented: And such as love to laugh at the *Theatre*, will probably miss him more than they now imagine.

SOURCE: *The Muses Mercury* (May 1707) pp. 123—4.

Alexander Pope (1737)

Some doubt, if equal pains or equal fire
The humbler Muse of Comedy require?
But in known Images of life I guess
The labour greater, as th' Indulgence less.
Observe how seldom ev'n the best succeed:
Tell me if Congreve's Fools are Fools indeed?
What pert low Dialogue has Farqu'ar writ!
How Van[1] wants grace, who never wanted wit!
The stage how loosely does Astræa[2] tread,
Who fairly puts all Characters to bed;
And idle Cibber, how he breaks the laws,
To make poor Pinky eat with vast applause!
But fill their purse, our Poet's work is done,
Alike to them, by Pathos or by Pun.

SOURCE: *The First Epistle of the Second Book of Horace*
(1737) ll. 282–95.

NOTES

1 [John Vanbrugh.]
2. [Aphra Behn.]

Theophilus Cibber (1753)

The general character that has been given of Mr. Farquhar's
comedies is, 'that the success of the most of them far exceeded the
author's expectations; that he was particularly happy in the
choice of his subjects, which he took care to adorn with a variety
of characters and incidents; his style is pure and unaffected; his
wit, natural and flowing, and his plots generally well contrived.

He lashed the vices of the age, tho' with a merciful hand; for his muse was good-natured, not abounding over-much with gall tho' he has been blamed for it by the critics: It has been objected to him, that he was too hasty in his productions; but by such only who are admirers of stiff and elaborate performances, since with a person of a sprightly fancy, those things are often best, that are struck off in a heat.[1] It is thought that in all his heroes, he generally sketched out his own character, of a young, gay, rakish spark, blessed with parts and abilities. His works are loose, tho' not so grossly libertine, as some other wits of his time, and leave not so pernicious impressions on the imagination as other figures of the like kind more strongly stampt by indelicate and heavier hands.'

He seems to have been a man of a genius rather sprightly than great, rather flow'ry than solid; his comedies are diverting, because his characters are natural, and such as we frequently meet with; but he has used no art in drawing them, nor does there appear any force of thinking in his performances, or any deep penetration into nature; but rather a superficial view, pleasant enough to the eye, though capable of leaving no great impression on the mind. He drew his observations chiefly from those he conversed with, and has seldom given any additional heightening, or indelible marks to his characters; which was the peculiar excellence of Shakespear, Johnson, and Congreve.

Had he lived to have gained a more general knowledge of life, or had his circumstances not been straitened, and so prevented his mingling with persons of rank, we might have seen his plays embellished with more finish'd characters, and with a more polish'd dialogue.

He had certainly a lively imagination, but then it was capable of no great compass; he had wit, but it was of so peculiar a sort, as not to gain ground upon consideration; and it is certainly true, that his comedies in general owe their success full as much to the player, as to anything intrinsically excellent in themselves.[2]

If he was not a man of the highest genius, he seems to have had excellent moral qualities, of which his behaviour to his wife and tenderness to his children are proofs, and deserved a better fate than to die oppressed with want, and under the calamitous apprehensions of leaving his family destitute: While Farquhar will ever be remembered with pleasure by people of taste, the name of the courtier who thus inhumanly ruined him, will be for ever dedicated to infamy.[3]

SOURCE: *The Lives of the Poets of Great Britain and Ireland* (1753) vol. III, pp. 136 – 7.

NOTES

1.   *Memoirs, ubi supra.* [Cibber there cites *Memoirs of Mr. Farquhar, before his Works.* The memoirs, by the actor Robert Wilks, first appear in the 1728 edition of Farquhar's works. – Ed.]

2.   [Richard Steele had observed in *The Tatler*, 26 May 1709, 'This evening was acted, *The Recruiting Officer*, in which Mr. Estcourt's proper sense and observation is what supports the play. There is not, in my humble opinion, the humour hit in Sergeant Kite; but it is admirably supplied by his action.' William Egerton also repeats this verdict in Anne Oldfield's memoirs (1731). – Ed.]

3.   [Cibber earlier relates that Farquhar sold his commission with the assurances of another from a 'certain noble courtier' who later reneged on his promise. Robert Jordan has recently questioned this popular account. – Ed.]

Oliver Goldsmith (1764)

William Congreve deserves also particular notice: his comedies, some of which were but coolly received upon their first appearance, seemed to mend upon repetition; and he is, at present, justly allowed the foremost in that species of dramatic poesy : his wit is ever just and brilliant : his sentiments new and lively; and his elegance equal to his regularity. Next him Vanbrugh is placed, whose humor seems more natural, and characters more new; but he owes too many obligations to the French entirely to pass for an original; and his total disregard of decency, in a great measure, impairs his merit. Farquhar is still more lively, and, perhaps, more entertaining than either: his pieces continue the favorite performances of the stage, and bear frequent repetition without satiety; but he often mistakes pertness for wit, and seldom strikes his characters with proper force or originality. However, he died very young; and it is remarkable, that he continued to improve as he grew older; his last play, entitled *The Beaux' Stratagem*, being the best of his productions.

SOURCE: *A History of England* (1764) pp. 89–90.

Elizabeth Inchbald (1808)

The Recruiting Officer

If the two last acts of this drama were equal to the three first, it would rank the foremost among Farquhar's works; for these are brilliant in wit, humour, character, incident, and every other requisite necessary to form a complete comedy. But the decrease of merit in a play, on approaching its conclusion, is, as in all other productions, of most unfortunate consequence.

The author was himself a recruiting officer, and possibly gathered all the materials for this play on the very spot where he has placed his scene – Shrewsbury. He has dedicated the piece 'to all friends round the Wrekin', and has thanked the inhabitants of the town for that cheerful hospitality, which made, he adds, 'the recruiting service, to some men the greatest fatigue on earth, to me the greatest pleasure in the world'.

He even acknowledges, that he found the country folk, whom he has here introduced – meaning those most excellently drawn characters of Rose, her brother, and the two recruits, – under the shade of that beforementioned hill near Shrewsbury, the Wrekin; and it may be well supposed, that he discovered Serjeant Kite in his own regiment, and Captain Plume in his own person. Certainly those characters have every appearance of being

copied from life – and probably, many other of his Salopian
acquaintance have here had their portraits drawn to perfection.

The disguise of Sylvia in boy's clothes, is an improbable, and
romantic occurrence; yet it is one of those dramatic events, which
were considered as perfectly natural in former times; although
neither history, nor tradition, gives any cause to suppose, that the
English ladies were accustomed to attire themselves in man's
apparel; and reason assures us, that they could seldom, if ever,
have concealed their sex by such stratagem.

Another incident in the *Recruiting Officer* might have had its
value a hundred years ago – just the time since the play was first
acted; but to the present generation, it is so dull, that it casts a
heaviness upon all those scenes whereon it has any influence.
Fortune-tellers are now a set of personages, in whom, and in
whose skill or fraud, no rational person takes interest; and though
such people still exist by their profession, they are so vile they are
beneath satire; and their dupes such idiots, they do not even
enjoy sense enough for their folly to produce risibility.

Perhaps the author despised this part of his play as much as the
severest critic can do; but having expended his store of entertainment upon the foregoing scenes, he was compelled to supply the
bulk of the two last acts from the scanty fund of wasted spirits, and
exhausted invention. . . .

The Beaux' Stratagem

It is an honour to the morality of the present age, that this most
entertaining comedy is but seldom performed; and never, except
some new pantomime, or other gaudy spectacle, be added, as an
afterpiece, for the attraction of an audience.

The well drawn characters, happy incidents, and excellent
dialogue, in *The Beaux Stratagem*, are but poor atonement for that
unrestrained contempt of principle which pervades every scene.
Plays of this kind are far more mischievous than those, which
preserve less appearance of delicacy. Every auditor and reader
shrinks from those crimes, which are recommended in unseemly
language, and from libertinism united with coarse manners; but
in adorning vice with wit, and audacious rakes with the vivacity

and elegance of men of fashion, youth, at least, will be decoyed into the snare of admiration.

Charmed with the spirit of Archer and Aimwell the reader may not, perhaps, immediately perceive, that those two fine gentlemen are but arrant impostors; and that the lively, though pitiable Mrs. Sullen, is no other than a deliberate violator of her marriage vow. Highly delighted with every character, he will not, perhaps, at first observe, that all the wise and witty persons of this comedy are knaves, and all the honest people fools.

It is said, that this play was written in six weeks — it is more surprising still, that it was written by a dying man!

Farquhar was a gentleman of elegant person and bewitching address, who, having experienced the vicissitudes of life, as a man of fashion, an actor, a captain in the army, an author, a lover, and a husband; and having encountered bitter disappointment in some of his adventures — though amply gratified by others — He, at the age of twenty-nine, sunk into a dejection of spirits and decline of health; and in this state, he wrote the present drama. — It had only been acted a night or two, when the author, in the midst of those honours, which he derived from its brilliant reception — died.[1]

As a proof that Farquhar was perfectly sensible of his dangerous state, and that he regained cheerfulness as his end approached, the following anecdote is told: —

The famed actress, Mrs. Oldfield, performed the part of Mrs. Sullen, when the comedy was first produced; and being highly interested in its success, from the esteem she bore the author; when it drew near the last rehearsal, she desired Wilkes, the actor, to go to him, and represent — that she advised him to make some alteration in the catastrophe of the piece; for that she was apprehensive, the free manner in which he had bestowed the hand of Mrs. Sullen upon Archer, without first procuring a divorce from her husband, would offend great part of the audience. 'Oh', replied Farquhar, gaily, when this message was delivered to him, 'tell her, I wish she was married to me instead of Sullen; for then, without the trouble of a divorce, I would give her my bond, that she should be a widow within a few days.'[2]

In this allusion he was prophetic; — and the apparent joy, with which he expected his dissolution, may be accounted for on the

supposition – that the profligate characters, which he has pourt-
rayed in *The Beaux Stratagem*, were such as he had uniformly met
with in the world; – and he was rejoiced to leave them all behind.

SOURCE: *The British Theatre* (1808) vol. VIII, pp. 2–5.

NOTES

1. [According to eighteenth-century tradition Farquhar died the
night of either the third performance (13 March) or a benefit
performance (29 April). Eric Rothstein suggests a later date between 18
May to 21 May – Ed.]
2. [W. R. Chetwood records this account in *A General History of the
Stage* (1749) – Ed.]

William Hazlitt (1819)

Farquhar's chief characters are also adventurers; but they are
adventurers of a romantic, not a knavish stamp, and succeed no
less by their honesty than their boldness. They conquer their
difficulties, and effect their 'hair-breadth 'scapes' by the impulse
of natural enthusiasm and the confidence of high principles of
gallantry and honour, as much as by their dexterity and readiness
at expedients. They are real gentlemen, and only pretended
impostors. Vanbrugh's upstart heroes are without 'any relish of
salvation', without generosity, virtue, or any pretensions to it. We
have little sympathy for them, and no respect at all. But we have
every sort of good-will towards Farquhar's heroes, who have as
many peccadillos to answer for, and play as many rogue's tricks,
but are honest fellows at bottom. I know little other difference
between these two capital writers and copyists of nature, than
that Farquhar's nature is the better nature of the two. We seem to
like both the author and his favourites. He has humour,
character, and invention, in common with the other, with a more
unaffected gaiety and spirit of enjoyment, which overflows and
sparkles in all he does. He makes us laugh from pleasure oftener
than from malice. He somewhere prides himself in having

introduced on the stage the class of comic heroes here spoken of, which has since become a standard character, and which represents the warm hearted, rattle-brained, thoughtless, highspirited young fellow, who floats on the back of his misfortunes without repining, who forfeits appearances, but saves his honour – and he gives us to understand that it was his own. He did not need to be ashamed of it. Indeed there is internal evidence that this sort of character is his own, for it pervades his works generally, and is the moving spirit that informs them. His comedies have on this account probably a greater appearance of truth and nature than almost any others. His incidents succeed one another with rapidity, but without premeditation; his wit is easy and spontaneous; his style animated, unembarrassed, and flowing; his characters full of life and spirit, and never over-strained so as to 'o'erstep the modesty of nature', though they sometimes, from haste and carelessness, seem left in a crude, unfinished state. There is a constant ebullition of gay, laughing invention, cordial good humour, and fine animal spirits, in his writings.

Of the four writers here classed together, we should perhaps have courted Congreve's acquaintance most, for his wit and the elegance of his manners; Wycherley's, for his sense and obser-vation on human nature; Vanbrugh's, for his power of farcical description and telling a story; Farquhar's, for the pleasure of his society, and the love of good fellowship. His fine gentlemen are not gentlemen of fortune and fashion, like those in Congreve; but are rather 'God Almighty's gentlemen'. His valets are good fellows: even his chambermaids are some of them disinterested and sincere. But his fine ladies, it must be allowed, are not so amiable, so witty, or accomplished, as those in Congreve. Perhaps they both described women in high-life as they found them: Congreve took their conversation, Farquhar their con-duct. . . .

The dialogue between Cherry and Archer, in the *Beaux' Stratagem*, in which she repeats her well conned love-catechism, is as good as this, but not so fit to be repeated any where but on the stage. The *Beaux' Stratagem* is the best of his plays, as a whole; infinitely lively, bustling, and full of point and interest. The

assumed disguise of the two principal characters, Archer and
Aimwell, is a perpetual amusement to the mind. Scrub is an
indispensable appendage to a country gentleman's kitchen, and
an exquisite confidant for the secrets of young ladies. *The
Recruiting Officer* is not one of Farquhar's best comedies, though it
is light and entertaining. It contains chiefly sketches and hints of
characters; and the conclusion of the plot is rather lame. He
informs us, in the dedication to the published play, that it was
founded on some local and personal circumstances that happened in Shropshire, where he was himself a recruiting officer;
and it seems not unlikely, that most of the scenes actually took
place at the foot of the Wrekin. *The Inconstant* is much superior to
it. The romantic interest and impressive catastrophe of this play I
thought had been borrowed from the more poetical and tragedy-
practised muse of the Beaumont and Fletcher; but I find they are
taken from an actual circumstance which took place in the
author's knowledge, at Paris. His other pieces, *Love and a Bottle*,
and the *Twin Rivals*, are not on a par with these; and are no
longer in possession of the stage. The public are, after all, not the
worst of judges. . . .

We may date the decline of English comedy from the time of
Farquhar. For this several causes might be assigned in the
political and moral changes of the times; but among other minor
ones, Jeremy Collier, in his *View of the English Stage*, frightened the
poets, and did all he could to spoil the stage, by pretending to
reform it; that is, by making it an echo of the pulpit, instead of a
reflection of the manners of the world. . . . The work is, however,
written with ability, and did much mischief: it produced those *do-
me-good*, lack-a-daisical, whining, make-believe comedies in the
next age, (such as Steele's *Conscious Lovers*, and others,) which are
enough to set one to sleep, and where the author tries in vain to be
merry and wise in the same breath; in which the utmost stretch of
licentiousness goes no farther than the gallant's being suspected
of keeping a mistress, and the highest proof of courage is given in
his refusing to accept a challenge.

SOURCE: *Lectures on the English Comic Writers* (1819)
pp. 163—75.

Leigh Hunt (1840)

. . . our author was a good-natured, reflective man, of so high an order of what may be called the *town* class of genius, as to sympathise with mankind at large upon the strength of what he saw of them in little, and to extract from a quintessence of good sense an inspiration just short of the romantic and imaginative; that is to say, he could turn what he had experienced in common life to the best account, but required in all cases the support of its ordinary associations, and could not project his spirit beyond them. He felt the little world too much, and the universal too little. He saw into all false pretensions, but not into all true ones; and if he had had a larger sphere of nature to fall back upon in his adversity, would probably not have died of it. The wings of his fancy were too common, and grown in too artificial an air, to support him in the sudden gulfs and great aching voids of that new region and enable him to beat his way to their green islands. His genius was so entirely social, that notwithstanding what appeared to be the contrary in his personal manners, and what he took for his own superiority to it, it compelled him to assume in his writings all the airs of the most received town ascendancy; and when it had once warmed itself in this way, it would seem that it had attained the healthiness natural to its best condition, and could have gone on for ever, increasing both in enjoyment and power, had external circumstances been favourable. He was becoming gayer and gayer, when death, in the shape of a sore anxiety, called him away, as if from a pleasant party, and left the house ringing with his jest.

In looking critically at Farquhar's plays in succession, nothing need be added to what has been said respecting the earliest one, *Love and a Bottle*, except that much of the talk is gratuitous, and that in this play, perhaps more than in any of the rest, is to be seen the 'pert low dialogue' which Pope accused him of writing; that is to say, brisk only, with a pretence of something better, and on that account wanting in an air of good breeding. Nor is Sir Harry Wildair without it in the *Constant Couple*, nor even Archer in his last play, the *Beaux-Stratagem*. It was probably owing to the conflict between the author's habits of personal reserve, and his sympathy in spirit with all that was the reverse. Goldsmith, who was a very diffident man, carried the same error into his Young Marlow in *She Stoops to Conquer*; or rather he would have carried it, had not the very intensity of his consciousness of the danger ingeniously converted it into a part of his comic intention. And Marlow, who in one of his situations is a copy of Archer, is, after all, really pert, and gives himself airs to the supposed chambermaid, beyond what a thorough-bred gentleman would have done. . . .

In the *Recruiting Officer* Farquhar . . . threw himself entirely upon his animal spirits, and produced accordingly one of his very best plays. In everything connected with it he was fortunate; for he went only upon grounds of truth and observation, and his own impulses. The humours were drawn from what he had seen while he was on [a] recruiting party; his hospitable friends 'round the Wrekin', to whom it was dedicated, furnished some of the characters; the play was written on the spot; his Colonel and his General liked it (Lord Orrery and the Duke of Ormond); the principal *dramatis personae* were represented by the best reigning performers (Wilks, Cibber, Estcourt, and Mrs Oldfield); and it gained that kind of success from which the author might have foreseen that it would retain possession of the stage. It has been stated by Nichols, on the authority of an old lady who remembered Farquhar and his recruiting party, that Justice Balance was Mr Berkeley, at that time Warden of Shrewsbury; that another of the Justices was a Mr Hill, of that city; Worthy, a Mr Owen of Russason; Melinda, a Miss Harnage, of Balsadine; and Sylvia, the Recorder's daughter.[1] Plume was, of course, pronounced to be 'himself'; but if the play, as it is asserted, and is probable, was written within a year of the *Beaux-Stratagem*, the gay Captain could only have been the imaginary Farquhar – gay enough, we doubt not, while so imagining, but in his own person, an anxious married man. Steele, who had a grudge against Farquhar, because he thought him wanting in sentiment, attributed the 'support' of the play to the admirable performance of his friend Estcourt. 'There is not', he says, 'in my humble opinion, the humour hit in Serjeant Kite; but it is admirably supplied by his action'. Succeeding times have not accorded with this criticism. Every character in the piece, of any prominence, is thought to be a genuine transcript from nature; and there is a charm of gaiety and good-humour throughout it, that enables us to put the best and least tragical construction upon certain anti-sentimentalities, which Steele perhaps was too much out of his customary good-humour to choose to consider in any light but one. We seem to breathe the clear, fresh, ruddy-making air of a remote country town, neighboured by hospitable elegancies. The sturdy male peasants will find their legs in life somehow, as the Serjeant has done; and the females will be taken more care of by the Captain himself, and by the good-natured Sylvia too, than the censor at first sight might suppose. The morals are not the best, we allow; and in the matter of *lying* (which always gives us a pang), they might be infinitely improved, as we doubt not they will, though not from the austerest quarters. When the best morals arrive, everybody will be as happily taken care of as the 'ladies' themselves – not the case certainly at present, nor provided for even by the prospective ethics of dear, excellent Richard Steele.

The sprightly success of the *Recruiting Officer* had probably the happiest effect upon the composition of our author's best and most successful production, the *Beaux-Stratagem* : an excellent play, which, like the one just mentioned, and the *Inconstant*, is always acted whenever actors can be found. Its plot is new, simple, and interesting; the characters various, without confusing it; the dialogue sprightly and characteristic; the moral bold, healthy, admirable, and doubly needed in those times, when sottishness was a fashion. Archer and Aimwell, who set out as mere intriguers, prove in the end true gentlemen, candid, conscientious, and generous. Scrub and Boniface, though but a servant and an innkeeper, are quotable fellows both, and have made themselves prominent in theatrical recollection – the former especially, for his quaint ignorance and sordid cunning. And Mrs Sullen is the more touching in her distress, from the cheerfulness with which she wipes away her tears. Sullen is an awful brute, yet not thoroughly inhuman; for he feels, after all, that he has no right to such a wife. The only fault in the termination, is what Mrs Oldfield objected to – that the law had provided no sanction for it; so that it became but a higher kind of sale by halter. But what a lesson did this very want imply! The footsteps of the gravest ultimate reforms are often found in places where they are least looked for. But Nature speaks there, and there they come. . . .

Of the four dramatists [discussed by Hunt] . . . it appears that Wycherley was the most reflective for reflection's sake, the most terse with simplicity in his style, the most original in departing from the comedy in vogue, and adding morals to manners, and the least so with regard to plot and character; that Congreve was the wittiest, most scholarly, most highly bred, the most elaborate in his plots and language, and most pungent but least natural in his characters, and that he had the least heart; that Vanbrugh was the readiest and most straightforward, the least superfluous, the least self-referential, mistrusting, or morbid, and therefore, with more pardon, the least scrupulous – caring for nothing but truth (as far as he saw it) and a strong effect; and that Farquhar had the highest animal spirits, with fits of the deepest sympathy, the greatest wish to please rather than to strike, the most agreeable diversity of character, the best instinct in avoiding revolting extravagances of the time, and the happiest invention in plot and situation; and, therefore, is to be pronounced, upon the whole, the truest dramatic genius, and the most likely to be of lasting popularity; as indeed he has hitherto been. He has far surpassed them all, we believe, in the number of editions; and is certainly ten times acted to their once. The *Confederacy*, on the strength of Brass and Dick Amwell and his mother, is the only play of Vanbrugh's that can compete, unaltered, with the quadruple duration of the *Constant Couple*, the *Inconstant*, the *Recruiting Officer* and the *Beaux-Stratagem*. . . .

But all the works of these dramatists are still read, though they are not all acted; and that they are no longer all acted is not to be wholly attributed either to their vices or to our virtues. Manners alone make some difference. Conventional pleasantries go out and cease to be understood; conventional virtues also change, and are not always converted into others more real. We are not of necessity the better or more moral for thinking the worst we can of freer modes of speech, or even of conduct. Our ancestors may not have been so bad as we suppose them, even upon our own principles. Animal spirits often say more than they mean; and in that case it is our dulness and want of spirits that misconstrue the speakers. Vanity pretends to more than it performs; and so does our own when it affects an extreme the other way. The balance is not always settled in our favour merely by our looking grave on the matter, and showing that our virtue makes us neither merry nor charitable.

Again, the drama is not a mere copy of nature – not a fac-simile. It is the free running hand of genius, under the impression of its liveliest wit or most passionate impulses, a thousand times adorning or feeling all as it goes; and you must read it, as the healthy instinct of audiences almost always does if the critics will let them alone – with a grain of allowance, and a tendency to go away with as much of it for use as is necessary, and the rest for the luxury of laughter, pity, or poetical admiration. Farquhar's, as well as Congreve's, rakes sometimes talk cruelly; but it is either towards imposture and trickery, or in the mere sting of the gusto of the will. They mean it to the letter as little as anybody; and we have seen that Farquhar himself died of anxiety for his family. There may have been a vanity in it, in his first productions; and very painful and startling it always sounds; but the very love of pleasure, in a heart like his, ended in making him humane, giving him a strong sense of the right of pleasure in others; and it was doubtless out of a sense of the desire and feasibility of this for all the world, and a suspicion of the world's paining itself overmuch and not wisely, that he talked on some subjects as carelessly as he did, and not out of any indifference to the happiness and real virtues of mankind. Read him, and his still freer spoken brethren, in the liberal spirit of that understanding, and you are safe in proportion to the goodness and cheerfulness of your own heart. If you feel neither generous nor blithe in the perusal, neither moved to correct the letter of the worst passages by the spirit of the best, nor to feel that the whole has some healthy end beyond itself, thus mistrusting the final purposes and good-nature of Nature herself, as they operate through the medium of a lively art, you may certainly need restraints which these holiday-going dramatists are as certainly not in a condition to supply. And lucky will you be if you get them in mirth-denouncing quarters, without their depriving you of the charity which such writers do not deny to anybody, and thus subjecting you to those hard and melancholy views of the world itself, which are the worst results of conduct the most vicious. Every book, it is true, even the noblest, is not a child's book, nor a guide to ordinary conduct; but a mind, candidly and healthily trained, may be suffered to grow up in almost any library; and you may put premature fears in it far worse than none. Nature approves of what is gradual, and loves a decent investment; but she is not fond of mutilated editions.

On the other hand, we are not to suppose that such a world as that of the very best of these dramatists is the best sort of world, or the cheerfullest, and the one to be most desired; much less such a suffocating region of fine heartless ladies and gentlemen as that of Congreve, who, in his passion for wit and a plot, thought of nothing but intrigue and lying, and saying two contrary things at once. It wanted all the poetry of the drama of the preceding ages, and had no fixed belief in any of the philosophy of the future; though the good nature of the better part of it was a kind of substitute for both. The best as well as worst of its women, for instance, are only fit to laugh and to perish. Perpetuity disowns them as thorough capable human creatures, such as Desdemona and Imogen – ready-made for being finally beautiful and moral, under the best conceivable dispensation; and yet the Sylvia and the Mrs Sullen of Farquhar have links with even women like these, by the force of their sympathy with whatsoever is kind and just. . . .[2]

SOURCE: extracts from the Introduction to *The Dramatic Works of Wycherley, Congreve, Vanbrugh and Farquhar* (1840) pp. *lvii, lviii–lix, lxii–lxiii.*

NOTES

1. [The British Museum has a letter to Bishop Percy from E. Blakeway written from Shrewsbury on 4 July 1765 that makes these identifications; see Stonehill, Rothstein or Jeffares – Ed.]

2. [The full version of Hunt's Introduction reprints Lamb's essay and also Hazlitt's entire lecture on the Restoration playwrights – Ed.]

William Archer (1905)

Farquhar has been, if not damned, at any rate gravely depreciated, by a single line of Pope's: 'What pert, low dialogue has Farquhar writ!' This casual remark has struck the keynote of criticism for more than a century and a half. It echoes in Professor Ward's assertion that

He is happy in the description of manners in a wider range than that commanded by Vanbrugh; but his dialogue is in general less gay and sparkling, and while his morality is no better than that of the most reckless of his contemporaries, he has a coarseness of fibre which renders him less endurable than some of these are to a refined taste.

We have here an indictment in three counts, which I shall attempt to meet one by one, but in inverse order. I submit, first, that Farquhar was much less nauseous in his coarseness than Wycherley, Congreve, or Vanbrugh; second, that he showed clear traces of an advance in moral sensibility, nowhere discernible in the other three; third, that the alleged lack of 'sparkle' in his dialogue in reality means a return to nature, an instinctive revolt against the sterilising convention of 'wit', 'Gaiety' Professor Ward must surely have denied him by inadvertence. His severest critics have contested the merit of his gaiety, but not the fact. . . .

. . . In Farquhar's . . . play, *The Recruiting Officer*, the conduct of Justice Balance and Silvia, on learning of the death of his son and her brother, seems incredibly unfeeling. To say that it belonged to the manners of the day is not, of course, to justify it; but another age may be as critical of our sensibility as we of the insensibility of the early eighteenth century. After all, there is nothing to show that the relation of Silvia to her brother had been at all intimate or tender. Perhaps they had seen very little of each other; perhaps they had been wholly unsympathetic. Mr Bernard Shaw's favourite thesis that near relatives always tend to hate each other, is flagrantly false; but the opposite belief, that they always and necessarily love each other dearly, is a superstition of modern sentimentality. The fact that Farquhar does not interrupt the course of his comedies with scenes of lamentation cannot fairly be taken as a proof that he was deficient in natural feeling.

The ethical standards of *The Recruiting Officer* and of *The Beaux' Stratagem* cannot, certainly, be called high; but there is in both a general tone of humanity which is far above the level of the age, and even above that of Farquhar's early plays, down to and including *Sir Harry Wildair*. Captain Plume, though a loose-living soldier, belongs rather to the company of Fielding's Tom Jones than to that of Wycherley's Horner or Manly, Congreve's Bellmour or Vainlove, Vanbrugh's Loveless or Worthy. As for Aimwell and Archer, adventurers though they be, they are neither brutal nor wholly unscrupulous. Aimwell, indeed, voluntarily forgoes the fruits of his intrigue, and confesses his personation, in the moment of its success – a trait of conscience inconceivable in the typical hero of the period. But it is not in definite and positive acts that the moral advance is chiefly to be noted. It is in the substitution of wholesome fresh air for the black, bitter, cruel atmosphere that weighs on us in the works of the three other playwrights. I shall try to show later that there are traces in *The Beaux' Stratagem* of an actual interest in moral problems, wholly different from the downright contempt for the very idea of morality which pervades the Restoration Comedy as a whole. In the meantime, it is sufficient to say that in all his plays, from *The Constant Couple* onwards, and especially in the last three, Farquhar gives a general preponderance to kindness over cruelty[1] and good over evil, which reverses the order of things prevailing in his contemporaries. . . .

We come now to the question of dialogue, which we shall find shading off into another and larger question. It may be admitted at once that Farquhar's dialogue has not the dry, hard polish – the 'sparkle', as Professor Ward justly calls it – of Congreve, or of Vanbrugh at his best. He is not, like Congreve, a virtuoso in style. There is perhaps no part in his plays so well written, in the literary sense, as that of Lord Foppington in Vanbrugh's *Relapse*. He was not, in fact, specifically a literary man. His verse is uniformly execrable, and his non-dramatic prose has far more ease than distinction. But we must note that if, in his dialogue, he did not achieve the glitter of Congreve, it is partly, at least, because he did not aim at it. Farquhar had plenty of wit; but he did not make wit the beginning and end of his endeavour. It would be a curious task for German industry (and by no means the idlest it has ever undertaken) to tell us how many times the word 'wit' occurs in the comedies of Congreve and Farquhar respectively. I would lay a heavy wager that the proportion would prove to be at least twenty to one. Congreve's characters, both the wise men (such as they be) and the fools, are always thinking and talking about their wit. Wit and intrigue are the sole objects of their existence. 'Leave business to idlers and wisdom to fools', cries Bellmour, on the first page of Congreve's first comedy; 'wit be my faculty, and pleasure my occupation'. No doubt it would be unjust to call this continual strain after similitude, paradox, and repartee a mere convention of the playhouse. There are social circles to-day in which the same self-conscious striving after brilliancy makes life an irritation and a toil. The great development of 'polite' intercourse which followed the Restoration begot a new Euphuism which, being unrestrained by decency or good nature, was an easily-acquired and highly infectious fashion. It is quite probable that the Dapperwit, the Sparkish, the Novel of Wycherley, the Brisk and Tattle and Petulant and Witwoud of Congreve, had their originals in real life, and were not even very grossly caricatured. But the world to which they belonged – the fast or 'smart' world, as we should nowadays call it – was a very small and superficial one. As the modern dramatist speaks of 'our little parish of St James's', so Congreve might have called the whole province of his genius 'our little parish of Covent Garden'. In his plays especially, but also in those of Wycherley and Vanbrugh, we have a constant sense of frequenting a small coterie of exceedingly disagreeable people. Their talk is essentially coterie-talk, keyed up to the pitch of a particular and narrow set. It is Farquhar's great merit to have released comedy from this circle of malign enchantment. Even in *The Constant Couple* and *Sir Harry Wildair* his characters have not quite the coterie stamp. We feel, at any rate, that they are studied from an outside point of view, by one who does not mistake the conventions of the coterie for laws of nature. In *The Twin-Rivals* the coterie tone is scarcely heard at all. With the return to a recognition (rather too formal to be artistic) of the difference between right and wrong, we have something like a return to nature in the tone of conversation. In the excellent little scene (1i) between Benjamin Wouldbe and the innkeeper Balderdash, there is nothing that can be called wit, but a great deal of humour; while Mrs Mandrake is a realistic life-study of extraordinary power. Finally, in *The Recruiting Officer* and *The Beaux' Stratagem*, Farquhar broke away altogether from the purlieus of Covent Garden, and took comedy out into the highways and the byways. When Congreve strayed into the country, it was only to present to us that amazing 'house party' of *The Double Dealer* – Lord and Lady Touchwood, Lord and Lady Froth, Sir Paul and Lady Plyant, Mellefont, Maskwell, Careless and Brisk – in a word, the coterie at its narrowest. When Vanbrugh went down to the shires, it was only to show Tom Fashion stealing away the daughter of Sir Tunbelly Clumsey. But Farquhar introduced us to the life of the inn, the market-place, and the manor house. He showed us the squire, the justice, the innkeeper, the highwayman, the recruiting sergeant, the charit-able lady, the country belle, the chambermaid, and half a score of excellent rustic types. He introduced the picaresque element into English comedy, along with a note of sincere and original observation. To have made the good folk of Shrewsbury and Lichfield express themselves with the modish, stereotyped wit of the London chocolate-house and boudoir would have been the height of absurdity. Farquhar reduced wit within something like the limits of nature, subordinating it to humour, and giving it, at the same time, an accent, all his own, of unforced, buoyant gaiety. And he had for his reward the line: 'What pert, low dialogue has Farquhar writ!'

That Farquhar widened the range of comedy is obvious and generally admitted. But critics have, so far as I know, overlooked a subtler distinction between his work and that of his con-temporaries, which seems to me real and important. If he was not specifically a literary man in the sense in which they were, he was specifically a dramatist in a sense in which they were not. That is to say, he was a dramatist and nothing else, whereas in Wycherley, Congreve and Vanbrugh the dramatist was as yet imperfectly differentiated from the social essayist. How often in their plays does the action stand still while the characters expatiate in reflection, generalisation, description and criticism of other characters; in short, in essays or leading articles broken up into dialogue! Comedy, as they conceived it, meant *the introspection of the coterie.* The business of the comic poet was to show the little circle, with which alone he was conversant, in the act of observing, analysing, and discussing its own manners and customs, humours and foibles. His characters were always intensely self-conscious, always perfectly aware that they were playing parts, under the critical eyes of their friends and acquaintances, upon the coterie-stage of 'the town'. There is scarcely a comedy of Wycherley, Congreve, or Vanbrugh from which long scenes of sheer generalisation or episodic portraiture could not be wholly excised, without leaving any sensible gap either in the action of the play or in the characterisation necessary to justify the action. As instances, let me mention in Wycherley the scenes between Lady Fidget, Mrs Dainty Fidget, and Mrs Squeamish (*Country Wife*, II i), between Horner, Sparkish, and Dorilant (*Country Wife*, III ii), between Olivia, Eliza, Novel, and Plausible (*Plain Dealer*, II i); in Congreve, the greater part of the Petulant and Witwoud dialogue in *The Way of the World*; and in Vanbrugh the scene between Lady Brute and Belinda (*Provoked Wife*, III iii), which opens in this characteristic strain of reflection:

LADY BRUTE   What hogs men turn, Belinda, when they grow weary of women!
BELINDA   And what owls they are whilst they are fond of 'em!

But whole scenes of this nature are, of course, comparatively rare. The essential point is that there is scarcely a scene in any of these writers wherein the characters do not pause, more or less frequently, to contemplate themselves or each other from what may be called the essayist's point of view, and to pass general remarks and theoretic judgments. There is scarcely a scene in which one could not find the text (and often a great part of the substance) of a *Tatler* or *Spectator* essay. The dramatist, in fact, was not merely a dramatist but a journalist as well. He suffered his characters not only to reveal themselves in action, but to explain and satirise themselves and each other, in undramatised or imperfectly dramatised disquisition. Even his valets and lady's-maids would not infrequently deliver themselves of neat little essays, wholly unnecessary to the progress of the plot.

When we come to Farquhar, we find the differentiation between the dramatist and the essayist rapidly completing itself. In *Love and a Bottle* it is still very imperfect, but from *The Constant Couple* onwards it is much more clearly marked than in any of the other three. His characters are not for ever feeling their own pulses, taking the social temperature, or noting the readings of the wit-barometer. It is impossible to prove a negative by quotation; I can but state what I think is the fact and leave the reader to verify it. Farquhar's plots are as conventional as those of his contemporaries, his technical devices as crude; but he confines his characters within the action, and keeps the action moving, better than they do. He is much less given to the elaborate portrayal of a Jonsonian 'humour' for its own sake. We do not find in his comedies that characters are minutely described before they appear, and then do nothing throughout the rest of the play but, as it were, copy their own portrait. I remember but one exception to this rule: Captain Brazen, in *The Recruiting Officer*, who is heralded by his full-length portrait, drawn by Worthy and Balance. The few lines of introduction which precede Sir Harry Wildair's entrance are scarcely a case in point; for Wildair is certainly a rounded character, not, like Dapperwit or Sparkish, or Tattle or Brisk, a mere incarnate 'humour'. This departure from the Jonsonian method is an additional evidence of the fact that the dramatist, properly so-called, was more highly developed in Farquhar than in his contemporaries.

Now history shows us that one of the chief literary phenomena of these years was precisely the differentiation of the journalist from the dramatist. Steele, who comes to the front as a dramatist two years later than Farquhar, and precedes him by a year in the movement towards a saner morality, presently abandons the stage (or nearly so) in order to devote himself to journalism. In other words, he distributes his essays and character-sketches in type through the coffee-houses and the boudoirs, instead of inviting the beaux, wits and ladies to come and listen to them in the theatre. Addison follows suit; and as the essay gains ground, comedy declines. This means that specifically dramatic endowment was rare, and that, as soon as the non-dramatic element in

Restoration Comedy was found readily separable from the dramatic framework, much of the talent which would otherwise have sought utterance in the theatre chose rather to express itself in a simple and natural than in a hybrid and highly artificial form. But Farquhar was the one man of the time who had dramatic talent highly developed and discursive talent scarcely at all. He had great fertility and facility; his last and best play he wrote in six weeks, while in the grip of mortal illness. Had he lived to sixty instead of dying before thirty, we can scarcely doubt that he would have kept the drama more nearly abreast of the essay and its successor, the novel, than it has ever been from his day to our own. We might have had in him a Fielding of the theatre.

Even as it was, in his brief literary life of eight or nine years, cut short before he can be supposed to have reached full maturity, he contrived to do work which makes him, far more than any other of his group, an influential precursor of Fielding. In humour and humanity the two are distinctly congenial; and, if we allow for difference of scale, Farquhar's power of character-drawing may quite well be measured with that of the 'Great Harry'. He had extraordinary ease in giving his personages individuality without caricature, or mechanical insistence or 'humours'. But what chiefly justifies us in regarding his too early death as one of the most notable of the many mischances that have befallen the English drama, is the steady growth we can perceive in him, not only of moral feeling, but of sober criticism of life. His first three comedies, as I have admitted, are entirely irresponsible; but in the last act of the last of them we come upon a passage which, in ironic form, strikes a note of sincere indignation. So, at least, I read the short scene in *Sir Harry Wildair* (V iv) between Sir Harry and Lord Bellamy. The almost savage scorn with which Sir Harry here spits in the face of 'smart' society – of what I have called the coterie – is not in his normal character. It reminds one of a tirade by one of the debauchee moralists of the younger Dumas. Farquhar is here uttering the bitterness of his own spirit; and from this time onward he is no longer irresponsible, not even in the semi-Elizabethan *Inconstant* which he borrowed from Fletcher. Especially noteworthy is the growth of his sympathy with the finer aspects of womanhood. Leanthe in *Love and a Bottle* is a romantic impossibility, Lucinda a very vulgar personage.

Angelica in *The Constant Couple* is a lay-figure, and in *Sir Harry Wildair* a convention; while Lady Lurewell is, in *The Constant Couple*, a melodramatic man-hater, not unlike Dumas's *Etrangère*, and has become, in *Sir Harry Wildair*, a vapourish, corrupt fine-lady. But in the later plays the heroines are always natural, agreeable women, with as much refinement as the atmosphere of the age would permit. I have already quoted an admirable saying of Aurelia's in *The Twin-Rivals*. Silvia, in *The Recruiting Officer*, in spite of the absurdity of her disguise and the coarseness of some of the episodes that spring from it, seems to me to have more than a touch of the free, generous, self-reliant womanhood of Shakespeare's heroines in the past and Mr Meredith's in the future. Dorinda, in *The Beaux' Stratagem*, is a pleasant figure, and even Mrs Sullen is not the ordinary female rake of Restoration Comedy. Professor Ward writes of this play: 'Some of the incidents are dubious, including one at the close – a separation by mutual consent, which throws a glaring light on the view taken by the author and his age on the sanctity of the marriage tie.' I venture to suggest that what is here set down to Farquhar's discredit is, in fact, a remarkable proof of the increasing earnestness of his outlook upon life. We have in this comedy (especially in the scenes between Mrs Sullen and Dorinda at the end of Act III, and between Squire Sullen and Sir Charles Freeman at the beginning of Act V) a serious and very damaging criticism of the conventional view that there can be no immorality in marriage save breach of the marriage vow. These scenes are, in fact, a plea for what Farquhar regarded, rightly or wrongly, as a more rational law of divorce. We may or may not think the plea a sound one; but it is certain that a serious discussion of the ethics of divorce was a homage to the idea of marriage which Wycherley, Congreve, or Vanbrugh would never have dreamt of paying. To them marriage meant nothing but a legal convention governing the transmission of property from (reputed) father to son. For the rest, it merely added a relish to libertinism. Where marriage constitutes no bond, divorce can have no function. When Farquhar seriously (and wittily) set himself to show that a certain type of marriage was loathsome and immoral, he broke once for all with the irresponsible licentiousness of his school. He admitted a moral standard, and subjected social convention, not to mere cynical presiflage, but to the criticism of reason. Having reached this point at twenty-nine, how far might he not have advanced if another twenty years had been vouchsafed him?

SOURCE: extract from *Fortnightly Review*, LXXVIII (new ser., 1905) 799–810; reprinted as introductions in Mermaid Series (London 1906) and Mermaid Dramabook (New York, 1959).

NOTE

1.   It may be said that *The Recruiting Officer* treats heartlessly of the cruelties perpetrated under the Enlistment Acts. But denunciation of these abuses was scarcely to be expected from an officer actually employed in the work of recruitment; and, on the other hand, though the comedy is gay and irresponsible in tone, it is no eulogy, but rather a satire, on the methods employed.

John Palmer (1913)

Farquhar is the last of the five principal figures in the half century of English comedy that began with Etherege. Facts continue to be kind. We have found in the lives and works of the four conspicuous predecessors of Farquhar an uninterrupted story of the development of a definite type of comedy. In Farquhar the story continues without a break. The comedy of manners, reaching perfection in Congreve, perceptibly droops in Vanbrugh, and in Farquhar is extinguished. It was no accident of history that Farquhar had no successor. Farquhar killed the comedy to which he contributed the last brilliant examples.

Farquhar's position in English comedy has not yet been historically considered. Critics have approached Farquhar from many points of view; never as the heir of Congreve. That Farquhar was the last of the comic dramatists, that he really succeeded Etherege and Wycherley, is one of those too obvious facts which invariably escape. Between the lines of most criticisms of the plays of Farquhar, more especially those which were written in the late nineteenth century – we detect an indulgence, a determination to make the most of his good, and the least of his bad qualities, which contrasts remarkably with the treatment usually bestowed upon his predecessors. The explanation of this is that Farquhar is invariably approached as a late nineteenth-century author, who, from youth, inexperience, hot blood, and high spirits, did not quite come off either morally or artistically. His heart is felt to be in the right place. He introduced, it is said, fresh air into the theatre. He took a serious interest in moral problems. The nauseous comedy of Wycherley; the heartless comedy of Congreve, is abandoned. Farquhar, in fact, has been treated as a reformer of the old theatre; and as the possible founder of a better type of play.

This is history inverted. When we come to consider his plays in detail we shall find in Farquhar precisely that acceptance of an outgrown convention which mars the comedy of Vanbrugh. Where the critics find in Farquhar humanity and fresh air we shall detect an emotional and romantic treatment of sex stifling the parent stem of a comedy whose appeal depended upon an entirely different system of moral and imaginative values. Farquhar's comedies are the direct result of an author, whose temperament and environment were not much unlike those of his nineteenth-century critics, trying to write comedies like Congreve. The consequent inconsistencies, often resulting in serious moral and artistic offence, are more patent than in Vanbrugh's case; for Farquhar was more careless a writer than his predecessor, and never really discovered in his art a neutral territory where the values he borrowed were reconciled with the values he contributed. . . .

Farquhar in . . . *The Recruiting Officer* sets off his comedy with the humours of country life and manners. Here definitely was Farquhar's opportunity to shake off the influences that thwarted him, and to find for himself a new convention. But the change of scene is all. Captain Plume is again Sir Harry Wildair – Congreve's libertine playing, in the teeth of his character, for the sympathy of Collier's parishioners. Having for a while consistently lived up to his reputation as the successor of Mr. Horner, he suddenly asserts for the comfort of his audience : 'I'm not that rake that the world imagines; I have got an air of freedom, which people mistake for lewdness in me, as they mistake formality in others for religion. The world is all a cheat; only I take mine, which is undesigned, to be more excusable than theirs, which is hypocritical. I hurt nobody but myself, and they abuse all mankind.'

Farquhar's last and best play, *The Beaux' Stratagem*, shows at their highest power all the qualities that make and mar his comedy. To pick holes is an ungrateful enterprise. This play is an act of splendid courage – a conspicuous triumph of the author over the man. Farquhar was dying, haunted with fears for his family left without provision. He was looking back upon a life of which the leitmotiv was hope unsatisfied:

AIM. But did you observe poor Jack Generous in the Park last week?

ARCH. Yes, with his autumnal periwig, shading his melancholy face, his coat older than anything but its fashion, with one hand idle in his pocket, and with the other picking his useless teeth; and, though the Mall was crowded with company, yet was poor Jack as single and solitary as a lion in the desert.

AIM. And as much avoided, for no crime upon earth but the want of money.

Jack Generous is the only spot of gloom in *The Beaux' Stratagem*. It is the sunniest of his plays. For the circumstances of its writing alone it deserves a high place in our regard. But we must not, therefore, falter in our analysis. The play shows no development upon any one of its predecessors. Archer is again Sir Harry Wildair, straight out of Congreve or Etherege. Archer delivers himself in a speech upon the five senses in the absolute manner of Sir Frederick Frollick:

Give me a man that keeps his five senses keen and bright as his sword; that has 'em always drawn out in their just order and strength, with his reason as commander at the head of 'em; that detaches 'em by turns upon whatever party of pleasure agreeably offers, and commands 'em to retreat upon the least appearance of disadvantage or danger! For my part, I can stick to my bottle while my wine, my company, and my

reason, holds good; I can be charmed with Sappho's singing without
falling in love with her face; I love hunting, but would not, like Actæon,
be eaten up by my own dogs; I love a fine house, but let another keep it;
and just so I love a fine woman.

This single speech is a perfect expression of the attitude which
determined the half-century of life and literature which preceded
its delivery. Nevertheless, in the same play are collected sentiments and motives which are directly contrary. Consider the root
question of marriage. Farquhar has been commended for his
insistence in marriage upon an alliance of spirit:

DOR.   But how can you shake off the yoke? Your divisions
don't come within the reach of the law for a divorce.

MRS. SUL.   Law! what law can search into the remote abyss of
nature? What evidence can prove the unaccountable disaffections of wedlock? Can a jury sum up the endless aversions that are
rooted in our souls, or can a bench give judgment upon
antipathies?

Farquhar here restores to English comedy the normal English
idea of sex-relationship. Restoration Society, as we have seen,
dissociated the act of sex from sentiments of friendship or the
transports of romantic exaltation. Farquhar has outlived the
influences which determined the Restoration attitude. His
comedy unhappily divides itself into scenes where the Restoration attitude is for the form's sake accepted, and scenes
where for the moral's sake it is condemned. It is significant that,
unconsciously torn between two irreconcilable alternatives, he
finally resorts, in his happiest manner, for refuge to his old device
of lightly skimming the surface of his theme for fear of tumbling
into a pitfall [quotes V iv 197 – 272] . . .

Everyway *The Beaux' Stratagem* is well fitted to close the story of
the fall of English comedy. The 'passionate and luscious'
treatment of sex which entered with Vanbrugh reaches a climax
in the interrupted bedchamber scene between Archer and Mrs.
Sullen. The lamentable obverse of this is Aimwell's fifth-act

repentance in the act of deceiving Dorinda [quotes V iv 21−43] . . .

To end upon a note so false as this would be flat injustice. Let us, as brief examples of a better Farquhar, read of Mr. Archer's 'Howd'ye,' and how the count nearly came to be hidden in Mrs. Sullen's closet. Archer was at this time a pretended footman:

MRS. SUL.   I suppose you served as footman before?

ARCH.   For that reason I would not serve in that post again; for my memory is too weak for the load of messages that the ladies lay upon their servants in London. My Lady Howd'ye, the last mistress I served, called me up one morning, and told me: Martin, go to my Lady Allnight with my humble service; tell her I was to wait on her ladyship yesterday, and left word with Mrs. Rebecca, that the preliminaries of the affair she knows of are stopped till we know the concurrence of the person that I know of, for which there are circumstances wanting which we shall accommodate at the old place; but that in the meantime there is a person about her ladyship, that, from several hints and surmises, was accessory at a certain time to the disappointments that naturally attend things, that to her knowledge are of more importance −

MRS. SUL. AND DOR.   Ha, ha ha! where are you going, sir?

ARCH.   Why, I haven't half done! − The whole howd'ye was about half an hour long; so I happened to misplace two syllables, and was turned off, and rendered incapable.

'The pleasantest fellow, sister, that I ever saw,' Dorinda's comment is justified. Foigard, the hero of the closet, is also a pleasant fellow − like Farquhar, an Irishman:

GIP.   What would you have me do, doctor?

FOI.   Noting, joy, but only hide the count in Mrs. Sullen's closet when it is dark.

GIP.   Nothing! is that nothing? It would be both a sin and a shame, doctor.

FOI.   Here is twenty Lewidores, joy, for your shame; and I will give you an absolution for the shin.

GIP.   But won't that money look like a bribe?

FOI.   Dat is according as you shall tauk it. If you receive the money beforehand, 'twill be, *logice*, a bribe; but if you stay till afterwards, 'twill be only a gratification. . . .

GIP.   But should I put the count into the closet —

FOI.   Vel, is dere any shin for a man's being in a closhet? One may go to prayers in a closhet.

GIP.   But if the lady should come into her chamber, and go to bed?

FOI.   Vel, and is dere any shin in going to bed, joy?

GIP.   Ay, but if the parties should meet, doctor?

FOI.   Vel den — the parties must be responsable. Do you be after putting the count in the closhet, and leave the shins wid themselves.

As with Vanbrugh we have been forced in reading the plays of Farquhar to dwell unduly upon the darker side. It has been necessary to insist that these two authors, accepting a comedy which expressed the society of the Restoration, were unable consistently to present life from the point of view of the men who served as their models. Their plays are pitted with inconsistencies. They never succeeded in bridging the gulf that separated their personal convictions from the moral and artistic conventions of the theatre into which they intruded. Nevertheless their positive merits must not be neglected. Vanbrugh reaches his height in scenes where humour and insight play tolerantly between two worlds. Farquhar is able to blind us to the worst of his faults in the happy running of his speech and fancy. He is perhaps the lightest of foot of all our comic authors. Farquhar was born too late. He should have come from Ireland in the 'sixties or 'seventies and have been accepted into the company of Etherege and Sedley. He might then have had for his share a more brilliant glory — to assist the rise of English comedy; actually he assisted the fall. It must be at the charge of Farquhar himself that no successor was found to continue the tradition.

SOURCE: *The Comedy of Manners* (1913; reprinted New York, 1962) pp. 242–4, 266–74.

Louis A. Strauss (1914)

Farquhar's position in English comedy is, historically, of far greater significance than is generally acknowledged. His work marks a turning-point in the drama so decided and meaningful that, without seeking to magnify his importance, I am disposed to mention him with such innovators as Lyly, Shakespeare, Jonson, and Etherege. As author of one of the last perfect specimens of comedy of manners and of the first two splendid examples of comedy of the balanced modern type, he emerges from the ranks of the Orange and Augustan comedians as the prophet of a new order. For while he introduced no comic principle hitherto unknown, he blended the essentials of character, plot, and situation in juster proportions than any previous writer of realistic comedy, lifting their interest to an equality with that of the dialogue, to which they had been subordinated in the wit-ridden comedy of manners. The result was a form of comedy unsurpassed for naturalness and fidelity to life : the form adopted and perfected by Sheridan and Goldsmith.

Mr. William Archer [see extract above], with a fine appreciation of Farquhar's genius, has lamented his early death as a great blow to the English drama – one of its many instances of unfulfilled promise. I would emphasize, on the other hand, the richness and completeness of Farquhar's personal achievement, and the unlikelihood of further achievement had his life been prolonged. . . .

Farquhar seems to have been unconscious, in his last two plays, of any departure from the prevailing type of comedy. There is no syllable, in dedication, prologue, or epilogue, to show that they pretended to be different from his early comedies. On the surface they seem to go back to the same style : his heroes have the free-and-easy bearing of rakes; Melinda and Mrs. Sullen are sophisticated women of fashion; and matters are lightly played with that *The Twin Rivals* treated seriously. The intrigue of Archer and Aimwell is of the kind on which comedy of manners flourished. And yet we are in sympathy with the men and their schemes, because we feel that at bottom they are good men and that their success can lead to no harm. Farquhar's rakes, it is

commonly admitted, have at no time been so thoroughly bad as
those of his teachers in art: but there is a world of difference
between Roebuck and Wildair, on the one hand, and Plume and
Aimwell on the other. Not that the latter have attained to the
angelic goodness of the modern leading juvenile: but that, thanks
to the assertion of Farquhar's kindly and wholesome nature, as
against the fashionable conventions of play-writing, we find a
deeper humanity beneath the rakish exterior. What influences
produced this change, and with what force each operated, are of
course impossible of discovery. Doubtless his marriage and the
struggle for a livelihood, his artistic growth, nourished by
reflection upon the failure of his intermediate plays, his illness,
with, perhaps, a mellowing and refining of his nature attendant
thereon, all were contributory.

Dr. Schmid has called attention to the fact that in these two
comedies Farquhar for the first time quits the purlieus of London
and sets his action in provincial towns.[1] Mr. Archer enlarges
upon this theme, pointing out its bracing effect upon the tone and
atmosphere of the plays, and the opportunity it afforded for fresh
observation and invention. In fact, though it were easy to leap to
rash conclusions and postulate romantic tendencies that do not
exist, it is almost impossible to overstate the effect of the change of
environment in these particulars. Farquhar brings much of
London manners into the country, in the train of his captains and
beaux. But he finds so much there that is new and fresh that
comedy of manners is completely sunk into a new something that,
by contrast, might well be called comedy of life. The stimulus it
furnishes his invention and spirits is astonishing; and the more so
when we reflect that this piece of good luck came to the English
stage through the happy accident of his recruiting visit to
Shropshire. Without this I believe he would have written no
more, or at best a bad comedy or two in his early manner.

For another thing we must give Farquhar credit at the outset. I
believe he felt as keenly as Steele or Cibber the impossible and
revolting state of court life and city morals, though, having no
liking for comédie larmoyante, he was less hopeful of a comedy
emancipated from them. He did, however, strongly resent the
evil tendency that his older contemporaries gleefully exploited.
To my mind, the lowest, though one of the cleverest comedies of

the age, is Vanbrugh's *Confederacy*. It shows the morals of the time at their worst, for here the fashionable vices have grown common, descended from the beaux and belles of the court to be the property of flunkeys and tradesmen's wives. In other words fashionable vice is vulgarized; but what is worse, it reveals corruption where virtue ought to persist. Farquhar satirizes this tendency again and again. In *The Beaux' Stratagem* Archer, the pretended valet, affects the spleen, which, 'like all other fashions wears out and descends to their (gentlefolk's) servants'. Farquhar alludes to 'the nice morality of the footmen' in the prologue to *Sir Harry Wildair* and again in the *Discourse*. The last two plays strike off sparks of satire now and again, sometimes hinting that the bitterness of poverty has won into the sweetness of Farquhar's temper, but oftener revealing a growing habit of thoughtfulness regarding manners and institutions. So here again, though much of the air of comedy of manners is preserved, we find the moral tone perceptibly altered.

The Recruiting Officer has its backbone in the recruiting scenes. If the play had no other merits it should live for these scenes alone, which opened a new field of legitimate comedy of the sprightliest kind. The two volunteers, Appletree and Pearmain, are notable creations, true to their kind, 'apprehensive, sturdy, brave blockheads'; in fact, the country characters of the play, Rose, Bullock, the justices, the butcher, and the smith, are a gallery of worthies hard to match, free from the traits of caricature that invariably accompanied the rustic in comedy. Justice Balance, in particular, is a fine, full-blooded picture of the country gentleman, anticipating the best work of Addison and Steele. The major characters, as more complex, are harder to deal with. Kite, a delightful relief from the clever valet of comedy of manners, is one of the most resourceful rascals in the English drama. He combines the shrewdness and wit of a confidential servant with the bluntness and authority of a petty officer, and is throughout faithful to his military character. He is the center of most of the striking passages of the play – the recruiting, astrologer, and court scenes – in each of which he surprises us afresh with his ingenious and spontaneous devices. Perhaps the part is somewhat overloaded; and it must be admitted that occasionally his cleverness is overdone. The same fault may be found with Lucy, Melinda's maid. Her stealing Melinda's signature to deceive Captain Brazen is an instance of over-elaboration that hurts the plausibility of the play.

The character of Captain Plume shows the undefined nature of the comedy in Farquhar's own mind. Plume is a rake and no rake. He is introduced to us at the outset as a Don Juan among bar-maids: witness Molly of the Castle and Kite's array of other wives. Yet he assures Silvia (Mr. Easy), in a tone of unquestionable sincerity, that he is not the rake the world believes him. He will 'give up a woman for a man at any time', and he does so in the case of Rose. At one moment he tells Worthy of his attempts to make Silvia his mistress: at the next he is furious at the gossips of the town for suspecting that he may have been successful. In short, he has not the petty virtue of consistency; but he has in abundance that quality of goodness of nature that Fielding so lovingly dwells upon. Altogether he is a likeable hero, brave, generous, and jovial, and not too profligate for redemption. He has magnetism for man and maid, gentleman and bumpkin, and is more nearly our notion of Farquhar himself than any other character of his creation. It is the very unsettled state of Plume's morals that gives the play at once its racy brightness and its ultimate wholesomeness.

Silvia, though a child of nature in the honesty of her love and her freedom from city affectation, is nothing of the coquettish ingenue which the comedy of the time invariably made the country girl. Her unflagging devotion to Plume, and his frank admiration of her sterling qualities, which he declares manly rather than womanish, give the play its firmest moral ground. Though her disguise takes her a step farther than masquerading heroines usually go, resulting in complications that are unfortunately free and suggestive, she remains the most healthful young woman of spirit in all the comedy of that period. Melinda is a vaporish creature, owing to her sudden accession of wealth, and an excellent foil to Silvia; but again, beneath all her caprice, there is an honest love, which asserts itself at the proper moment. For sheer originality of conception and faultless execution, Brazen is undoubtedly the cleverest creation in the play. To derive him from Vanbrugh's Captain Bluff and Congreve's Tattle is distinctly unjust unless we are to identify all foolish captains with one another. His refreshing audacity, mendacity, and self-conceit, his wonderfully inventive memory, above all his brisk sanguiness of success in his amours, make him the most engaging of rattle-pates. The supposed similarity to Bluff rests, I believe, in the employment of the common old masking trick to cheat him into marriage.

The characters in *The Beaux' Stratagem*, though not more vivid and original, are more finished than those of *The Recruiting Officer*. The minor persons are invested with a distinction almost Shakespearean. Boniface is become the accepted type of English innkeeper, and his name is a part of our everyday language. Of Scrub, the factotum, it is sufficient to say that it was a favorite part with Garrick, who frequently exchanged for it the more important rôle of Archer. Cherry, the pert bar-maid, was voted adorable by eighteenth-century audiences. In Lady Bountiful, the medicine-dispensing old country lady, Farquhar has exalted a humour into a character. Her matter-of-fact common sense completely redeems her from the conventional. The unconscious humour of her diagnosis of Aimwell's malady furnishes one of the richest bits of Farquhar's comedy. 'Wind, nothing but wind!' she interjects, after each grandiose flight of his description of the symptoms of love. Sullen, the impossible country husband, is the middle-step between Jerry Blackacre and Tony Lumpkin, while Gibbet, Foigard, and Gipsey all have more than a touch of individuality. In Dorinda, Farquhar has given us something better than the lay figures of his earlier plays; she is genuine and charming. While Mrs. Sullen, albeit somewhat oversensuous, is probably his best drawn and most highly-colored heroine. Aimwell is an admirable lover : his confession of the cheat in the moment of victory is a capital stroke, and saves him the true gentleman.

But Archer is Farquhar's most masterly creation. Some one has well said that in Mercutio Shakespeare anticipated all the wit and gaiety of the seventeenth-century cavalier. In Archer Farquhar has perfectly drawn the same cavalier of a later generation, when devotion had given place to pleasure-loving egoism, wit grown hard and brilliant, and poetry vanished to make way for showy prose. In place of Mercutio's free-flowing poetic fancy, we have the art of compliment in high-sounding rhetorical outburst, an echo of the heroic play at the only point where that type of drama really touched court-life. We find all the dashing adventuresomeness of the seventeenth-century rake combined with the circumspect worldliness of his eighteenth-century successor. 'Look ye, madam, I'm none of your romantick fools that fight giants and monsters for nothing; my valour is downright Swiss; I'm a soldier of fortune, and must be paid.' And so fixed is his determination to get what he wants, that the modern reader is fairly aghast at the lengths of realism to which he leads his author. Thwarted in his design upon Mrs. Sullen, he fights and captures the house-breakers – then coolly asks her for her garter to bind the rogues! 'The devil's in this fellow', she ejaculates. 'He fights, loves, and banters, all in a breath!' And so it is: courage, sensuality, and wit are his leading qualities, and one is perpetually crowding another out of the fore. When he engages in a project, it is to the bitter end. Had he been in Aimwell's position, no such lover-like compunction would have caused him to reveal the 'stratagem' that was to gain a wife for one and funds for both. 'I can't stop,' says Aimwell, before matters were critical, 'for I love her to distraction.' ' 'Sdeath', Archer retorts, 'if you love her a hair's-breadth beyond discretion, you must go no farther.' So much for love leading to matrimony; but in the pursuit of an illicit amour, Archer's intensity knows no bounds. It is a pity that the best-rounded comedy since Fletcher should be hurt by finding its climax in a scene too salacious for modern representation; and especially since that scene is so logically the outgrowth of the plot and characters that to excise or change it is to kill the play. But it is indeed so. Archer is true to himself in this scene; fortunately, in a better sense of the phrase, Mrs. Sullen is also true to herself. But this scarcely mends the matter, for Farquhar has gone as far as he could and much further than he should.

This brings the question of morals once more to the front. I have said that Farquhar wrote his last plays more or less in the same light mood of comedy of manners that characterized his early work. This means that he wrote them merely to entertain, and if the result, morally, is better than in his earlier plays, it is because the changing taste of the times and the growth of his own character have made themselves felt. Of serious moral or satirical purpose there is (I am tempted to say 'fortunately' when I think of *The Twin Rivals*) not a trace. Of satire there is abundance, and of excellent quality, but it comes in occasional flashes and strikes at all sorts of things—the dishonesty of constables, the confederacy between innkeepers and highwaymen, the pensioning of army officers' illegitimate offspring, and ever and again the heartlessness of fashionable society. On the whole, the tone of *The Recruiting Officer* is anything but vicious; careless it certainly is. *The Beaux' Stratagem* is freer from indecency, but is, as we have observed, deplorably voluptuous in one vital scene. On the other hand, to find fault with the close of the play as seriously countenancing divorce by mutual consent is really basing grave conclusions upon very trifling grounds. Farquhar was thinking only of the case before him—of a beautiful, clever woman mismated with a sottish and surly clown—and he certainly presents a sound argument for that particular case. He was not addicted to the envisagement of broad social questions or to attacking legal institutions; accordingly criticism has no business to generalize this case and praise or blame him for his views. It is a mistake to judge so light-hearted an author on so serious grounds. It is equally wrong to blame Farquhar for the little grief shown by Balance, Silvia, and Aimwell, for the death of their near relations. A near relation, in the comedy of that age, was a mere conventional barrier between a hero or heroine and a fortune. The removal of that barrier was no occasion for tears and hysterics, and to introduce them would have been far worse than the apparent indifference shown. This sort of criticism, and it is very common, really deserves no answer, but if answer must be made I would point to the scene in the last act of *The Constant Couple* in which young Clincher tells of his brother's death. Here Farquhar himself pays his respects to a convention that was none of his making.

That 'manners' remain an important ingredient in these plays is apparent from both the dialogue and the characters. Wit is still a strong factor—as it must be in all comedy: and Farquhar is not entirely above sacrificing even his characters at the altar of the seventeenth-century goddess. Thus Kite and Lucy, to say nothing of those to the manner born, are much too clever. Sullen spars with his wife in the last act with the finished ease of a

habitué of Covent Garden. Scrub goes so far out of his own
character as to quote Latin. The dialogues between Archer and
Aimwell, as well as the picture scene, are unduly protracted to
permit the exchange of clever broadsides. In the case of Love's
Catechism, by having Cherry speak her part by rote Farquhar
escapes sacrificing the character; a clever device but one that
could not be used again. However, in general Farquhar makes
his persons speak in character and the well contrived plots are
allowed to work themselves out without delays.

Again, as regards plot, these two plays, by the care and skill
employed in their construction, depart radically from the loose
habits of comedy of manners. Internally they are totally unlike.
The Recruiting Officer has the more elaborate and intricate plot,
crowded with incident and striking situations, and with business
enough for several comedies. That of *The Beaux' Stratagem*, while
simpler and more open, loses nothing, by contrast, in point of
strength and effectiveness. The impressive fact in this connection
is that however Farquhar may yield to tradition, he never goes so
far as to allow dialogue to destroy our interest in the developing
action. It is this that enables him to produce an admirably
balanced and truly natural comedy.

Accordingly, we may well say that, despite the impress that
comedy of manners left upon all his work, Farquhar has in these
plays left that form of art far behind him. Exalting both plot and
character above dialogue, and humour of situation above wit,
escaping largely the conventional and typical of manners and
humours, he gave the world two comedies of unsurpassed
freshness, deriving their interest from no passing fashion of the
day but from their deep-grounded perception of human nature,
their liveliness from the ingenious invention of a really creative
imagination, and their charm from the playfulness of a buoyant,
happy spirit at large in a new, untrodden field. Farquhar is at
heart neither Cavalier nor Puritan, neither rake nor ascetic. He
entered joyously into the game the former were playing without
insight into its meaning or care as to its consequences. Troubled
by the obviously just reproaches of the latter, he reacted upon this
stimulus with little appreciation of its value. He was neither
Cavalier nor Puritan, but a happy-go-lucky Celt who entered the
world of warring conventions without prejudice as to forms of

discipline, but with a mighty propensity for free living and the enjoyment of life. That is why he, of all the dramatists, could for a brief space bring comedy into the mood of a joyous representation of life, unhampered by the chronic English pretensions to moralism or satire. He could not reform comedy, for in him there was nothing of the reformer; but by giving his healthy nature free play he allowed comedy to re-form itself, rid of its tyrant, humours, and its mistress, manners, true to the larger life of the English people for the first time in a century. Emulating the playful buoyancy of Farquhar's spirits and preserving his balance of the comic elements, two other light-hearted Irishmen, Goldsmith and Sheridan, gave us all we have of distinguished excellence in later English comedy to 1880.

SOURCE: *A Discourse upon Comedy*: *'The Recruiting Officer'* and *'The Beaux' Stratagem'* (Boston, 1914) pp. *xiii–xiv, xlv–lvi.*

NOTE

1. [David Schmid, *George Farquhar, Sein Leben und Seine Original-Dramen* (1904) – Ed.]

Bonamy Dobrée (1924)

So long as men write in a certain form (inside sufficiently large limits) and with a similar artistic purpose, it is possible to measure them against one another, or to compare them with some fixed standard. Thus Vanbrugh may justifiably be measured against Congreve. But when comedy comes to be written with a totally different intent, from, as far as can be judged, a quite different impulse, the comparison is invidious. We do not try to compare a hollyhock with a tulip, and it is just as absurd to compare the work of George Farquhar with the bulk of Restoration comedy. It is true that in his earlier plays Farquhar accepted Restoration themes and the Restoration manner, but in his last two, and even in *The Twin Rivals*, he broke away from them. Certainly to the end he worked the same line as Vanbrugh, but it is that line most removed from Etherege or Congreve, namely that of the domestic drama. For the rest, he went back to Shakespearian times. We may say that at the beginning of the eighteenth century comedy split into two courses, on the one hand to the sentimental comedy of Cibber and Steele; on the other, back to the Elizabethans with Vanbrugh and Farquhar.

Farquhar, it is true, commented upon manners, but such criticism was only a side issue with him. He was more intent upon lively action and the telling of a roguish tale. It is all fun and frolic with him, a question of disguises and counterfeits, the gaining of fortunes, and even of burglarious entries. 'He lies even further from literature than Vanbrugh', says Mr. Gosse, 'but he has a greater knowledge of life'. And if his intellect was rather humdrum, he had flashes of insight. Leigh Hunt said of him that 'he felt the little world too much, and the universal too little . . . his genius was entirely social'. But this criticism will only hold if he is regarded as Congreve's successor, rather than as an original who projected his disappointments in life – or 'expectorated his grief', to use a phrase from his single ode – on to the stage in the form of light-hearted comedy. In his dramatic world very little is impossible; it is full of Rabelaisian gaiety touched with a satire that is as light as a feather.

A reference has been made to his disappointments, which were these: he failed to realize a competence, and was never accepted among the gentlemen and wits. All his plays contain at least one person who needed at all costs to marry money, and his heroes were more fortunate than he was. The bride who was to have brought him seven hundred pounds a year, proved to be penniless.

Like a true writer of critical comedy he pricked the bubble of pretensions, and did so by thrusting at the wits who would not make him one of them. There are continual strokes at the pretenders to and usurpers of the title of gentleman, or at the false standards by which others recognize them.

When Clincher in *The Constant Couple* is charged with murder and robbery, the constable cries out, 'Murder and robbery! then he must be a gentleman'. But the best touch of all is, 'The gentleman, indeed, behaved himself like a gentleman; for he drew his sword and swore, and afterwards laid it down and said nothing.' There are many hits in the same vein.

The most surprising thing about him is his extreme modernity: many passages might have been written yesterday. He was two hundred years ahead of his time, in the Butler – Shaw tradition when he wrote, 'The patient's faith goes farther toward the miracle than your prescription'; or ''Tis still my maxim, that there is no scandal like rags, nor any crime so shameful as poverty'. On one of the very few occasions when he is at all heavy, he urges that to pay one's tradesmen's bills is more honourable than to pay one's 'debts of honour' incurred at the gaming table. But honour is a prerogative of the wealthy; 'Lack-a-day, sir, it shows as ridiculous and haughty for us to imitate our betters in their honour as in their finery; leave honour to the nobility that can support it.' But what must appeal to us with peculiar force at the present day are the arguments circling around the question of how much licence soldiers may be allowed at home in return for risking their lives abroad in defence of their countrymen:

COLONEL STANDARD   Had not these brave fellows' swords defended you, your house had been a bonfire ere this about your ears. Did we not venture our lives, sir?
ALDERMAN SMUGGLER   Did we not pay you for your lives, sir? Venture your lives! I'm sure we ventured our money.

Are not we too, bitterly familiar with the subject of 'war sacrifices'? Or again, there is the scene between Justice Scale and Justice Balance, of which the context is self-evident:

SCALE   I say, 'tis not to be borne, Mr. Balance.
BAL.   Look 'ee, Mr. Scale, for my own part, I shall be very tender in what regards the officers of the army, they expose their lives to so many dangers for us abroad, that we may give them some grain of allowance at home.
SCALE   Allowance! This poor girl's father is my tenant; and if I mistake her not, her mother nursed a child for you. Shall they debauch our daughters to our faces?

BAL.   Consider, Mr. Scale, that were it not for the bravery of these officers, we should have French dragoons among us, and that would leave us neither liberty, property, wife or daughters.

How often in recent times did a similar controversy ring in our ears!

The divergence from his predecessors that has received most attention from commentators, is in the matter of love. Mr. Palmer decides that he finally ruined the Restoration tradition by carrying still further than Vanbrugh the 'luscious' treatment of sex. Mr. William Archer, relating the change to modern sentiment in the matter rather than to the earlier, finds Farquhar's cleaner and more rational. His point was that the marriage of bodies, whose joys he would be the last to consider non-important, did involve also a marriage of minds. 'You and your wife, Mr. Guts', Sir Charles Freeman says to Boniface, 'may be one flesh, because ye are nothing else; but rational creatures have minds that must be united', and the end of the play, *The Beaux' Stratagem*, turns upon the separation of the Sullens for incompatibility of temper. Farquhar may have been a gay rogue, but he had common sense, and a tie involving a cat and dog existence such as that led by the Sullens – his rather less literary version of Sir John and Lady Brute – had nothing sacred for him. Separation was certainly better than the brazen cuckoldry practised by the gallants, and used as material by the comic writers of the previous century. The reason, of course, is that social conditions had changed; the assumption that passion and social exigencies could be squared had broken down.

In truth, Farquhar was an advanced rationalist, and this trait comes out again and again in little, subtle touches. He was not to be paid in abstract ideas, or with conventional lies. He realized, for instance, that 'with the estate to back the suit, you'll find the law too strong for justice'. And in this last play there is a touch as good as it can be. Archer has captured the thief Gibbet, and threatens to shoot him rather than send him for hanging:

ARCHER   Come rogue, if you have a short prayer, say it.
GIBBET   Sir, I have no prayer at all; the government has provided a chaplain to say prayers for us on these occasions.

One would not be surprised to find the remark in a page of Voltaire, and indeed Farquhar was always something of a pre-Voltairean Voltairean, for when at Trinity Dublin he was told to comment upon the episode of Christ walking upon the water, he did so by an allusion to those born to be hanged.

His real divergence, however, consists, as has been hinted, in a return to the Elizabethans. After *The Twin Rivals*, at the period when he saw, and said, that comedy had become but 'an agreeable vehicle for counsel and reproof', he sought for something different. There are passages where one might be reading, if not Shakespeare – although his recruiting court is not far removed from that of Falstaff, and 'profound master Shallow' – at least Massinger or Marlowe in his burlesque moments. He scarcely touches on the humours of Jonson, his Boniface and his Mrs. Mandrake have too much diversity of character. This is not, of course, to belittle Jonson, his is a different and more universal method. Yet listening to Sergeant Kite we might well be hearing some actor of a hundred years before:

Yes, sir, I understand my business, I will say it – You must know, sir, I was born a gipsy, and bred among that crew till I was ten year old. There I learned canting and lying. I was bought from my mother, Cleopatra, by a certain nobleman for three pistoles; who, liking my beauty, made me his page; there I learned impudence and pimping. I was turned off for wearing my lord's linen, and drinking my lady's ratafia, and then turned bailiff's follower : there I learned bullying and swearing. I at last got into the army, and there I learned whoring and drinking : so that if your worship pleases to cast up the whole sum, viz. canting, lying, impudence, pimping, bullying, swearing, whoring, drinking, and a halberd, you will find the sum total will amount to a recruiting serjeant.

He has an atmosphere of exaggeration that is indeed akin to that of Jonson, but it is of another kind. He is influenced, but he is not imitative. We sometimes feel Bobadill, or Parolles, or Wilson's astrologer, but he is always original except in his failures to adapt Restoration treatment. We may take the passage where an old woman has come to Lady Bountiful for medicine for her husband, but is intercepted by Mrs. Sullen, who impersonates

her mother-in-law. It begins in the Restoration manner, but flies
off to the heights of a robust tomfoolery:

WOMAN   I come, an't please your ladyship – you're my Lady
Bountiful, an't ye?
MRS. S.   Well, good woman, go on.
WOMAN   I come seventeen long mail to have a cure for my
husband's sore leg.
MRS. S.   Your husband! what, woman, cure your husband!
WOMAN   Ay, poor man, for his sore leg won't let him stir from
home.
MRS. S.   There, I confess, you have given me a reason. Well,
good woman, I'll tell you what you must do. You must lay your
husband's leg upon a table, and with a chopping knife you must
lay it open as broad as you can; then you must take out the bone,
and beat the flesh soundly with a rolling pin; then take salt,
pepper, cloves, mace, and ginger, some sweet herbs, and season it
very well; then roll it up like brawn, and put it into the oven for
two hours.

This is the real spirit of Farquhar, a huge gust of laughter. Life
was a discoloured and painful thing to him, and the only remedy
was to treat it as a game, not the delicate intellectual game of
Etherege, but a good Elizabethan romp. He is like his own Mrs.
Sullen, who 'can be merry with the misfortunes of other people
because her own make her sad', but he can laugh at himself as
well. Even on his death-bed, where he wrote his last play, this
fierce determination to defeat life, to rise superior to its
restrictions and find an unconditioned freedom, manifested itself
in bursts of boisterous laughter. Pope said that he wrote farce,
and if we accept Dryden's definition that 'Farce entertains us
with what is monstrous and chimerical', this is to some extent
true. But he had a most amazing dexterity of touch. He is
continually surprising us into laughter with a sudden turn of
expression, as when Lurewell in *Sir Henry Wildair* says:

Look ye, girl, we women of quality have each of us some darling
fright – I, now, hate a mouse; my Lady Lovecards abhors a cat; Mrs.

Fiddlefan can't bear a squirrel; the Countess of Piquet abominates a frog; and my Lady Swimair hates a man.

What irresistible 'go'!

This real Farquhar does not laugh the satiric laugh of the social creature, but the laugh of the child at the unaccountability of things, a laugh that had he lived might have developed into something very deep. His freedom is visible not only in his plots and scenes, but also in his verbal play. This shows itself, not as antithetical wit, but in puns. Here, for instance, we have the meeting between two recruiting officers:

BRAZEN   Have you any pretensions, sir?
PLUME   Pretensions!
BRAZEN   That is, sir, have you ever served abroad?
PLUME   I have served at home, sir, for ages served this cruel fair — and that will serve the turn, sir.

Or we have a passage where Silvia, disguised as a man, exhibits both the Elizabethan exuberance and the verbal play:

BALANCE   Pray, sir, what commission may you bear?
SILVIA   I'm called captain, sir, by all the coffeemen, drawers, whores, and groom porters in London; for I wear a red coat, a sword, a hat *bien troussé*, a martial twist in my cravat, a cane upon my button, piquet in my head, and dice in my pocket.
SCALE   Your name, pray, sir?
SILVIA   Captain Pinch: I cock my hat with a pinch, I take snuff with a pinch, pay my whores with a pinch. In short, I can do anything at a pinch, but fight and fill my belly.

'He makes us laugh from pleasure oftener than from malice', Hazlitt wrote. 'There is a constant ebullition of gay, laughing invention, cordial good-humour, and fine animal spirits in his writings.' It is for that we should go to Farquhar. If we search for a poet, for a profound critic of life, for a close thinker of the Restoration type, or for a finished artist, we shall not find him. To approach him for a torrent of semi-nonsensical amusement, mingled with that clear logic which also is the Irishman's heritage, and to ask no more, is to obtain a refreshing release from the conditioned social universe in which we are forced to live. . . .

SOURCE: *Restoration Comedy, 1660–1720* (Oxford, 1924) pp. 161–9.

PART TWO

Modern Studies

Vincent F. Hopper and Gerald B. Lahey

CHARACTER-DIFFERENTIATION AND 'PROBLEM-PLAY' FEATURES IN *THE BEAUX' STRATAGEM* (1963)

. . . Farquhar's wit has affinities with both that of Wilde and Shaw, yet it is basically different. Shaw's is the rational, intellectual wit exploring the pathology of the social tissue. Wilde's is the mental costume of the dandy, the finely tailored epigram. Farquhar's wit is more varied and ample but less precisely aimed or formulated. It is the wit of the alert, ironic, yet wondering observer contemplating with inner amazement the absurdity of things, yet without any formula for renovation or any posture of cynical detachment.

The Beaux' Stratagem as a comedy of wit and sex intrigue presents Aimwell, younger and impecunious brother of a Lord, and Archer, his resourceful and needy companion. Their alternating role of man and servant, both in search of a beautiful heiress, is a plot sufficiently appealing that Mr. P. G. Wodehouse reissued it in his novel *French Leave*, in which masquerading ladies are substituted for men in pursuit of romance and fortune. In Farquhar's plot, at the outset both are philanderers and amorists, adventurers and fortune-hunters descending upon the provinces in search of their pleasing heiress. They are men of fashion, given to love and drink, formerly of some affluence but now of exhausted fortune. With regret and half-bemused nostalgia, they recollect vanished happiness.

The complications attendant upon their quest introduce a growing differentiation in character. Although in Archer the Restoration beau is preserved for the most part, Aimwell undergoes a romantic and edifying change of heart. Conscience transforms the predatory rake of Restoration tradition into the sentimental hero of the New or Sentimental comedy: a man suddenly given to virtuous idealism born of the unexpected influence of virtuous female beauty. Hence we have preserved in Archer the older tradition of satire and realism; in Aimwell we look forward to the Sentimental comedy of edification and propriety, discreetly attended by substantial financial success.

In characterization Archer and Aimwell are like two rivulets which, beginning from the same hill-top, diverge increasingly as they move along their forward journey. Both begin as philandering, fortune-hunting adventurers. Unlike Archer, Aimwell is transformed by female beauty of character as well as person. He undergoes a radical moral conversion and shifts to the side of the angels. Farquhar, stretching to the limit his desire for diversity, thus combines in one comedy those elements kept separate by his Restoration predecessors: sex and marriage, love and loyalty, amorous delight and domesticity. This divergence of Aimwell from Archer is suitably expressed at the end of the comedy in a rather Shavian predicament. Aimwell, still under his original obligation to Archer to divide any booty resulting from their expedition, presents the latter with a dramatic choice between Dorinda (the fair lady) and the fair lady's fortune. The offer is not belittling to Dorinda since the now regenerated Aimwell knows that the old unrepentant sinner Archer will take the cash and let the moral credit go.

Then in the almost inevitable manner of what eventually came to be the New or Sentimental comedy, Aimwell's brother dies. He has been living offstage in apparently flourishing health but evidently with an exquisite sense of time and occasion. By means of his sudden death, Farquhar promptly subsidizes morality with the title and fortune to which the hitherto unredeemed Aimwell had been merely the idle pretender. The union of material reward and moral endeavor was already present. The cash-nexus between honor and its consequences was eventually to taint with suspicion the morality of the Sentimental comedy. From the start, however, the heirs to the kingdom of heaven approached their reward in a coach and six. The equivocal nature of this spirit of reform in the Sentimental hero is evident not merely in the grandiose rhetoric of regeneration but likewise in subsequent reflections upon it.

Aimwell's sudden moral rebirth is presented in his reflections upon the virtuous nature of the beautiful lady he is about to

deceive: 'Such goodness who cou'd injure; I find myself unequal
to the task of Villain; she has gain'd my Soul, and made it honest
like her own . . . judge of my Passion by my Conversion.' Only
slightly later he confides to Archer: ' . . . methought she receiv'd
my Confession with Pleasure'.[1] Noble sentiment is promptly
blessed by the god of expedience. Presently, Dorinda enters – in
obedience to stage directions 'mighty gay'. And rightly so. For
she brings news of Aimwell's succession to title and fortune to
which she adds her own readiness to forgive and enjoy. Not only
does good fortune ensue readily upon Aimwell's apparent
renunciation of base impulse, but he has in a way obscurely
anticipated the practical benefit of higher ones.

Aimwell's change from predatory rake to man of moral
probity and high feeling is underlined in that his spiritual rebirth
takes place at a crucial moment in the rake's progress. He is
simultaneously implicated in two of the standard devices of
seduction resorted to by Restoration stage-rakes on the make for
money: 1) the 'clandestine' and 2) the 'tricked' marriage.

As to the first, Aimwell plans to marry Dorinda outside of
canonical hours. Foigard is to officiate although he is not a priest
of the Anglican succession nor an authorized representative of
the Church. Secondly, Aimwell has falsely presented himself in
name, title, and fortune. Hence his sudden renunciation of his
lower self marks the rejection of a well-defined practice of the
Restoration rake. Despite this sudden display of exquisite feeling,
Aimwell is curiously insensitive to the loss of a brother, whose
name and memory he had so nearly betrayed. His dry crust of
repentance and severely controlled brotherly sorrow are transformed easily into the manna of jubilation. He might have been
perfectly at home in *The Importance of Being Earnest*, except for the
gravely limiting factor that he *was* in earnest.

Aimwell thus stands near the beginning of what is to be the
grand succession of the Sentimental hero as he appears first in
stage and eventually in fictional tradition. The shadows of Tom
Jones, Charles Surface, Young Marlowe, etc. are already cast
upon the screen of the future. All are typical of those dashing
young rips of easy morals whose tarnished souls are miraculously
brightened and made radiant by contact with exquisite female
goodness enshrined in beauty of person – yet not without a

favorable cash balance. The kind of love relationship in which this tradition ultimately culminated is expressed with subtly humorous grace by Lord David Cecil: ' . . . a tender sentiment for a virtuous object, founded largely on esteem, precious for its power to elevate life and sweeten character but always under the ultimate control of reason and virtue.' It is perhaps significant that Farquhar has Dorinda fall in love with Aimwell at Church service.

Archer as a representative of the older comic tradition of satire and realism is quite otherwise. In Farquhar's first play *Love and a Bottle*, a hero of comedy is described as being among other things: 'A Compound of practical Rake, and speculative Gentleman, who always bears off the great Fortune in the Play.' It suits Archer. As amorist and fortune-seeker, Archer has a touch of the picaresque rogue as well as that of the Restoration rake. Like the latter he pursues the pleasures of drink, play, and love. But like the rogue, he is the resourceful and witty rascal who is totally indifferent to the well-being of others when his own interests are at stake. He warns perpetually against committing matrimony without benefit of a substantial dowry. He is also a man of quixotic pride, rejecting the pert and winsome Cherry not only because of her insufficient dowry but because she is a servant. Crossing moral boundaries does not trouble him, but class lines are sacred. Besides acquiring money, his one ambition is to treat all attractive females as Alexander Pope accused Mrs. Aphra Behn of doing with her stage characters. Referring to her as Astrea, Pope wrote:

> The stage how loosely does Astrea tread
> Who fairly puts all characters to bed.

For all of that, Archer is more than a thoughtless irresponsible child of laughter and delight. He is a philosophical and rational rake:

Give me a man that keeps his five senses keen and bright as his sword; . . . detaches 'em by turns upon whatever party of pleasure agreeably offers . . . I can stick to my bottle while my wine, my company, and my reason, holds good; I can be charmed with Sappho's singing without falling in love with her face . . . I love a fine house, but let another keep it; and just so I love a fine woman.

Archer's statement might stand as the obituary of the Restoration rake who retired before the chilling blasts of Jeremy Collier in 1698. By 1707 the moral climate had so altered that Archer's manifesto is almost 'reactionary'. Indeed, the icy touch of Collier is not absent from Archer's career. Despite his reckless pursuit of Cherry and Mrs. Sullen, he remains at the final curtain desirous of both but having enjoyed neither. Indeed, Archer's most human, if not his most edifying or most characteristic expression, is his cry: 'Rot the money; I've lost my wench.'

Yet it was money that Archer sought primarily, despite moments of transient weakness. Farquhar's immediate predecessor Vanbrugh wrote for one of his characters a line often quoted as both symptomatic and prophetic of the change in the *ethos* of the Restoration hero and stage: '. . .to be capable of loving one, doubtless is better than to possess a Thousand'. Archer doubtless felt that it was much preferable to possess a Thousand, provided they be pounds, and thereby be free to love many.

In character he is a mixture of Shakespeare's Mercutio and Shaw's Captain Bluntschli of *Arms and the Man*. Like Mercutio, he thinks of love as a game and a sport, not to be taken seriously. Hence Archer keeps alive the light-hearted, frivolous attitude toward love of the older stage tradition, the tradition that went underground during the Sentimental period to reappear so brilliantly in *The Importance of Being Earnest*. The somewhat artificially introduced 'catechism of love' by Archer and Cherry preserves this spirit. In his encounter with Cherry as with Mrs. Sullen, Archer's wit and high-spirited gaiety are in contrast with the fulsome rhetoric of the sober-hearted lover, the sentimental-sublime that characterizes so many of the exchanges between Dorinda and Aimwell.

Like Captain Bluntschli, but without his Olympian competence, Archer possesses a whimsically realistic and anti-romantic wit. In the bedroom scene, having been the valiant protector of Mrs. Sullen's virtue, Archer turns arch-seducer and demands favors for services rendered. To considerations of gallantry and chivalry placed before him as an impediment, he retorts: 'Look 'ye, Madam, I'm none of your Romantick Fools, that fight Gyants and Monsters for nothing; my Valour is down right Swiss; I'm a Soldier of Fortune and must be paid.' We might be listening to a Restoration Chocolate Soldier chiding his Raina for offering only chocolates.

Dorinda and Mrs. Sullen, the female opposites to Aimwell and Archer, are like their male counterparts a contrast: the idealistic and edifying set off against the realistic and sardonic. But with this difference. Mrs. Sullen more than any of the other characters in the play is an individualized, complex human being who cannot be easily labelled.

Mrs. Sullen is a sophisticated lady of fashion and pleasure transplanted from London to a provincial town. Her pointed and invidious comparisons do not allow us to forget the social distance she has travelled. Dorinda of the four is the only representative of the country gentry. Besides being a 'feeder' of lines to Mrs. Sullen, allowing the latter to voice her marital distress and desolation, Dorinda is an attractively fresh and convincing character in her own right. Although idealized, she is not merely the virtuously self-conscious, demurely proper, moralizing heroine who reclaims wild and wayward young men for the more tame satisfactions of domestic society. There is much in her lively spirit that is a foreshadowing of Goldsmith's Kate Hardcastle.

When we first see Dorinda, she is uneasy about Mrs. Sullen's possibly straying into intimacy with visiting male charmers. But after falling in love herself with Aimwell, Dorinda acknowledges an increased susceptibility to the elemental attraction of sex. She does not hesitate to say that she no longer finds it unnatural to actively contemplate man as a bedfellow: ' . . . while the Mind is conversant with Flesh and Blood, it must conform to the Humours of the Company', she puts it whimsically. The remark elicits from Mrs. Sullen one of her most human comments: 'How a little Love and good Company improves a Woman.' Far from being merely a frigid advocate of the sobering qualities of chaste love, Dorinda is quite susceptible to a little lush flattery: 'My Lord has told me that I have more Wit and Beauty than any of my Sex; and truly I begin to think the Man is sincere.' Perhaps the most sprightly expression of Dorinda's charm and animation

is her rapturous vision of the anticipated delights of marriage:
' . . . the Park, the Play, and the drawing-Room, Splendour,
Equipage, Noise and Flambeaux — Hey — my Lady Aimwell's
Servants there — Lights, Lights to the Stairs — My Lady
Aimwell's Coach put forward — Stand by, make room for her
Ladyship — ' The country girl's dream of the Town.

If Farquhar's portrait of Dorinda is that of a delightful young
lady brought painlessly to the threshold of felicity, his characterization of Mrs. Sullen is less simple. Obviously we are
conscious of her at first as the wife of Squire Sullen. As such, Mrs.
Sullen's mode of existence is variously described in metaphors
ranging from war to animal husbandry. She tells Count Bellair
that she is a 'Prisoner of War' and in the best battle-of-the-sexes
tradition comments that in marriage 'a Woman must wear
chains'. Mrs. Sullen dejectedly asks of Dorinda: 'And must the
fair Apartment of my Breast be made a Stable for a Brute to lie
in?'

The quality of the 'Brute', her husband the Squire, was
adequately expressed in another context when Mrs. Sullen was
contemplating the world of instinct and feeling in relation to the
rigidity of law: 'What Law can search into the remote Abyss of
Nature?' The phrase unwittingly descriptive of her husband is
'Abyss of Nature'. He has not even the redeeming trait of being
remote. The chasm of his deficiency, his yawning emptiness,
presents every impediment not merely to the marriage of true
minds but even of amiable mindlessness.

In herself Mrs. Sullen is a character of varying whims, moods,
sentiments, and urges. She is not the traditional female rake of
Restoration comedy to be found, for example, in *The Country Wife*
or *The Way of the World*. She tends that way by inclination, but
the impulsion is checked by scruple. In comparing her existence
to that of a prisoner of war, she adds that she is restrained likewise
from freedom of decision by 'Parole of Honour'. Nor is she the
ordinary, bored London-bred wife of a sottish country squire.
Her boredom gives rise at times to a distinctly prickly bitterness,
one at times sadistic enough to satisfy even Hedda Gabler. But
along with this bitterness, softening and humanizing it, is a
wistful quality, a languorous pessimism and melancholy that
arouse rather than alienate our sympathy. It is the interplay of

these qualities of mind that makes Mrs. Sullen hardly a comic character, for Farquhar is evidently too much in sympathy with her to preserve the detachment necessary for laughter.

Mrs. Sullen's sense of helplessness is complicated by a strain of irony. Early in the play, she says to Dorinda that she is ready to go to Church: 'Anywhere to Pray; for Heaven alone can help me . . . ' Quickly she spices her sadness with the astringent afterthought: 'But, I think, Dorinda, there's no Form of Prayer in the Liturgy against bad Husbands.' At the same moment, Mrs. Sullen, despite her own desolation of spirit can take a sympathetic view of Dorinda's inexperience in regard to love, saying: 'You like nothing, your time is not come; Love and Death have their Fatalities, and strike home one time or other.' It is a line that might have been spoken by the tragic Duchess of Malfi. At other times, her reflective melancholy modulates into a Keatsian pathos, something vaguely reminiscent of the gentle despair of the *Ode to a Nightingale*. After Dorinda's hour of romance has arrived and she is rapturously imagining the pleasures of married life with Aimwell, Mrs. Sullen exclaims: 'Happy, happy Sister! your Angel has been watchful for your Happiness, whilst mine has slept regardless of his Charge. – Long smiling Years of circling Joys for you, but not one Hour for me! (*Weeps*).'

Alternating with this moody discontent is a strain of bitterness, now wryly amusing, again almost Swiftian in its malevolence. All of the pleasures for which she married the Squire have been denied Mrs. Sullen. In their stead she is offered only 'Ditches . . . Stiles . . . drinking Fat Ale . . . smoaking To-bacco . . .' and soliciting the butler as dancing partner if he will condescend. After a day of oppressive boredom, Mrs. Sullen notes that '. . . my whole Night's Comfort is the tuneable Serenade of the wakeful Nightingale, his Nose. – O the Pleasure of counting the melancholy Clock by a snoring Husband!' But her bitterness is sharper, for instance, when she retorts upon her husband's invitation to acquire a lover provided she does not make him a cuckold: '. . . you would allow me the Sin but rob me of the Pleasure'. Her advice to the needy, forlorn woman whose husband has an ailing leg and who is applying to Lady Bountiful for aid and advice has a sadistic twist: '. . . lay your Husbands Leg upon a Table, and with a Choping-knife, you must lay it open as broad as you can; then you must take out the Bone, and beat the Flesh soundly with a rowling-pin . . . season it very well; then rowl it up like Brawn, and put it into the Oven for two Hours'.

It is this alternation of melancholy with gaiety, humor with bitterness, and pathos with wit that makes Mrs. Sullen too complicated a human being for laughter only. In still another way, she is a departure from the traditional Restoration female with an unsatisfying husband. Whereas in the plays of Wycherley and Congreve the dissatisfied wife had no hesitation in making a cuckold of her husband, Mrs. Sullen, a voluptuous but hesitating beauty, balances inclination and scruple. For all of her insinuating confidences and erotic innuendo, she remains the conventional wife in behavior, passionately yearning but prudently unyielding. In this conflict, she marks a break with the character of traditional comedy, in which adultery was simply another convention alternative with fidelity to the marriage vow. Mrs. Sullen's attitude is not so coolly simple and straightforward.

The difference makes her vulnerable to criticism as a satisfactory character. Instead of the tartly witty sex-comedy of cuckoldom, we now have a 'busom-heaving', tormented, sighing spirit, tempered with inconvenient but obstinate scruples. Gone is the easy, unhesitating, light love of the old Utopia of Restoration gallantry. Mrs. Sullen's attitude is passionate and lusciously languishing. She begins thinking Archer 'a very pretty Fellow', next decides, 'I like him', then proceeds to wish him 'in a Design upon my self'. To Archer's light-hearted flattery and artificial rhetoric, she responds not with witty repartee but with a longing sigh: 'Had it been my Lot to have match'd with such a Man!' She then drifts to the languishing stage: 'I do love that Fellow; – and if I met him . . . undrest . . . Look 'ye Sister . . . I can't swear I cou'd resist the Temptation . . .' Unable to dismiss this particular form of erotic yearning, Mrs. Sullen approaches the frontiers of swoondom when she is questioned by Dorinda. The latter casually asks her whether, if Archer were in her bedchamber, she might not capitulate. On a flood-tide of longing which submerges wit and imagination, Mrs. Sullen returns to her obsession: 'Here! what, in my Bed-chamber at two a Clock o'th' Morning, I undress'd, the Family asleep, my hated Husband abroad, and my lovely Fellow at my Feet – O gad, Sister!' This O-gad-Sister attitude inclines towards the sentimental, romantic adultery of enchantment, not the Restoration adultery of comic detachment.

As such, it might look better in the sober costume of serious domestic drama, unadorned with the cap and bells of jesting comedy. Notwithstanding, it is just this snarled, complicated gathering of human emotions that makes Mrs. Sullen, if not the ideal character of comedy, an ideal role for the actress. The part remains to this day the favorite of actresses and perhaps the principal role of the play.

The Play as 'Problem' Play

Although not listed under the *Dramatis Personae*, the shadowy presence of John Milton inhabits the world of *The Beaux' Stratagem*. Milton is the ghost-writer of parts of the more impressive dialogue denouncing the indissoluble marriage contract that binds antagonistic personalities in spiritual squalor. Farquhar has pieced out his dialogue with odds and ends stolen out of Milton's holy writ *The Doctrine and Discipline of Divorce*. The cathedral cadences of Milton's voice invade momentarily even the dense breast of Squire Sullen. He merely quotes Milton when he says of the plight of the incompatible couple, 'One Flesh! rather two Carcasses join'd unnaturally together.' In the same idiom Sir Charles Freeman preaches to Boniface on the difference between the union of mere 'Guts' and that union of 'rational Creatures' who 'have minds'.

When Mrs. Sullen sonorously declaims against an irrevocable marriage-bond, she at times almost quotes Milton's attack upon the social will to shackle the supple, shifting life of instinct by the rigid artifice of human law : 'Law! what Law can search into the remote Abyss of Nature? what Evidence can prove the unaccountable Disaffections of Wedlock? – Can a Jury sum up the endless Aversions that are rooted in our Souls . . . ?'

When Dorinda (to provide an opening for one of Milton's main preoccupations) suggests that the law 'meddles' only in cases of adultery or 'uncleanness', Mrs. Sullen again echoes Milton; 'Uncleanness! O Sister, casual Violation is a transient

Injury, and may possibly be repair'd, but can radical Hatreds, be ever reconcil'd? – No, no, Sister, Nature is the first Law-giver, and when she has set Tempers opposite, not all the golden Links of Wedlock, nor iron Manacles of Law can keep 'um fast.' Notwithstanding, in the course of the play, Mrs. Sullen (helped by Dorinda) is much busier avoiding 'casual Violation' even though only a 'transient Injury' than in meditating upon the marriage of true minds. It was Farquhar who had read and admired Milton, not Mrs. Sullen – who would have sympathized with Milton's wife.

The casual reader could and the careful one would note that this lofty judicial voice must have been tuned to an instrument other than the mind and spirit of the pleasure-seeking Mrs. Sullen. Her own normal style of allusion to her husband and matrimonial problems is expressed as follows : 'O Sister, Sister! I shall never ha' the Good of the Beast till I get him to Town; London, dear London, is the Place for managing and breaking a Husband . . . No, no, Child 'tis a standing Maxim in conjugal Discipline, that . . . when a Lady would be arbitrary with her Husband, she wheedles her Booby up to Town . . . O Dorinda, Dorinda! a fine Woman may do anything in London.' It is locality that disturbs Mrs. Sullen, not law.

Quite obviously Mrs. Sullen does not approach her own problem in the spirit of a Mrs. Alving – by reading 'advanced' literature. Her private doctrine of conjugal discipline for dealing with 'Booby' and 'Beast' is not that of Milton's *Discipline.* Her voice is that of the disgruntled stage-wife in a disaffected mood, the conventional voice of the theatre of her time. Her occasionally borrowed voice, that of Milton, is the revolutionary voice of the radical and turbulent seventeenth century. All the harmonizing skill of Farquhar barely reconciles the austere elevation of the Miltonic inflection with the racy vernacular idiom of the thwarted lady of pleasure and fashion.

We have already dwelt on the bleak situation of the dying Farquhar as he bent close to his life's brief candle for light enough for one more play. In such a plight, it is not surprising that he needed literary help as well as financial. Wilks supplied the latter; Milton the former. Yet Farquhar also vividly retouched important elements of plot and situation borrowed from his successful predecessor Sir John Vanbrugh. Farquhar's mind naturally reverted in his last extremity to his days of high hope when he first arrived in London, when the plays in vogue were Vanbrugh's *The Relapse* and *The Provok'd Wife*.

Whereas in *The Relapse* the bedroom sex-comedy scene ends in successful seduction, Farquhar using the same situation forbears Midnight burglars enter as the fortuitous custodians of virtue. From *The Provok'd Wife* Farquhar appears to have borrowed important elements of plot and character. Besides the basic resemblance of the main characters in both plays, Farquhar's Dorinda and Aimwell are a revision and re-issue of Vanbrugh's romantic and non-married couple Bellinda and Heartfree – only they are no longer treated in the tradition variously known as the Gay Couple or the Love Game. Farquhar introduces the newer note of sentimental reformation of heart and makes the relation more solemn and serious. Last night's wild oats are sown. But the harvest yields wholesome and nutritious porridge for next morning's breakfast. Farquhar takes his couple to the altar not in lightness of heart but in a mood of lofty sobriety. Rather obviously Vanbrugh's Sir John and Lady Brute are an early version of the married couple living in the same state of reciprocal torment in which we find Squire and Mrs. Sullen, except that London is exchanged for the country. Dorinda, too, is the agreeable confidante to Mrs. Sullen as is Bellinda to Lady Brute. But Dorinda is more the moral counsellor, warning against sexual transgression.

In handling the relation between the Squire and Mrs. Sullen, however, Farquhar had to take into consideration not only the necessary variation upon Vanbrugh to escape the suspicion of servile imitation. He had also to refrain from contaminating unduly the newly purified atmosphere of the theatre, the new climate of feeling brought in by the provoked parson Collier.

As to the first point, Farquhar has consciously varied significant details. Indeed he almost appears to have used a method of negative variation for secondary matters. For example, Vanbrugh's Lady Brute solemnly disavows any recourse to the expedient of artful coquetry as an amorous potion to arouse the sluggish emotions of a negligent husband. Not so Mrs. Sullen. She arranges the most elaborate plot for just such a purpose. Or again, when Sir John Brute quite by accident discovers the attentions of another to his wife, he is unwilling to accept the challenge of a duel. Squire Sullen, deliberately tricked into the triangle situation, is all for the arbitrament of the sword, despite the fact that he cherishes only his honor of husband-proprietor, openly disdaining any interest in either his wife's virtue or person.

Secondly, Vanbrugh leaves it passingly clear that Constant who pursues the married Lady Brute (he is the prototype of Archer) will succeed, that Lady Brute's husband will be cuckolded not long after the final curtain. Such solutions by 1707 are less tolerable. Indeed, so astonishingly has the climate of feeling changed that Anne Oldfield, the actress 'discovered' by Farquhar in a local tavern, objects even to the presumably purified arrangement whereby Mrs. Sullen achieves her freedom. Anne Oldfield objected to the makeshift device whereby Mrs. Sullen was returned again to green pastures. Obviously she did not believe in the 'divorce' and felt that it was merely a blind for a possible future adulterous relationship, that it was a clumsy makeshift concocted by Farquhar for a happy curtain.

We have already seen that Farquhar is careful not to allow Archer to seduce Mrs. Sullen in the bedroom scene. Besides the new climate of morality, Farquhar has to reckon with an element of plot — Mrs. Sullen's rural isolation. If Archer is not to prevail against her virtue, neither can she be left alone in the sole company of the Squire, her husband. Farquhar's sense of comedy required a happy ending. Vanbrugh's Lady Brute was in London. As Mrs. Sullen enviously reflected, in London a wife 'may do anything'. But not in the provinces. Archer even as an interim lover would soon be on his way. A genuine opportunist and adventurer, Archer would not tarry long in Lichfield, especially now that he had acquired a small fortune with which to invest in the pleasures of London. What then was Farquhar to do as an alternative to returning his favorite character to the abhorrent and abhorring husband?

What he did was to borrow from Paul to pay the interest due on the sum previously borrowed from Peter. From Milton could be borrowed what was needed to vary the borrowing from Vanbrugh. Milton's *Doctrine and Discipline* would supply the

ready-made phrases and a device of plot whereby the Restoration comedy of *The Provok'd Wife* could be transformed into
the nearly sentimental comedy of the unyoked wife. The device
was to introduce divorce or separation by 'mutual consent'.

That the Miltonic borrowings are an expedient for a happy
curtain (and not a new social epoch) is evident in the supreme
hurry and carelessness with which Farquhar introduces the
question, quite without any of the early and careful preparation
of an Ibsen. Sir Charles Freeman is the *deus ex machina* who, at the
last minute, descends upon the play from the empty spaces over
the stage. He arrives as a plausible means for awarding Mrs.
Sullen her 'divorce' and her liberty. He too has gotten up his
Milton and talks about the union of true minds although neither
Mrs. Sullen nor the Squire has the slightest interest in the sort of
mental union celebrated and desired by Milton. Equally unpre-
pared for is the introduction at the last moment of something
called Squire Sullen's 'writings' which can presumably be used to
coerce his consent although there has been talk about 'mutual
consent'.

Sir Charles Freeman, a brother of Mrs. Sullen, is neither a
member of Parliament, a representative of the Church, nor a part
of the judicial system. That is, he belongs to no portion of the
governing order which would be responsible for evaluating and
passing judgment on the proposals he is to make. He has been
simply waiting off-stage, Milton in hand, for his cue. Even
Archer, who stands to gain most from the transaction, refused to
regard 'mutual consent' seriously. He treats it as an uproarious
joke. Despite his drafting of Miltonic phrases and attitudes for
service in *The Beaux' Stratagem*, Farquhar is very unlikely to have
had in mind the role of a proto-Ibsen. Almost certainly he was
not using the stage as a platform for sensational social reform,
heroically expounding the evils of a too rigid matrimonial law.
Milton might be regarded as a forerunner of Ibsen, not
Farquhar. To vary a notable metaphor in its application, what
Farquhar admired in Milton's divorce pamphlet was the
gorgeous plumage, not the dying bird. He merely wanted a few
colorful feathers for the nest of a happy ending.

In *Lady Windermere's Fan*, Oscar Wilde presumably borrows
from Cardinal Newman's 'Autobiographical Memoir' the ma-

terials for philosophizing on the 'evangelical conscience'. He uses these materials to give flavor to his play and point to his plot, not because he has embraced the moral philosophy of the High Church movement. Farquhar was not more seriously interested in adopting and establishing Milton's philosophy of divorce than was Wilde in renovating England with Newman's theory of conscience. Milton's volcanic outpouring, fired by a personal and domestic tragedy, could be used to ornament and conclude a social comedy. With his gift for felicitous handling of improbable materials, Farquhar did just that.

Much, if not most, of the standard criticism of Farquhar's comedy is contrary to the foregoing. Milton's presence in the play, however tenuous, has given it a thematic character in the eyes of many contemporary critics of note. Not to notice such a tradition of interpretation would be a culpable negligence in any serious account of the play and its place in the tradition of English comedy. . . . In one way or another the views of many varying critics point to Farquhar as a prototype of Ibsen: depending upon the individual enthusiasm, something in between the cautious, moralizing Ibsen of Professor Joseph Wood Krutch and the fervent, crusading Ibsen of Bernard Shaw. At any rate, Farquhar's treatment of the wrangling and abusive relation of the Sullens is to such critics not so much a highly qualified variation of the comedy of Vanbrugh as an unqualified anti- cipation of the comedy of Ibsen. The Quintessence of *The Beaux' Stratagem* is a bold assault upon the unduly rigid and stifling regulations governing marriage.

Despite the impressive names ranged upon the other side of the question, it seems to us that Farquhar no more sought to use his play to liberalize the laws governing divorce than he sought to insinuate socialism with the phrases concerning poverty which Shaw found convenient to borrow from him. For all of that, *Ghosts* are now confidently reported as wandering about the midnight terrain of early eighteenth-century Lichfield.

Actually, both internal and external evidence is contrary to such a conception. First there is the fact of contemporary silence concerning any such introduction, 'boldly' or otherwise, of so serious a proposition into drama. We all know of the angry buzz and flutter of excitement that greeted Ibsen's handling of the theme in *The Doll's House* and *Ghosts*, of the angry agitation surrounding Milton's bulky tract. Indeed, we have seen that not even Anne Oldfield could quite take it seriously. Clearly she considered the 'mutual consent' merely a sophistical device for escaping Squire Sullen. Apparently Farquhar did himself, for he is reported to have consoled her by promising to give her a 'real' divorce. One cannot imagine Milton or Ibsen light-heartedly setting aside their passionate polemics as a joking matter.

The critics who regard the drama as presenting the divorce-by-mutual-consent thesis attempt to make much of Farquhar's marriage. They insist that he married in hope of capturing an heiress, that the lady deceived him, and that his consequent disappointment prompted in part his plea for more liberal divorce laws. Certainly there was passionate personal prompting behind Milton's tract. But all of the tradition of the time that has reached us is to the effect that Farquhar and his wife handsomely suited each other and lived in mutual sympathy.

Internally the evidence is even more dubious. The idea of divorce is most casually introduced at the last moment and has on the face of it the appearance of a mere improvisation of plot, not an improvement of the human lot. Nor do the characters in any way illustrate the kind of situation which Milton had in mind when writing the tract from which Farquhar borrowed phrases. What Milton was contemplating was the union of a Samuel Taylor Coleridge with a Sara Fricker — the tormented romantic genius tethered irrevocably to a plump suburban matron permanently in front of a television set. The only issue between Squire and Mrs. Sullen is drink, tavern, and horses as opposed to teas, gossip, and cards. This is not Milton's dramatic struggle in which 'spirit' is hobbled and fettered by union with gross 'matter'. Mrs. Sullen is neither a Nora Helmer nor a Mrs. Alving.

But to conclude the matter. If one wished to discover Farquhar's purpose — or that of any other eighteenth-century dramatist — where would he apply but to the Prologue and Epilogue of the play? And there one is confronted with a desolating silence. As likewise by the 'Advertisement'. The discovery of Archer and the elaborations of subsequent critics seem not to have touched the mind of author or audience. If Farquhar, so conscious of addressing himself to so momentous a

question, was really so engaged, why is there complete silence
about this intention in the Prologue? Why, to the contrary, does
the Prologue contain lines such as the following:

> When thro' Great Britain's fair extensive Round,
> The Trumps of Fame the Notes of Union sound;
> When Anna's Scepter points the Laws their Course,
> And Her Example gives her Precepts Force:
> There scarce is room for Satyr, all our Lays
> Must be, or Songs of Triumph, or of Praise.

Surely so witty a man as Farquhar would have sensed the
ironic equivocation of Trumps of Fame sounding 'Notes of
Union' when writing a stage plea for divorce. Never did Prologue
so totally abdicate its function if this murmur of general
complancency was intended to be a trumpet call to matrimonial
reform. Epilogue and Advertisement stress but one point:
Farquhar hoped that his play would be successful entertainment.

Dr. Johnson said that much could be done with a Scotsman if
he were caught early enough. England has done well with her
Irishmen of talent and wit from Farquhar to Wilde. But not even
Queen Anne's England could Miltonize George Farquhar. The
critics are interpreting Farquhar as one might have interpreted a
well-known remark of Dr. Johnson's if it had been found as a
pencilled note in the fly-leaf of his copy of Milton's *Doctrine and
Discipline:*

It is so far from being natural for a man and woman to live in a state of
marriage that we find all the motives which they have for remaining in
that condition and the restraints which civilized society imposes to
prevent separation, are hardly sufficient to keep them together.

In such a supposed context the passage might be regarded as an
expression of dignified sarcasm in behalf of Milton's views.
Rather it merely reflects Johnson's sturdy, unsentimental realism
of mind, his frank view of a system which he accepted with an
almost fatal resignation.

Farquhar too knew that he lived in an age in which it was rare
for even a powerful nobleman to pass his private Parliamentary

bill for a divorce. The notion of making such an exclusive prerogative as accessible as the country air of Lichfield was hardly thinkable. But where Dr. Johnson was realistic, Farquhar was whimsical. To grace a final curtain with a pleasing vista, Farquhar would create over the ruined site of the Restoration's Utopia of gallantry the transitory vision of a Utopia of easy divorce.

SOURCE: Introduction to *The Beaux' Stratagem* (Great Neck, N. Y., 1963) pp. 20 – 37, 40 – 4.

NOTE

1.   [Hopper and Lahey are, of course, using their own text throughout this essay – Ed.]

Ronald Berman

THE COMEDY OF REASON (1965)

Restoration comedy provokes familiar and confusing responses. You can call it satire and spend the rest of the day looking for the standards it invokes. You can call it lechery and wonder why it has no sensual affectiveness. You can go along with Knights and Krutch and dismiss it as insufficiently serious, or with Bredvold and Underwood and call it dramatized Pyrhhonism. You can appeal to Hobbes (materialism), Montaigne (scepticism) or simply stick with Lamb and Hazlitt on the 'comedy of manners'. Eventually the antis appeal to morality, and *aficionados* are left holding the bag of art for art's sake. I think that Restoration comedy is one of the great forms of the drama of ideas, and I'd like to consider how one play brings this out. *The Beaux' Stratagem* is not the best Restoration comedy, but it has a characteristic kind of logic. It does not argue for liberation from moral demands; in fact it imposes them, although in a special sense. It explains why men should submit to Reason, Nature, and their social embodiments. This sounds chilly and dialectical, but the Restoration was like that. We might begin by taking a look at the final cause of the play, the sum of ten thousand pounds. The efficient cause is only the attempt to get it. The ten thousand is mentioned at least once in each act and has particular powers of definition. The first time we see it Archer talks about 'the Ten Thousand we have spent' and says simply, 'so much Pleasure for so much Money'. He says this as if he were talking about a consensus. He would like to think that 'we are the Men of intrinsick Value, who can strike our Fortunes out of ourselves, whose worth is independent of Accidents in Life', but if there is anything that is uncertain in this play it is the whole concept of intrinsic value. In fact, Archer knows well enough that he is what he is only by virtue of having the money. Without it he literally is not himself, even to himself. His disguise is no disguise, but an identity. That is what men without money are like. They are now men of two hundred pounds, which is to say men who disappear from the social scene. Life is a rational and especially a transactional affair; if they had a million they would take it 'to the same Market'. Prudentially, however, they reserve one of their last two hundred for a last journey, to the battlefields of the Low Countries. It is all beautifully and coldly accepted, the transactional alternatives of 'Pleasures' in London and extinction in Belgium. The ideal is a million, the last reality a hundred, and the object ten thousand pounds. The relationship of one sum and one idea to another is very nearly Aristotelian; the mean is a compromise between nothingness and the supreme good.

The ten thousand and 'Pleasures' are closely connected; when one is mentioned the other appears and completes a context. In the second act Mrs. Sullen says, 'I brought your Brother Ten thousand Pounds, out of which, I might expect some pretty things, called Pleasures.' The pleasures are not necessarily sexual – opposed are 'Country Pleasures' and 'the Pleasures of the Town'. That is to say, those of the flesh and those of the mind, although plenty of leeway ought to be allowed in the distinction. The town *may* be sexual, but it is above all rational. As a matter of fact the town pleasures are conceived of in so refined a way that we literally fail to get a sense of their concrete reality. Certainly 'Country Pleasures' are associated with the breaking of limits: indiscriminate eating, drinking, and fornication. The country is the place of sensual exaggeration and the town of sensual decorum. The husband comes to bed 'dead as a Salmon into a Fishmonger's Basket; his Feet cold as Ice, his Breath hot as a Furnace, and his Hands and his Face as greasy as his flanel night-cap'. Both sacrament and sexuality are burlesqued in the evocation of 'two Carcasses join'd unnaturally together'. Adultery is conceived of here as a mode of humanization. It isn't the corrosive image of men and women in bed that Iago had made Othello see, or the vision of the mindless lust of Restoration quasi pornography, but a sense of abstract *value* that is involved: 'Women are like Pictures of no Value in the Hands of a Fool, till he hears Men of Sense bid high for the purchase'. Part of the wit consists of *doubles entendres*, but I think the central meaning is that reason, operating in transaction, defines the 'natural' human relationship.

Act III has its ten thousand also:

AIMWELL   O *Archer*, I read her thousands in her Looks, she look'd like *Ceres* in her harvest, Corn, Wine and Oil, Milk and Honey, Gardens, Groves, and Purling Streams, play'd on her plenteous Face.

ARCHER   Her Face! Her Pocket, you mean; the Corn, Wine and Oil lies there. In short, she has ten thousand Pound, that's the English on't.

The goddess of this play, to be sure, is not Venus but Ceres, now patron of income. When Mrs. Sullen talks in Act IV about 'Pleasures' Dorinda responds with the idea of ten thousand pounds, which 'may lie brooding here this seven Years, and hatch nothing at last but some illnatur'd Clown'. It is the sum of money the beaux have spent, the sum they are after, the dowry of Mrs. Sullen, the dowry of Dorinda, and, in the ultimate sense, the signature of fertility itself. Eventually it assumes the form of liberator of the flesh, allowing Mrs. Sullen to participate in 'the Pleasures of an agreeable Society'. It is of some interest, though I wouldn't press it too far, that when she gets her money she leaves her 'prison' and has a stab at Archer, who in name and function unites money and Eros.

The last act brings out a good deal of intrigue, all focussed on the vital ten thousand and its transfer. But there is even a subplot about money – the unseen protagonist, ten thousand, has a supporting cast of smaller bankrolls. There is the elusive two hundred pounds deposited with Boniface by the beaux and linked consistently with the 'natural' sensual vitality of Cherry. It gives us a renewed sense of the vitality of cash. And, from the first, it is conceived of in terms of transactional power of a familiar kind:

CHERRY   Father, would you have me give my Secret for his?

BONIFACE   Consider, Child, there's Two hundred Pound to boot.

He makes an admirable pun on 'mind your Business'. But this subplot, if anything, is even more rational than the main plot. Cherry does in fact come to be worth a certain sum and status – she even conceives of herself in that sense – proving that Boniface is only stupid, not evil. In the mode of the senile pastoral the swain sings out 'Death and Fire! her Lips are Honey-combs'. When he regains his town composure the two hundred pounds (now augmented to the two thousand Cherry proposes to steal) weigh far more than the 'Pleasure' he describes: 'what need you make me Master of yourself and Money, when you may have the same Pleasure out of me, and still keep your Fortune in your Hands'. Again there is the coupling of money and 'Pleasure', but there is a hierarchy of values, and, in this least sensual of comedies, the pleasure that never transpires continually subserves the vivifying, inhibiting power of money. At the end of the play Cherry sends a strongbox with a note that she might have accompanied it, but the two hundred she returns must be measured by the ten thousand to whose rank it gives precedence. There is a marvellous sense of sanctions imposed by the durable nature of cash. It holds ranks apart; imposes valuation; determines how much a servant shall be bribed for and for how much a highwayman will bribe. Eventually, apart from its almost mythical function as the cause of 'Pleasure' it accounts for the concept of relationship itself. By the end of the play whatever order is being asserted is very plainly determined by cash and contract. One of the most useful of *dei ex machinae* is the dead Lord Aimwell, out of whose happy demise comes the means to free the men from social and the women from sexual extinction. The play ends with a dissolution, a kind of *komos* in reverse. Instead of union and reconciliation quite the opposite occurs. But money endures, is celebrated, and makes the dissolution possible and even creative.

The dominant mode of language and conception is transactional, and this can most easily be brought out by a summary of the modes of rational commerce. I have listed this by acts:

Act I

Boniface is almost the cash nexus personified. He defines Lady

Bountiful as a woman of a thousand a year; Dorinda as 'the greatest Fortune' in the country; Sullen as a 'Man of great Estate' who 'values no Body', his own life as 'a good running Trade'; the French as men who pay double for everything they get. In addition, much about taxes, rent, how much he can give his daughter. Archer and Aimwell have the dialogue about ten thousand pounds and talk about sexual pleasures the way that Crusoe talks about God: 'and I think your kind Keepers have much the best on't; for they indulge the most Senses by one Expense. There's the Seeing, Hearing, and Feeling, amply gratify'd; and some Philosophers will tell you, that from such a Commerce there arises a sixth Sense that gives infinitely more Pleasure than the other five put together.' The show of money to the landlord provokes the spontaneous guess that Archer and Aimwell are in politics, evidently the cash relationship *par excellence*.

Act II

Begins with Mrs. Sullen complaining about the bad exchange of her ten thousand pounds. Dorinda asks why poets always picture pastoral bliss, and she responds 'Because they wanted Money, Child, to find out the Pleasures of the Town. Did you ever see a Poet or Philosopher worth Ten thousand Pound?' Women are conceived of as 'of no Value in the Hands of a Fool' but of great price when bid for by wits. The next scene confirms and modifies this when Aimwell says 'no Woman can be a Beauty without a Fortune'. Gibbet enters, a connoisseur of valuation – even to assaying a sad story worth half a crown. The issue of love between Cherry and Archer is resolved when he prudently decides that 'the Fortune may go off in a Year or two, and the Wife may live – Lord knows how long'. This leads to the central paradox that there is nothing so durable as money, but that itself is not durable.

Act III

The vision of Ceres and the ten thousand pounds. Scrub ventures that virtue is more durable than beauty but that it is generally imaginary. Archer makes himself understood within what are evidently the terms of a consensus: 'Madam, the Ladies pay best; the Honour of serving them is sufficient Wages.' In the last act 'pay' becomes much more clearly defined. Bellair talks about his love for Mrs. Sullen. She asks 'why shou'd you put such a Value upon my person'; they throw back and forth *doubles entendres* on 'the Value of the Jewel' which is 'unregarded' except by the lover-merchant who 'takes you up'. Sullen asks his wife to 'contrive any way of being a Whore without making me a Cuckold' and she replies that she wants both the pleasure and the sin. She doesn't shrink from the full meaning of the transaction.

Act IV

Gipsey is assured that money before the act is a bribe, but after only a gratification. She resolves to sin with 'security'. She is bribed to betray her mistress, and Scrub is bribed to betray her. The beaux invoke their fate, the sordid evasion of debts in coffeehouses. Money is not so much the payment for as the sign of sexual life – their 'impotent Pockets' prevent any female interest.

Act V

There is a good deal of talk about 'principal', 'interest' and 'services', the last of which is rewarded at the 'expense' of honor. Archer: 'I'm none of your *Romantick* Fools, that fight Gyants and Monsters for nothing; my Valour is downright *Swiss*; I'm a Soldier of Fortune, and must be paid.' Cut-throat dispute between the beaux for Dorinda's dowry. Lord Aimwell's death received with financial thanksgiving. Boniface absconds with the money, which is immediately returned by Cherry. Poignant and realistic 'I wou'd have deliver'd my self into your Hands with a Sum that much exceeds that in your strong Box.' The ten thousand resurfaces and dominates the ending.

The play centers on an idea of what is durable. The significance of this for comedy is that its nearly Platonic sense of the oneness of money has to subsist with money's other meanings. The most fundamental thing that can be said of this play is that it challenges all life to be defined by a standard universally acknowledged to be relative. Until the last act, which is, I think, intentionally sentimental, it relies on a standard which is as likely to break down distinctions as it is to create them. The standards which dominate the play can best be understood by looking over the substructure. The dialogue is intensely generalized – not so much a scattering of epigrams as a system of assertions. They have the force of axioms, and, like axioms, their fate is to be deduced and demonstrated. The fundamental verity in the play is money; the fundamental metaphor involves commerce; the fundamental axiom is that poverty is nonexistence. The last is restated at least three times in the first dialogue of Archer and Aimwell:

> There is no Scandal like Rags, nor any Crime so shameful as Poverty.
> No Crime upon Earth but the want of Money.
> Men must not be poor; Idleness is the root of all Evil.

These sound like the most deadening formulations of the Protestant ethic. In fact, when we hear that 'Men of Sense are left to their Industry' we wonder whether it was Farquhar who wrote this or perhaps Defoe. It is not precisely a parody that is involved; these statements are evidently taken seriously enough to provoke the play's action. They are taken seriously enough, in fact, to lead to a demonstration of the nature of human relationship.

At the simplest, human relationships seem to be viewed satirically and traditionally. The scattered vignettes of successful sharpers and destitute *honnêtes hommes* are based on commonplaces that go back at least as far as Euripides: 'I know that all/A man's friends leave him stone-cold if he becomes poor' (*Medea*). Jack Handycraft 'keeps the best Company in the Town while Jack Generous 'is single and solitary as a Lion in a Desert'. The stock figures are here; the footman who sets up as dancing master and carries off a fortune, the gigolo, the friends in prosperity who are strangers in adversity. But these characters who people the dialogues and who constitute the outer reality within which the drama occurs are not treated satirically. The peculiar force of this play lies in its cool acceptance of the principles of buying and selling. This is not to say it is decadent – most of the errors made in criticizing Restoration comedy are based on the assumption that the plays achieve their effect because they glorify the amoral. They only understand it. They understand too that it may be one of the ultimate sources of precedent, and hence of ethics. In Restoration comedy in general and in this particular play there is an absolute distinction between traditional satire and social logistics. When Archer tells Cherry his biography it takes only three lines: 'I went to *London* a younger Brother, fell into the Hands of Sharpers, who stript me of my Money, my Friends disown'd me, and now my Necessity brings me to what you see.' The important word is 'Necessity', for it is unconsciously diagnostic. Everyone involved in society (and these comedies have a unique sense of the social) agrees to the necessity, even the victims. It is a kind of Calvinism in burlesque: the providential scheme works so clearly that all may discern it, participate in it, and confirm it. The extraordinary precision with which each agent fixes his condition demonstrates this. Surely no other play portrays so exactly an intricate system of valuation and acceptance. Under the law of things Cherry knows that she is 'worth' two hundred pounds; Sullen is convinced that a man 'of Three thousand Pound a Year' deserves the good life of insensibility; the beaux, Mrs. Sullen, and Dorinda are all eloquent on the meaning of ten thousand a year; Gibbet, without complaint, knows how much is due to bribe his captor and how much should remain to bribe the judge; Scrub is a two-guinea man; Gipsey will settle for a benediction followed by a gratification. This is not to say only that every man has his price; it means that the price is the function of a system. The strongest evidence for this is the satisfaction of the dramatic agents when contemplating the system. That it *works* is really the comic issue.

If the intensely rational nature of the play is admitted the question of love and passion remains. Two things may be asked: is the ending merely sentimental? does the love that is generated invalidate the analytical structure? I think the answer to the first is 'no' and to the second 'yes'. Certainly the passions are expressed in the unspeakably soapy manner the Restoration reserved for amorous seriousness: 'the teeming Jolly Spring Smiles in her blooming face, and, when she was conceiv'd, her Mother smelt to Roses, look'd on Lillies'. It is hideous, but not much worse than even the best of Restoration tragedies. The point, I think, is that it represents a new availability. This play is like Dryden's *Secular Masque*, which was also a farewell to mores. In that play the age is summed up in a *locus classicus*:

> MOMUS 'All, all of a piece throughout:
> > *Pointing to* Diana.
> > Thy chase had a beast in view;
> > *To* Mars.
> > Thy wars brought nothing about;
> > *To* Venus.
> > Thy lovers were all untrue.
> JANUS 'Tis well an old age is out:
> CHRONOS And time to begin a new.

It is a magnificent comment on an age by a man who helped create it. *The Beaux' Stratagem* is a comment much less intense but much to the same point. The confrontation of social laws which are inexorable, rational, and transactional by passions which, after all, invalidate them, is a cultural comment. In the most general sense it marks a move from the world of Hobbes to that of Shaftesbury.

Aimwell says that beauty has 'won me from my self' and, in a rejection of the whole scheme by which the play has operated, he adds, 'I prefer the Interest of my Mistress to my own.' The play is dishonest to the extent that such a change is not really accounted for. There is no real tension in the opposition of selfish, transactional reason and altruistic passion – only the statement that reason loses. Somewhere in this play is the outline of a much greater play in which the battle might have been somewhat more exhausting. At any rate, we are left at the end not merely with the spectacle of social and sexual integration, but of a theory of human relationship that has proved invalid. So has its alternative. The central crux of Restoration and Augustan thought on sexuality is unconsciously delineated: the body social offers laws of relationship as immutable and necessary as those of gravity, and they are broken by passions so easily aroused as to have no possible relationship to offer as a substitute. The play has stated that nothing is durable but money, and we can see that money is not durable. It then offers the statement that nothing is necessary but passion, and we already have a sense of how far that is durable. One world-view founded on a relativity is replaced by another. Farquhar has tried to solve this issue, but he has been able only to exploit it.

SOURCE: 'The Comedy of Reason', *Texas Studies in Literature and Language*, VII (1965) 161–8.

Albert John Farmer

'A NEW MORAL DIMENSION' (1966)

. . . Farquhar's last two plays show a remarkable advance on all his preceding work. It is already evident in *The Recruiting Officer*, directly inspired by his experiences when recruiting in the West of England. Dedicated 'To All Friends Round the Wrekin',[1] the comedy was born, says Farquhar in his preface, 'from some little turns of humour that I met with almost within the shade of that ancient hill', and he goes on to admit that some of his characters were painted from life. Needless to say, this admission has brought forth any number of speculations as to the originals, and a number of identifications with local notabilities have been proposed, without it being possible to substantiate the claims. In any case, the interest of the work lies elsewhere. The play is characterized by a light-hearted gaiety which is apparent already in the opening scene, where we see the astute Sergeant Kite beginning his recruiting campaign in the market-place of the country town, and meditating his stratagems to bring the rustics into the Queen's army. This gaiety runs through all the love scenes, in which the sprightly Captain Plume, one more version of the familiar Farquhar hero, with the added prestige of uniform, is engaged with the no less sprightly Silvia, daughter of Justice Balance, who has disguised herself as a young man to be near her too versatile lover. The episode in which Kite, made up as an astrologer, arranges his own affairs, and those involving the countryman Bullock and his pretty sister Rose, with skillful impudence, are highly amusing. The appearance of the rustic recruits, enrolled without their being aware of it, before the court presided over by the local justices, gives rise to laughable dialogue. Captain Brazen, Plume's fellow-officer, is an original remaking of the stock character of the *miles gloriosus*: he has been everywhere, seen everything, knows everybody and is ready, on the slightest pretext, to enlarge on his adventures which are always, of course, unique. In this comedy, there are no displeasing characters, no conflicts other than those of young love. The provincial world Farquhar evokes is free of all care, delightful in every way: Leigh Hunt defines it well when he notes that 'we seem to breathe the clear, fresh, ruddy-making air of a remote country-town, neighboured by hospitable elegancies'. Critics have been quick to point out analogies between *The Recruiting Officer* and plays in which soldiers appear, like Fletcher's *Humorous Lieutenant*, Shadwell's *Woman Captain* and even Steele's *Funeral*; the only one to present a real similarity is Shadwell's in which Mrs Gripe, the woman captain, enlists, like Silvia, in the army, but in order to get away from her husband. Otherwise, the characters and situations are Farquhar's own. The constant high spirits, and the brisk light-heartedness with which the play moves along, testify to a newly-found assurance, after the uncertainty and hesitation of the preceding works.

The same gay and confident atmosphere envelops the last and best of his comedies, *The Beaux' Stratagem*. It takes place in Lichfield, and tradition has it that Farquhar visited this little country town first on his recruiting campaign; at the old George Inn there, the room in which he is supposed to have stayed is still displayed. We are at the inn when the curtain rises, in company with the eccentric landlord Boniface and his pretty daughter Cherry. The arrival of the two 'beaux' from London, Aimwell and Archer, sets the action moving. The two young men hope to repair their sadly compromised fortunes by a rich marriage in the country. Their introduction into local society, Aimwell in the role of his titled elder brother and Archer masquerading as his servant, will be followed by rapid consequences: Aimwell will win the heart of the heiress Dorinda, while Archer will have found his way into the good graces of Mrs Sullen, the wife of the local squire, and will presumably marry her, and her ten thousand pounds, once she has obtained a divorce from her impossible spouse. In the meantime, we have been carried through a series of diverting scenes at the inn, and in the manor house, the home of Dorinda as well as of her brother Squire Sullen and his wife. At the inn, we have met Gibbett, the highwayman and his acolytes, Foigard who gives himself out as a Flemish priest and is revealed as an Irishman, a 'Teague', and

Count Bellair, a French officer on parole (captured in the war
which had begun in 1702) who has begun to court Mrs Sullen. At
the manor house, the Squire's man Scrub and the maid Gipsey
provide the comedy, and a late arrival on the scene, Sir Charles
Freeman, Mrs Sullen's brother, will bring about, in the last act,
the peaceful separation of the warring couple. All these characters are deftly presented, each with his marked and picturesque
individuality, but it is naturally towards the principal figures that
we look. Farquhar has differentiated his two 'beaux': Aimwell
has about him a touch of the romantic, Archer is closer to the
witty Dorimants and Mirabels of Restoration tradition; Aimwell
will be smitten with remorse before Dorinda's trustfulness, and
will confess his imposture, whereas Archer will refuse to forego
the advantages gained with Mrs Sullen by his transparent
disguise as a servant. Squire Sullen, in his perpetual ill-temper,
has his moments of humour, Dorinda is wholly charming,
romantic yet sensible, while Mrs Sullen has more depth than
most stage wives: she is, in reality, the most interesting character,
full of wit, vivacity and intelligence. Here are the two women
talking of their admirers:

MRS SULLEN   How a little Love and good Company improves
a Woman; why, Child, you begin to live – you never spoke
before.

DORINDA   Because I was never spoke to. – My Lord has told
me that I have more Wit and Beauty than any of my Sex; and
truly I begin to think the Man is sincere.

MRS SULLEN   You're in the right, *Dorinda*, Pride is the Life of a
Woman, and Flattery is our daily Bread; and she's a Fool that
won't believe a Man there, as much as she that believes him in
any thing else – But I'll lay you a Guinea, that I had finer things
said to me than you had.

DORINDA   Done – What did your Fellow say to ye?

MRS SULLEN   My Fellow took the Picture of *Venus* for Mine.

DORINDA   But my Lover took me for *Venus* her self.

MRS SULLEN   Common Cant! had my Spark call'd me a *Venus*
directly, I shou'd have believed him a Footman in good earnest.

DORINDA   But my Lover was upon his Knees to me.

MRS SULLEN   And mine was upon his Tiptoes to me.

108 ALBERT JOHN FARMER

DORINDA Mine vow'd to die for me.
MRS SULLEN Mine swore to die with me.

But a moment later the banter has ceased: a sudden melancholy
falls on Mrs Sullen as she realizes that hers is perhaps an empty
dream:

MRS SULLEN Happy, happy Sister! your Angel has been
watchful for your Happiness, whilst mine has slept regardless of
his Charge. — Long smiling Years of circling Joys for you, but not
one Hour for me! (*Weeps.*)
DORINDA Come, my Dear, we'll talk of something else. (IV i)

The scene, with its mingling of light raillery and emotion,
illustrates the sureness with which Farquhar now handles
character and dialogue. In a droller vein, the conversation
between Archer and Cherry, the scenes in which, in turn,
Boniface, Gibbet and Scrub try to penetrate the secret of Archer's
identity, and the final debate between Mrs Sullen and her
husband are marked by an ease, a spontaneity and a flow of
humour that go beyond anything to be found in the earlier
comedies.

The play has another particularity: it presents the picture of an
ill-assorted couple, constantly at strife. The theme was not a new
one; for Restoration comedy is full of such couples. But Farquhar
sees their situation differently from his fellow-dramatists. For
them, the normal solution was that the dissatisfied partner,
usually the wife, should seek consolation elsewhere. Wycherley's
Country Wife, to take perhaps the most striking example, shows us
a whole series of discontented wives hastening to throw themselves into the arms of lovers. Closer to Farquhar, Vanbrugh's
Provoked Wife paints a couple whose position is almost identical
with that of Squire Sullen and his wife. Lady Brute, unhappily
married, has long resisted the temptation to turn for solace to her
faithful admirer Constant, but the end of the play will see her
ready to yield, for such is, in her eyes, the only redress for the
unjust treatment she receives at the hands of her husband. In
part, the divorce laws were to blame: separation could only be
granted by the ecclesiastical courts, and in rare cases; incom-

patibility of temperament was not an admitted ground. With smiling earnestness, Farquhar pleads for a more humane view:

DORINDA But how can you shake off the Yoke – Your Divisions don't come within the Reach of the Law for a Divorce.

MRS SULLEN Law! what Law can search into the remote Abyss of Nature, what Evidence can prove the unaccountable Disaffections of Wedlock – can a Jury sum up the endless Aversions that are rooted in our Souls, or can a Bench give Judgment upon Antipathies. (III iii)

Marriage, as Squire Sullen hears to his stupefaction, is not merely a union of bodies, but of minds:

SIR CHARLES You and your Wife, Mr. Guts, may be one Flesh, because ye are nothing else – but rational Creatures have minds that must be united.

SULLEN Minds. (V i)

What Farquhar would wish for in such cases is separation by mutual consent, and the final scene, in which the Squire and his wife, at last in accord, join hands, pictures amusingly, but with an underlying gravity, the solution he proposes:

SQ. SUL. These hands joined us, these shall part us – away!
(V v)

It has been noted that his ideas on marriage and divorce echo those set out by Milton in a famous series of pamphlets more than half a century before, and it is certain that Farquhar had read these works carefully. This alone suffices to indicate the difference of his outlook from that of the other playwrights of the time. There is thus a serious note in this light-hearted comedy, where Farquhar's gifts find their best expression.

Highly popular in their century, both *The Recruiting Officer* and *The Beaux' Stratagem* have met with considerable success in recent revivals on the London stage.

Farquhar's career is a short one – some eight or nine years in all – but it shows a distinct evolution. His early plays, close to the Restoration model, are licentious in tone, and it is largely because of them that his morality has been brought into question. But, even in these works, the licentiousness is in the language rather than in the thought. The time was not over-nice in expression, as is evident in the work of his fellow-playwrights, Vanbrugh in particular, who is his direct contemporary. The later plays show a gradual improvement, due in part, no doubt, to the new standards which, in the opening eighteenth century, make for more refinement and decency in speech. If, in *The Recruiting Officer*, the dialogue has still that 'pert, low' touch which Pope stigmatized, there is little to offend, and much to please, the taste of the modern reader or playgoer in the verbal exchanges of *The Beaux' Stratagem*. It is true that, down to the end, Farquhar keeps a certain liberty of expression: but the frank outspokenness does not cover, as with so many of his predecessors, a fundamental indifference to morality. 'Farquhar', writes Edmund Gosse, 'succeeds in being wholesome, even when he cannot persuade himself to be decent'.

More important, the characters themselves have moved away from their prototypes of the older theatre. Out of the Restoration rake, the fickle and heartless libertine of Etherege and Wycherley, he has made a new type. Roebuck and Wildair, gay, vivacious, open, if wild and unpredictable in their behaviour, have a good deal in common with Fielding's Tom Jones: together with his heedless flightiness, they have his warm heart. More restrained, Mirabel the inconstant and Captain Plume are of the same complexion; they can be moved by a sincere sentiment and hasten to repair any wrong their thoughtlessness may have caused. Aimwell and Archer, young and easy-going, show themselves bold in the cause of their love; they are adventurers, like all Farquhar's heroes, and practise deception, but it never goes very far. Comparing them with Vanbrugh's creations, Hazlitt observes:

Farquhar's chief characters are also adventurers, but they are of a romantic, not a knavish stamp, and succeed no less by their honesty than by their boldness . . . They are real gentlemen and only pre-

tended imposters. Vanbrugh's upstart heroes are 'without any relish of
salvation', without generosity, virtue, or any pretensions to it. We have
little sympathy for them, and no respect at all. But we have every sort of
goodwill towards Farquhar's heroes, who have as many peccadilloes to
answer for, and play as many rogue's tricks, but are honest fellows at
bottom.

In a well-known essay, Lamb affirmed that the characters of
Wycherley and Congreve inspire no particular sentiment in us
because they belong to a world which has no connection with
reality. Allowing for the paradox innate in the critic's conception
of the 'artificial comedy', we can admit that we feel we have little
in common with such creations. If they were translated into real
life, we should be repelled by the inhumanity of a Horner or even
of Congreve's Mirabel. About Farquhar's heroes there is an
absence of calculating cynicism and a fundamental generosity
that appeal to us.

The same applies to Farquhar's heroines. Some are merely
stage *ingénues* innocent and trusting, and destined to be rescued
by their lovers from dishonour or from undesired marriages; such
are Isabella in *The Stage Coach*, Constance and Aurelia in *The
Twin-Rivals*. Others, more characteristic, are determined and
resourceful; Leanthe, Oriana and Silvia are ready to affront
difficulties and danger, if necessary, in order to remain by their
lover's side; witty and audacious, they have been compared to
the Rosalinds and Violas of Shakesperian comedy. Like their
predecessors, they gain a new charm disguised as young men. In
them, there is a kind of naturalistic philosophy: men are not
considered as enemies, as is the case in so many Restoration plays.
Lurewell represents an exceptional case: if she sets out to use her
beauty to entrap men, it is to revenge her sex for the unjust
treatment she herself has received, or believes she has received, at
men's hands. But nowhere, among Farquhar's women, do we
find a character like the lying, licentious and vindictive Olivia of
Wycherley's *Plain Dealer*. His conception of womanhood is best
illustrated in his last play, with Dorinda, charming, unaffected,
direct in thought and speech, and with Mrs Sullen, a woman who
has not been embittered by her unhappy experience and can still
believe in happiness.

Precisely because these characters are closer to humanity than most creations of Restoration comedy, we are the more ready to take into serious account the author's presentation of the problem which more than any other preoccupied the writers of the time : that of the relations of men and women in the contemporary social structures. It was seen by Farquhar's predecessors essentially from the man's point of view, with his age-old right to pleasure, and Farquhar's first plays reproduce this conception, illustrated by Roebuck and Wildair. But, as he proceeds, he moves towards the woman's standpoint. It is expressed directly by Oriana, in *The Inconstant*; and Silvia, in *The Recruiting Officer*, rises against the conventional attitude which allows men a privileged position in the pursuit of love. Already there is a sense of the equality of the sexes and, in the concluding scene of *The Beaux' Stratagem*, we see Squire Sullen and his wife discussing calmly and as admitted equals a situation which they agree is due to faults on both sides. One might imagine such a dialogue in Shaw, and it is no doubt with this in mind that Bonamy Dobrée thinks that, had Farquhar lived to continue his development, he might have been the Shaw of his time. As it is, we are with him on the way to the new 'sentimental' comedy of Steele and Cibber, which was to insist on a view of the relationship of the sexes more acceptable to us than that pictured in the Restoration theatre.

The new moral dimension in Farquhar's plays is directly linked to his incursion into provincial life and society. Here, too, a significant change is to be noted. One remembers the ridiculous figure cut by the country gentry in the plays of his predecessors. Vanbrugh, in *The Relapse*, had poured scorn on country life, showing us the grotesque Sir Tunbelly Clumsey, his boisterous daughter Hoyden and their uncouth household. In Farquhar's portrait of Squire Mockmode, and that of young Clincher, some traces of this attitude remain. But, in *The Recruiting Officer*, the Shropshire worthies appear in a completely different light: Balance, Simple and Worthy are men of culture and good breeding, and Balance's daughter, Silvia, unconventional and outspoken as she is, has nothing in common with Hoyden. Squire Sullen is a reversion to the Restoration type, but without the ridicule attached to him in Wycherley or Congreve; his shortcomings result from temperament rather than from his rural upbringing. In a general way, provincial life is portrayed agreeably; the characters are seen in a sympathetic light. Lady Bountiful is a pleasing figure, for whom Restoration comedy offers no equal. Farquhar thus breaks the link binding comedy to fashionable London life, with its narrow outlook; he takes us into a pleasanter world, where life is simpler. In *The Beaux' Stratagem*, the young gentlemen from London seem like intruders; finally, they are conquered by the charm of country existence. Farquhar thus takes us back to the joyous, open-air atmosphere of Elizabethan comedy, and he opens the way to Goldsmith whose inspiration, in *She Stoops to Conquer*, owes not a little to Farquhar.

Farquhar's plays have not the robust construction we admire in Wycherley, nor the intricacy which makes Congreve's comedies an intellectual delight. This indifference to a highly mechanized plot Farquhar shares with Vanbrugh. In both cases, the story told is full of unexpected turns, but it is rarely complicated. The effects Farquhar seeks are often obtained by the use of all the current, often hackneyed devices of the stage: disguises, hidden identities, unexpected encounters. But he shows great skill in his timing. Cherry, for instance, has been pressed by Boniface to employ all her wiles to persuade the pseudo-footman Archer to reveal his real identity and that of his master; left alone, she indignantly soliloquizes: 'This Landlord of mine . . . would betray his Guest, and debauch his Daughter into the bargain, – and by a Footman too!' And, as she ends, Archer enters. Or Scrub, anxious to deceive Foigard in whom he detects a rival for Gipsey's favour, tells him: 'Gipsey . . . she's dead – two Months ago.' Whereupon Gipsey makes her appearance.

His dialogue lacks, no doubt, the glitter and polish of Etherege or Congreve, and the power of Wycherley, but it has an unaffected ease and naturalness often lacking in the work of these writers. It has vivacity and a colloquial ring. The constant straining after wit is replaced by an engaging humour, presented with zest, as Mrs Sullen's description to Dorinda of life with the squire shows:

He came home this Morning at his usual Hour of Four, waken'd me out of a sweet Dream of something else, by tumbling over the Tea-table, which he broke all to pieces, after his Man and he had rowl'd about the

Room like sick Passengers in a Storm, he comes flounce into Bed, dead as a Salmon into a Fishmonger's Basket; his Feet cold as Ice, his Breath hot as a Furnace, and his Hands and his Face as greasy as his Flanel Night-cap. – Oh Matrimony! – He tosses up the Clothes with a barbarous swing over his Shoulders, disorders the whole Oeconomy of my Bed, leaves me half naked, and my whole Night's Comfort is the tuneable Serenade of that wakeful Nightingale, his Nose. – O the Pleasure of counting the melancholly Clock by a snoring Husband! . . . (*The Beaux' Stratagem*, II i)

All the plays, even the earliest ones, are full of such passages, and their cheerful spontaniety more than makes up for the lack of dazzling repartee. . . .

SOURCE: extract from *George Farquhar* (London, 1966) pp. 23–34.

NOTE

1. The Wrekin is the hill north of the River Severn, overlooking Shrewsbury.

Eric Rothstein

THE RECRUITING OFFICER (1967)

With *The Recruiting Officer* we come to the first of the two late comedies on which Farquhar's reputation rests. The legerdemain of *The Constant Couple* and the adroit experimentalism of the middle plays, which might well fan hopes for what would come, now led to and was superseded by a new kind of comedy. Without losing the complexity and sureness that had increasingly marked his work, Farquhar left behind the harsh moral melodrama that had permeated *The Twin-Rivals* and *The Inconstant*. This is not to say that his moral interests were abandoned; they were reassessed and placed in a more comprehensive context. His powers of development and control suddenly grew, and he was enabled to write comedies among the finest and most original in English.

Since Farquhar's enlarged abilities permitted him to elaborate upon and ripen the incidents of his plot as never before, he found it relatively less important to invent striking and novel incidents. *The Recruiting Officer* in particular merely chooses a fertile situation, rich in dramatic conflict and skulduggery upon which comedy could thrive : it makes use of something perfectly familiar to Farquhar and probably to his audience, without having to contrive a set of original circumstances.

If we look at the actual recruiting act under which Farquhar himself had been working, Anno 2° and 3° Annae Reginae (March, 1703 – March, 1705), we can see at hand the matrix for almost all the public military matters in the play. Cap. xix empowers three Justices of the Peace – Balance, Scale, and Scruple in the play – to 'Raise and Levy such Able-bodied Men as have not any lawful Calling or Employment, or visible Means for their Maintenance, and Livelihood, to serve as Soldiers.' In recompense, 'the respective Officer who shall Receive such new Raised Men, shall out of the Levy-Money pay to every Person so raised, Twenty Shillings, and to the Constable, or other Parish-

Officer employed in the Raising of them, any Sum not exceeding Ten Shillings a Man'. This makes explicable the constable's setting a bribe of 11s. a man in Farquhar's play: as Silvia explains, 'he said that the Act allows him but ten, so the odd Shilling was clear Gains' (v v 105).[1] Volunteers were to be paid twice as much, forty shillings, so that Kite's attempt to enlist the bumpkins for only 23/6 must be regarded as governmental economy, and Plume's gift to each of two guineas – then worth a pound apiece – more strictly proper. But volunteers or press-gang, after receiving money 'and Reading the said Articles of War [against mutiny and desertion], every Person so Raised, shall be deemed a Listed Soldier to all Intents and Purposes, and shall be subject to the Discipline of War, and in case of Desertion, shall be punished as a Deserter'. The punishment was death. If they did not desert, they were allowed to fight for their queen and be paid a maximum of 4d. a day for 'Diet and Small-Beer'. *The Recruiting Officer* exploits all of this – the two parts of recruiting (getting volunteers and impressing the jobless); the legal bribes and threats; even the hardships of army life, implicit in the tricks needed to lure men otherwise faced with vagrancy or a fourteen-hour workday. Farquhar's basic plot is almost a comic documentary.

If the military affairs have been plucked from real life and then developed, Farquhar's characters come directly from contemporary fiction. They are intricate developments of well-tried prototypes. As in his earlier plays, Farquhar contrived two couples, following his practice in *The Twin-Rivals* of using one sprightly and one subdued pair. As in three of his earlier plays, he supplied a 'breeches part', a role in which an actress dressed as a man. Silvia's military disguise, although new in Farquhar, might have been borrowed from any number of works: Scarron's *Comical Romance*, for instance, incorporates the story of an heiress named Sophia who disguised herself as the cavalier Don Hernando, and rose to become Viceroy of Valencia under Charles V.[2] Kite's masquerade as Copernicus the astrologer – or 'Coppernose', as the Smith calls him, perhaps as Farquhar's mischievous reminiscence of Tycho Brahe's famed golden nose – has such dramatic antecedents as Foresight in Congreve's *Love for Love*, or for that matter Face and Subtle in Jonson's *Alchemist*.

Brazen, of course, can trace his family tree through a dense foliage of Restoration fops; Justice Balance, through a thinner group of crusty Restoration fathers, whose function as 'blocking characters' he nominally maintains.

One of the reasons for the conventionality of the characters, besides his audience's conservatism, may be that Farquhar wrote the play rapidly. The evidence indicates that he did, whether because canvassing and cajoling for Her Majesty's Army exhausted him or because the attractions of Shrewsbury enticed away his will to write. For whatever reason, he left the play – at least the published copy – marked by carelessness. In the second act, the bumpkins change names: the first has been Costar, the second Thummas throughout the scene of their recruitment (e.g., on p. 63), but when they finally give their names to Plume at the end of the act, the first gives his as Thummas Appletree, the second his as Costar Pearmain. There is no indication in the stage directions that each indicates the other at this final moment; and to assume that Farquhar was deliberately having the men muddle their names so as to suggest their inseparability, seems like a strained reading, even in a play in which both male friendships and changes in identity recur as themes. Nor is this the only instance of Farquhar's carelessness.

Plume knows the disguised Silvia as Jack Wilfull in III ii and IV ii. But in the last act, he enlists her in court as Pinch, the name that she gives Justice Balance, and shows no sign of ever having seen the brisk young man that he had enlisted, with great pains, the previous day. Conversely, in the last scene of the play, Justice Balance speaks of Silvia as 'Mr. *Wilfull*', although he has only known her as Pinch. Even if one supposes that she tips Plume a wink in the courtroom scene, her father's new knowledge cannot be explained. Still a third slip comes in IV ii. When Melinda signs her name to verify the signature given the astrologer, Lucy borrows the slip of paper 'for my own Affairs', and later uses it to write Brazen her note of assignation, pretending to be her mistress. But shortly thereafter, Farquhar lets us know that Lucy, posing as Melinda, has been writing to Brazen in her own hand. Brazen then must think that Lucy's hand, 'no more like *Melinda's* Character than black is to white', is Melinda's; and for Lucy to use Melinda's real writing at this point ought to alert Brazen, not fool him. In short, it seems hard not to agree that *The Recruiting Officer* 'was probably hastily written and never thoroughly reviewed by the author, a man usually careful about such details'.[3]

Given the casualness with which the comedy was put together, it is theoretically possible that Farquhar's use of the country, perhaps the finest stroke of inspiration in the play, may have been first prompted by an attempt to compliment the Shrewsbury folk, who had given the recruiting playwright their hospitality. Before Farquhar, provincials had almost always been treated with contempt on the Restoration stage. Congreve's Millamant, for instance, can dismiss the Shrewsbury squire Sir Willful Witwoud as a 'Rustick, ruder than *Gothick*'. In *The Relapse*, Vanbrugh's Sir Tunbelly Clumsey is a West-country fool whose name displays his character, just as his daughter Hoyden's displays hers. But Farquhar, masterfully, blots off the predictable contempt of the audience for the country, by bringing in the bumpkins to absorb contempt at the beginning. He thus can treat Justice Balance, who is no bumpkin, with respect. A man of the same standing and city as Sir Willful, of the same standing and familial situation as Sir Tunbelly, has been transformed into a charming and sensible gentleman, the equal of a Londoner. Justice Balance does not, of course, challenge the excellence of London, or vie with London urbanity. But the traditional bluffness and candor of the provincial melt into an engaging personality. Along with Balance, Shrewsbury itself moves out of the realm of stage caricature. All the variety and sense of real life that enhanced the traditional London scene are transferred to Shrewsbury; and Shrewsbury values become the normative values of the play. By rehabilitating the country as an analogue to, rather than as an intruder within, the world of London, Farquhar gave *The Recruiting Officer* the freshness that has captivated critics ever since. He also empowered himself to portray a wide social range of characters without at the same time having to broaden the focus of his plot.

The flower of Farquhar's Shrewsbury is Silvia. She is a kind of cross between the bumptious Hoyden Clumsey type and the gay young lady of Restoration comedy. As she says, she is 'troubled with neither Spleen, Cholick, nor Vapours[;] I need no Salt for my Stomach, no Hart's-horn for my Head, nor Wash for my Complexion; I can gallop all the Morning after the Hunting Horn, and all the Evening after a Fiddle: in short, I can do every thing with my Father but drink and shoot flying; and I'm sure I can do every thing my Mother cou'd, were I put to the Tryal' (1 iii 52).

To prepare the audience for this 'natural' woman, Farquhar skillfully begins the scene with a depreciation of Melinda, who speaks first: 'Welcome to Town, Cosin *Silvia* [*Salute.*] I envy'd you your Retreat in the Country; for *Shrewsbury*, methinks, and all your Heads of Shires, are the most irregular Places for living; here we have Smoak, Noise, Scandal, Affectation, and Pretension; in short, every thing to give the Spleen, and nothing to divert it.' The effect here is a bit like that achieved by Swift in creating Lilliput, or by Pope in the diminished world of 'The Rape of the Lock.' Melinda's fashionable complaints echo fashionable complaints about London, and reinforce the treatment of Shrewsbury as analogue to London; but the self-importance of this comparison would also be ludicrous to a London audience, amusing them with Melinda's own 'Affectation, and Pretension'. Since the audience has been told five or ten minutes earlier that Melinda's airs result from her new riches, she seems even sillier. Within this context, the declaration of candor and good health from Silvia comes as a sympathetic corrective rather than rude excess: Silvia is accepted in the act, the necessary act, of rejecting Melinda. Silvia's values are accepted at the same time.

Thematically, Silvia binds together the two worlds of the play, Shrewsbury and the army. But before we can explore her function in this regard, we must understand the dramatic position of the army, as we have begun to understand that of Shrewsbury. *The Recruiting Officer* is a pro-war play, characterized by the same dry-eyed patriotic militarism that appears in Farquhar's other plays, and in poems like 'General Schomberg' and 'Barcellona'. The militarism is presumed by the boast in his dedication: 'The Duke of *Ormond* encourag'd the Author, and the Earl of *Orrery* approv'd the Play – My *Recruits* were *reviewed* by my *General* and my *Colonel*, and could not fail to *pass Muster.*'

A minor token of it even appears, cleverly, in his epigraph, 'Captique dolis, donisque coacti' ('captured by tricks and urged on by gifts'), referring to the methods of recruitment. In fact, Virgil's line (*Aen.* II 196) is 'captique dolis, lacrimisque coactis', or 'captured by tricks and forced tears'. The misquotation leads one to look at the epic context: Sinon, a Greek sent to deceive the Trojans into making way for the Horse, has tearfully begged for his life and promised victory for Troy if the Horse should be taken within the city walls. Looking back much later on this treachery, Aeneas remarks: 'By such stratagems and Sinon's skillful perjury was the lie believed, and that nation was captured by tricks and forced tears, whom neither Diomedes nor the Larissian Achilles, neither ten years of siege nor a thousand ships, could defeat.' Ingeniously, Farquhar has reversed the situation. His alert reader is referred to the foolish trust and disarmament of Troy as testimony for the necessity of English armament, and as a justification for Kite's stratagems. At the same time, the heroic comparison between beleaguered Troy and beleaguered Tummas Appletree is so grotesque as to indicate Farquhar's limited sympathy for the victims of recruitment.

Granted our historical knowledge of Farquhar's professed attitudes and his belittling the familiar distresses of recruits, we must still ask how *The Recruiting Officer* defines within itself its militaristic attitude.[4] Although Farquhar's dramatic technique forced him to be deeply aware of appraisal and judgment, he concealed neither the chicanery of recruitment nor the dangers of war. He evidently felt that he had made the army's position strong enough to withstand such realistic touches. Some of his rhetoric to this end is general. Farquhar makes his officers sprightly and clever, like Plume and Kite, or (at worst) rattle-brained, like Brazen. These men do not seem ruthless or oppressive. Furthermore, they resemble stock figures – the wit, the adroit valet, the fop – from other plays of the time, so that the audience accepts them and their tricks easily. The civilian characters within the play accept them too. However reluctant to join the army Farquhar's bumpkins are, they huzza for the Queen and declare her 'greater than any King of 'em all', with a patriotic zeal that reflects upon her recruiting agents (II iii 60). No one really challenges Plume's procedures; in fact, they have support from the vivacious and sensible Balance.

The rhetoric and tone of good feelings, with which *The*

Recruiting Officer keeps brimming over, soften the effect of Farquhar's candor in the particular scenes of recruiting and impressment. For instance, the enlistment of Appletree and Pearmain (II iii) is shaped like a little comedy. The two enter singing 'Over the Hills and Far Away', cast themselves in fantasy as a Justice of the Peace and as the Queen, find themselves with a Carolus apiece, and then in a sudden reversal, are condemned to comic confinement: 'I place you both Centinels in this place for two Hours,' Kite commands them, 'to watch the Motion of St. *Mary's* Clock you, and you the Motion of St. *Chad's*' (61 – 62). As they reach this nadir of mechanism and stasis through their trust in their own illusions, Plume enters as the representative of a benevolent government to right them in the name of justice and the Queen. Kite is beaten off the stage and the men properly paid, as their fantasies about being a Justice and the Queen come true, at least by proxy. As the men voluntarily enlist and go off singing 'Over the Hills and Far Away' once more, the action of the first part of the scene finds itself translated into terms of free will and free movement. Perhaps the scene as a whole is ironic, for it offers the pleasures of trickery, so familiar from other comedies of the time. In another sense, however, it is not ironic. The bumpkins are happy; they have been dealt with justly; they are enlisted for country and queen. Plume has gotten what he wanted, but he has given them a version of what they had wanted too.[5]

Impressment seems crueler than trickery to a modern audience, and may have to Farquhar's also. Here, in the courtroom scene (V v), he uses tone and rhythm to guard against misplaced pity. The scene begins and ends with encounters between Kite and the Constable, framing three cases before the court. The third is Silvia's, and as a result the audience has a focus of attention that prevents it from taking the other events of the episode very seriously: a comic tone is set in anticipation, then in actuality, by Silvia's amusing trial. Although the two cases preceding hers both involve the court's stretching the law, each is so arranged that the impediment is stated first, then ingeniously or comically dismissed. One victim cannot be legally impressed, for his wife and five children depend on him; but he is discovered to be a poacher, and then his wife disqualifies herself by declaring that 'the Parish shall get nothing by sending him away, for I won't loose my Teeming Time if there be a Man left in the Parish' (102). The other victim cannot be legally impressed, for he has a job and a wife; but Kite wittily suggests that the man, a collier, 'has no visible means of a Livelihood, for he works under-ground' (103). While this piece of wit holds everybody's judgment in suspense, the collier's position is completely undercut by his 'wife's' admission that 'We agreed that I shou'd call him Husband to avoid passing for a Whore, and that he shou'd call me Wife to shun going for a Soldier.' The whoremongering rogue who shirks his duty to public and private morality alike immediately loses all sympathy. And the legality of his exemption has now been slurred over by his having felt it necessary to pretend marriage so as to dodge the draft.

Silvia, the third conscript, joins Farquhar's military myth to the traditional romance. In her father and Plume, she loves the central representatives of town and army both; and she herself, through her impersonation, can partake of both worlds. Her volunteering and impressment seem to represent her being handed over to the army by the two respective agents of civil power, the individual citizen and the state. In fact she reverses this process by drafting her father and Plume from the army to forward her romance. She is a recruiting officer in recruit's clothing: the title of the play ends up by describing her, not Plume. As things turn out, she joins the army in the one position of command that neither her Captain nor her Sergeant had thought it possible to offer as an enticement while in the midst of securing their smiths and musicians, drummers and doctors.

Thematically, her double function leads Farquhar to present Silvia hermaphroditically from the start. The girl who 'can do every thing with my Father but drink and shoot flying' (I iii 52) 'think[s] a Petticoat a mighty simple thing, and I'm heartily tir'd of my Sex', and then begins 'to fancy [her] self in Breeches in good earnest' (53); her actions are 'noble and generous, Manly Friendship' so that 'her Sex is but a foil to her' (51, 50). This whole train of images points to her eventual assumption of her brother's clothes, London swagger, and sexual prowess, as well as his inheritance.

If Silvia is a sort of hermaphrodite, the army itself is sexless.

(Again, I am speaking in terms of themes and images, not accusations or innuendoes.) Stonehill, in a note to III ii 77, brings together a group of relevant passages, with an ominous silence about their import:

SIL.   What! Men kiss one another!
KITE.   We Officers do, 'tis our way; we live together like Man and Wife, always either kissing or fighting.

'In the same scene,' says Stonehill, 'Plume offers the "recruit" as final temptation, "You shall lie with me, you young rogue," and kisses him. In Act IV i, of this play, there is another such scene. [Plume seals his enlistment of Silvia with a kiss, and comments, ' 'Sdeath! there's something in this Fellow that charms me.'] In the final scene of Act V, Bullock offers himself to Plume in the place of his sister.' Besides these instances, Brazen and Plume embrace several times, call each other 'Dear', and at least once (v iv 99) exchange 'a Buss.' But it would be silly, I think, to read this sort of thing as a continuing reference to homosexuality. Not that the Restoration stage was deeply averse to amusing an audience with sexual perversion – the subplot of *Venice Preserv'd* and the character of Coupler in *The Relapse* testify otherwise; rather that the rest of this play proves that Kite, Plume, and Brazen simply are not 'sexually maladjusted,' as the polite jargon of today would put it. The lying together and 'bussing' of *The Recruiting Officer* are a recasting, in the idiom of the army, of the forms of civilian romance. Their function is different, because the basic social unit in the army is a platoon rather than a family, but their formal position in the military world is analogous with that of romantic gestures in the civilian world.

Once one realizes this, it becomes clear that Farquhar is furthering the analogy between military and civilian life that the dual role of Silvia suggests. War and marriage are parallel, as in Kite's comment quoted above. Earlier, Kite speaks of the '*Bed of Honour*', an analogue to, and antidote for, the marriage bed (I i 45–6). 'Over the Hills and Far Away' comes directly from a popular song of blighted romance, 'Jockey's Lamentation': ' 'Twas o'er the Hills, and far away,/ That *Jenny* stole my Heart away.'[6] Plume's fathering a bastard also becomes a form of recruiting, like Kite's marriages (I ii 47 – 8), just as Worthy's suit becomes a siege later in the same scene. Here Plume specifically makes the parallel about which I am talking:

PLUME   Shake hands Brother, if you go to that – Behold me as obsequious, as thoughtful, and as constant a Coxcomb as your Worship.
WOR.   For whom?
PLUME   For a Regiment.

Later, Balance makes it: 'For shame, Captain – You're engag'd already, wedded to the War, War is your Mistress, and it is below a Soldier to think of any other' (II i 55). And in line with this, Plume can declare that though he always refuses to fight for a lady, 'for a Man I'll fight Knee deep' (III ii 77).

Farquhar is, on one level, making comedy out of various conventions, like the soldier's reduction of all matters into military jargon, or like the metaphor of sex as war. He is providing himself with a store of amusing *double-entendres*. But on a second level, he is tightening the structure of the play, an exchange of characters between the two valid worlds presented. Both care for the stability of England, the army in its way, Justice Balance's world by its concern for law and inheritance. Socially productive sexual life jars with the army's way, but is compatible with Balance's. Therefore, Farquhar estranges sex from the army. Since the audience expects army life to be bawdy – everyone knows what scandalous things these soldiers do – Farquhar includes the Molly episode at the very beginning. But such tribute-money to the popular stereotype need not be paid, and is not, after he has made plausible the hilarious and thematically useful parodies that we have been discussing.

While Roebuck and Sir Harry Wildair must be converted to virtue by learning, Captain Plume must be reclaimed by our discovery that he really never was much of a rake at all. His women are only magnets to draw recruits, he informs us. 'No, Faith, I am not that Rake that the World imagines; I have got an Air of Freedom, which People mistake for Lewdness in me, as they mistake Formality in others for Religion' (IV i 82). Critics have complained that this speech is artistically crude and inconsistent, or that it marks Farquhar's selling out to the new morality and sentimentalism. Both accusations may be true – the former surely is – but they are also superficial in their failure to understand that Plume's self-defense is thematically necessary. It is not a sudden sop to prudes, but the result of Farquhar's zeal to exculpate the army. To allow the army to corrupt, rather than merely to parody, the civil proprieties would be to undermine the strength of social order that the whole play justifies, and that makes the whole play work. If Farquhar seems to indict the army along with Plume at the beginning, in deference to the popular notion of scandal and danger, he quickly turns to a rhetoric that reverses original expectations and reclaims the honor of his army.

Silvia's dual role, we have said, suggests the analogy between military and civilian life in terms of the complex war-sex metaphor or parody. There is a second set of parallels and parodies between the army and the city, suggested by what one might call Silvia's 'formal hypocrisy'. By 'formal' I do not mean to emphasize that her 'hypocrisy' is not to be condemned, although of course it is not. I mean that in playing her dual role, she exploits social forms and social rituals such as recruitment or perhaps even wenching by participating in their letter and not their spirit. Farquhar shows us that Silvia's temperament thrives on such equivocal irony by giving her a first scene in which she subverts a quiet afternoon tea with her cousin. She is perfectly equipped to carry on her own recruiting as Plume and Kite carry on theirs, and with very much the same impish will.

In one sense, she levies a mock justice against an army that practices 'hypocrisy' like hers; and in Plume's capture, Farquhar uses the standard comic plot of the cheater cheated. ' 'Tis the sport', as Hamlet says, 'to have the enginer/ Hoist with his own petar.' The army, in recruiting, takes advantage of the analogy between the military and civil orders, subverting in one way or another a whole series of normal civilian relationships so as to transfer people from the Shrewsbury society into the regiment. The Rose episode alone exploits marriage, which Plume promises; courtship, which Rose will use to enlist her swains; the relationship between brother and sister; and the relationship between buyer and seller. In the same way, Pearmain and Appletree are marked for likely recruits by their friendship, which can be converted into the *cameraderie* typical of the military men in the play. They are eventually caught through the empty form of giving out recruiting money and Plume's rendering the forms of justice. Later in the play, Kite points out that the trades of butcher and smith can be translated into the military idiom as surgeon and gunwright, and uses the empty forms of prediction and promise to catch his men. In each case, analogies between natural civilian relationships and military ones offer victims for recruitment, who are trapped by that abuse of relationships which I have called 'formal hypocrisy'.

The army, by strict moral logic, should be punished in some way for these offenses against the natural order. But Farquhar and his audience approve of the army's methods; and besides, the army should not in any case be attacked. He resolves this pair of opposed claims by making Plume the happy scapegoat or surrogate for whatever moral censure the audience may care to levy against the tricks of recruiting. Silvia dupes Plume and her father, who has connived in the recruiting procedures, by turning their own methods against them. Ordinarily in comedy it is the villain who is swept away at the end by having his schemes boomerang; here Plume, and to a lesser extent Balance, 'suffer' a kind of token punishment, nominally in the villain's place. As surrogate characters, standing in for the 'erring' forces of government, Plume and Balance are being used by Farquhar in the same way that Pearmain and Appletree are used at the beginning of the play to absorb the audience's scorn for the provincial and thus to make possible an unprejudiced view of Shrewsbury and the Balances.

Farquhar employs other kinds of surrogacy in *The Recruiting Officer*, too. His skill with the device suggests a remarkable advance in his ability to unify his work despite the difficulties of dealing at once with three plots and a wide range of social types and situations. Silvia's disguise as Owen Balance/Jack Wilfull stands, as one might expect, as the most interesting as well as the most prominent example of surrogacy. Farquhar sets it up by including the dramatically irrelevant death of Owen. Thus robbed of a brother, she re-creates him, physically, socially, and financially. Like Viola in Shakespeare's *Twelfth Night*, she brings to life through an act of will what nature has taken away. Like

Viola too, her volitive must come true.[7] Justice Balance's discovery of her hermaphroditic role, in which she is at once his hidden son and daughter, restores his daughter to him; but Balance also, in admitting Plume as Silvia's husband, restores his son and heir. Balance thus executes an act of paternal justice that stands parallel to the act of social justice executed in the courtroom scene, each one validating its own brand of recruiting.

Another surrogate relationship is that between Melinda and Silvia. This relationship depends on parallelism, but it goes beyond the simple sort of parallelism represented by, say, Plume and Worthy, in that Melinda is made to exculpate her cousin as Plume and Balance exculpate the army. I discussed above the way in which Farquhar allies the audience with Silvia at her first appearance (I iii) by opposing her fresh candor to Melinda's pouting airs. Melinda must be made worse so that Silvia can look better. The development of the parallelism, first mentioned by Worthy (I ii), continues to amplify this relationship: the girls are cousins, both heiresses who have been the subject of 'wicked Insinuations, artful Baits, deceitful Arguments, cunning Pretences, . . . impudent Behaviour, loose Expressions, familiar Letters, [and] rude Visits', as Melinda says (V iii 98). But the foolish and passive cousin has first wavered at the brink of capitulation, and then, upon inheriting £20,000, grown insufferably haughty. The other cousin, who has announced to her suitor that 'she wou'd have the Wedding before Consummation', has remained constant, and she gets what she wants without posturing or pain. Her service as recruit matches and mocks Melinda's service to Brazen, as her sexless night with Rose does the others' impotent flirtation. While Silvia can be the recruiting officer of the play, Melinda must eventually be recruited, as indeed, through Kite's recruiting disguise, she is. Furthermore, Melinda begins to act as she should only after being duped by the disguised Kite through her credulity about the pretended absolutism of planetary law; in the parallel situation, confronted by the actually absolute law of the state, Silvia holds to her complete supremacy and free will. Farquhar arranges each of these instances to belittle Melinda, and so to reaffirm the central position of Silvia in the play.

We may observe that in all this talk about the arrangement of affairs in *The Recruiting Officer*, nothing has been said about a process of education, such as goes on in one form or another in the early plays and *The Inconstant*. There really is no such process of education in late Farquhar. While characters may learn to mend their ways, as Melinda does or as Aimwell does in *The Beaux' Stratagem*, the plays do not turn upon individual reform. They are more interested in exhibiting an ideal system of social relationships in tune with reason and moral law. Faulty characters are not so much purged as reestablished in proper positions. The foppish Brazen, for instance, almost suffers a marriage with the maid Lucy. In many Restoration plays, in Farquhar's *Love and a Bottle* for that matter, the sloughing of the fop in marriage to a servant or whore comes at the end of the play and is looked upon as a piece of poetic justice. *The Recruiting Officer* treats it only secondarily as poetic justice. Primarily, it is a way of pushing Brazen firmly into place. Once he accepts his proper role, he not only is entrusted with all the recruits but also is allowed for once to be perfectly accurate in spouting a genealogy, that of Balance's 'Unkle that was Governour of the *Leeward* Islands' and 'play'd at Billiards to a miracle' (V vi 109). Such treatment is more heavily social in orientation than the usual tucking-in of loose ends with a comic resolution. Here, as we shall see in the discussion of *The Beaux' Stratagem*, Farquhar was moving toward a kind of comedy that went beyond the individual to the relational patterns of law.

SOURCE: *George Farquhar* (New York, 1967) pp. 128–41.

NOTES

1. [*The Complete Works*, ed. Charles Stonehill (London, 1930) is the edition used throughout this essay – Ed.]

2. *Scarron's Comical Romance of a Company of Stage Players*, Part II, Ch. 14, in *The Whole Comical Works of Mons'. Scarron*, trans. Thomas Brown, *et al.* (London, 1703) pp. 176–200. This is one of several editions of Sophia's story, 'The Judge in her own Cause', that would have been available to Farquhar.

3. Two articles by Robert L. Hough in *Notes and Queries* discuss all

these errors save the bumpkins' change of names: 'An Error in "*The Recruiting Officer*"' and 'Farquhar: "*The Recruiting Officer*",' in CXCVIII (1953) 340–41, and CXCIX (1954) 474, respectively.

4. William Gaskill's otherwise excellent production of *The Recruiting Officer* at the National Theatre in London (1963) tried to stress skeptical anti-heroic elements, even to the extent of minor tampering with Farquhar's text. One proof of Farquhar's deep militarism is that Gaskill's careful changes of stress and text seemed discordant and failed of their effect.

5. Farquhar's handling of this scene may be contrasted with that of Bertolt Brecht, who adapted *The Recruiting Officer* in 1955 as *Pauken und Trompeten* (*Trumpets and Drums*). Brecht, who turns the play into a piece of pacifistic zealotry, ends the scene with Kite's herding the recruits into the barracks, in a rigid repetition of the action of confinement. Without Farquhar's rhetoric of good feelings, the only pleasure in the scene is cruel. A general comparison of *Pauken und Trompeten* with *The Recruiting Officer* illustrates much about Farquhar's methods; unfortunately, it is outside the scope of this study. [See Wertheim's essay below – Ed.]

6. *Pills to Purge Melancholy*, V 316–21.

7. I am indebted to Professor John Anson for pointing out to me the possibility of reading Viola's disguise as a central creative act.

Eric Rothstein

THE BEAUX' STRATAGEM (1967)

The audacity of Farquhar's innovations in the three full-length plays preceding *The Beaux' Stratagem* was masked, in part deliberately. *The Twin-Rivals*, a brilliant if imperfect assault upon the assumptions of Restoration comedy, was supposed to be shielded by its Christian Collierist principles. This shield turned out to be flimsy, but the mishap came from miscalculation, not blind daring. In a less spectacular way, *The Inconstant* attacked the same assumptions of Restoration comedy, by sapping the ornamented parterres of Fletcher with highly individualized characters and moral seriousness. Here the deviation from Fletcher increases as the play goes on, so that Farquhar's audience was eased unwitting into the new dimension of judgment. Lastly, *The Recruiting Officer*, with its novelties of structure and technique, followed its pair of predecessors in its use of conventional plots and character types. As a practicing playwright, Farquhar must have felt himself obliged, for his own sake if not for the company's, to tone down the new and ingenious for an inertial public taste. When he began *The Beaux' Stratagem*, however, he was a dying man, and knew it. Given the state of early eighteenth-century medicine, he would have had to have been a fool not to know it, and also to know, given the state of the eighteenth-century theater, that no matter how well or how poorly his new comedy did, the want of his family could not be long assuaged. Perhaps it is this that enabled him to write so independent a play, to dress to such advantage the ideas and attitudes that had concerned him since the failure of *Sir Harry Wildair*.

When I talk about the 'independence' of *The Beaux' Stratagem*, I mean that its intellectual and formal structure is openly novel. I do not mean to imply that the play spins about its own axis only, free from the constant gravitation of other plays and changing audiences. After spending years at his profession, always writing within the dramatic grammar of his time, Farquhar could not have practiced wilfulness even if he had wanted to. And there is no sign that he wanted to. On the contrary, his Aesopian theory of comedy, as he described it in the 'Discourse', would have led him to conceive of comedy as a mode of rhetoric. Rhetoric has to communicate, and it can communicate only in language that people can understand, therefore a language that (in the case of plays) has been developed and refined by dramatic experiences. *The Beaux' Stratagem* has and uses a context of dramatic experiences, and, as I shall point out, a context of contemporary ideas, that provide much of the motive force behind its rhetoric.

Before discussing these contexts, however, it may be useful to discuss another kind of source, this one genetic. Shrewsbury, its setting and its people, provided the models for *The Recruiting Officer*. We know this because of Farquhar's dedication to the play, which alerts us that he has written a *roman à clef* (or *drame à clef*), and which therefore makes credible the Blakeway letter that offers the key to translate art into life. Farquhar remained silent about similar sources for *The Beaux' Stratagem*, either because of his incapacitating illness or because there were none; but equivalents of the Blakeway letter have claimed that he followed an analogous procedure, and that the characters in the play are based on actual Lichfield townspeople. Some of the early biographers make unsupported claims to this effect, but the earliest piece of evidence comes from an obituary in 1759 for Thomas Bond, 'servant in Sir The. Biddulph's family great part of his life'. It remarks that Bond was 'said to be the original from whom Mr. Farquhar took his character of Scrub in the Beaux Stra[ta]gem'. A later book, Thomas Harwood's *The History and Antiquities of the Church and City of Lichfield* (1806), elaborates: '[In Bridge Street] stands the George Inn, the landlord of which, in 1707, Farquhar, in his comedy of the *Beaux Stratagem*, has drawn in the character of *Boniface*. . . . Lady Biddulph, who then occupied the Bishop's Palace, was supposed to have been personated in the character of *Lady Bountiful*. *Cherry* was the daughter of one Harrison, who kept the George.'[1]

These identifications, even if they are accepted (and there is no strong reason why they should be), could add to the meaning of the play only for Lichfield antiquarians; they do not even have the same mild rhetorical significance as do those for *The Recruiting Officer*, since Farquhar did not feel that courtesy urged him to spare the feelings of innkeeper Harrison as he spares those of Justice Berkley. Nor is either Cherry or Scrub sufficiently striking a character to have gained much by having been modeled on a real person, even if the creator of Mandrake and Old Mirabel had needed that sort of artistic push. What the hypothesis of living models does indicate, whether it is true or not, is a public consciousness of Farquhar's having broken with the ideals of Restoration comedy. In Etherege and Wycherley, even in Vanbrugh and Cibber, lower-class characters exist in a conventional anonymity. Sometimes they are buffoons and sometimes ornaments of their masters' equipage, but almost never people. No one, I suspect, would accuse or credit any of those playwrights with using real men and women as Farquhar is said to have used them, as models for lower-class characters independent of their dramatic superiors and of the taint of the provinces. *The Beaux' Stratagem* follows the tack taken by *The Recruiting Officer* in lessening the social and geographical bias of Restoration comedy, and in this sense both plays look forward to Fielding rather than back to the King Charles wits.

The wits, his predecessors and contemporaries, do serve Farquhar by providing a context within which his works may be read. *The Recruiting Officer* amiably shared characters and conventions with the wits; *The Twin-Rivals* inverted and parodied their values with a vengeance. *The Beaux' Stratagem* found Farquhar going back to the method of *The Twin-Rivals*, but with more subtlety. In the earlier comedy, he had stressed a moral point through direct parodic comparison, to make clear his discontent. He now preferred to stress his aesthetic superiority to his colleagues, and thereby to win his audience to the moral position that they had found dramatically most satisfying. But so as to avoid talking in a vacuum, let me move to specific examples.

Partly because of the Collier controversy, partly because of the temper of the times that made Collier possible, the subject matter of comedy had undergone change in the decade or so before *The Beaux' Stratagem*. Playwrights dealt less and less with the dashing rakes who had enthralled the Restoration stage, and had begun to consider more specifically social matters, such as marriage. Vanbrugh's *Relapse* and *Provok'd Wife*, Cibber's *Love's Last Shift* and *Careless Husband*, Burnaby's *Reform'd Wife* and *Modish Husband*, and Steele's *Funeral* and *Tender Husband* take marital troubles as their focus, in a way that none of the comedies of Etherege or Wycherley or Congreve do.[2] Farquhar was quite in vogue. He takes advantage of this by tipping in allusions to other plays, to other men's resolutions of the problems with which he is concerned. Thereby he can implicitly call attention to the aesthetic ingenuity and moral rectitude of his own resolution, the divorce of the Sullens.

For instance, Berinthia's seduction scene with Loveless in Vanbrugh's *Relapse* probably served to prompt Mrs. Sullen's seduction scene with Archer (v ii). The rectitude of *The Beaux' Stratagem* demands that Archer be interrupted, as Loveless and Berinthia are not; the rectitude of Mrs. Sullen demands that she refuse illicit advances, even though she has earlier told Dorinda: 'Tho' to confess the Truth, I do love that Fellow; – And if I met him drest as he shou'd be, and I undrest as I shou'd be – Look'ye, Sister, I have no supernatural Gifts; I can't swear I cou'd resist the Temptation, – tho' I can safely promise to avoid it; and that's as much as the best of us can do' (IV I 70).[3] Now, at the height of desire and of opportunity, temptation has been unavoidable. In a similar situation, Berinthia calls out 'Help, help, I'm Ravish'd, ruin'd, undone.' – but she calls, as the stage direction tells us, '*Very softly*'.[4] The humor of Vanbrugh's scene comes from Berinthia's hypocrisy; but in Farquhar, where Mrs. Sullen's 'Thieves, Thieves, Murder' bursts out with real conviction, the joke cannot be at her expense. Instead, Farquhar builds the scene on an incongruity that is at once funny and significant. Mrs. Sullen's cries turn out to be unexpectedly accurate, for thieves have broken into the house. The effects of the tension between Berinthia's words and motives are picked up in the tension between Mrs. Sullen's words and their undesigned meaning. By this twist, Farquhar not only keeps the joke but also unifies two plots brilliantly. Archer and the thieves are compared with each other so as to clarify Archer's moral position; but as the comparison incriminates him, his bravery simultaneously makes his crime seem milder. Farquhar's scene achieves everything its unwitting competitor could, and more. It is morally purer, and argues for its moral purity by its aesthetic superiority.

Or, to take another example of a slightly different sort from *The Relapse*, Berinthia remarks that she and her late husband lived

> Like Man and Wife, assunder;
> He lov'd the Country, I the Town.
> He Hawks and Hounds, I Coaches and Equipage.
> He Eating and Drinking, I Carding and Playing.
> He the Sound of a Horn, I the Squeak of a Fiddle.
> We were dull Company at Table, worse A-bed.
> And never agreed but once, which was about lying alone.

Farquhar picked up the speech for the countercharges of the Sullens:

> MRS. SUL. In the first Place I can't drink Ale with him.
> SUL. Nor can I drink Tea with her.
> MRS. SUL. I can't hunt with you.
> SUL. Nor can I dance with you.
> MRS. SUL. I hate Cocking [cock-fighting] and Racing.
> SUL. And I abhor Ombre and Piquet [fashionable card games]. . . .
> MRS. SUL. Is there on Earth a thing we cou'd agree in?
> SUL. Yes – to part. (v iv 189 – 90)

Berinthia's pert antitheses, suggesting both her wit and her having the formulated situation well in hand, become a more emotional set of contrasts in the Sullens' exchange. The third person pronouns of the first pair of lines warm to the direct 'you's' of the next and to the more vehement verbs of the pairs after that. The final solution is an aesthetic as well as an argumentative climax, made more striking by its sudden brevity. Beyond this immediate effect, Farquhar offers divorce as a natural and meaningful resolution to the discord, while Vanbrugh has mustered up nothing better than killing off Berinthia's husband before the play itself begins, and has left himself no way of resolving the marital tensions that the play itself develops. Such handling accords with Vanbrugh's declaration that the pleasure and moral of comedy 'lies much more in the Characters and the Dialogue, than in the Business and the Event'.[5] Farquhar, the lover of Aesop, rejected such theory, and used allusion to make the audience reject it too.

The treatment of divorce leads to consideration of an allusion that operates at the dramatic and ideological core of *The Beaux' Stratagem*. After much grave nodding in approval of his advanced discussion of ideas, scholars were confounded to learn that Farquhar had merely excerpted his thoughtful speeches about marriage from Milton's *Doctrine and Discipline of Divorce*.[6] For example, the Sullens'

SUL.   You're impertinent.

MRS. SUL.   I was ever so, since I became one Flesh with you.

SUL.   One Flesh! rather two Carcasses join'd unnaturally together.

MRS. SUL.   Or rather a living Soul coupled to a dead body. (III iii 156)

comes from Milton's saying of a discordant couple, 'instead of beeing one flesh, they will be rather two carkasses chain'd unnaturally together; or, as it may happ'n, a living soule bound to a dead corps' (II xvi). When Mrs. Sullen complains of 'the golden Links of Wedlock' and 'Iron Manacles of Law', she is recalling not the proverbial 'Chains of gold are stronger than chains of iron', but Milton's eloquent revision of it, 'To couple hatred, therefore, though wedlock try all golden links, and borrow to her aid all the iron manacles and fetters of Law, it does but seek to twist a rope of sand' (II xxii). Given verbal parallels as close as these – and these are not the only ones – we can safely assume that the coincidences in thought and argument between Farquhar and Milton are not fortuitous, but derivative.

Willard Connely provides one explanation for this extensive borrowing by bringing in biographical suppositions:

Then Farquhar got down to the question that was really on his mind: what to do with a man and wife who were mutually and hopelessly antipathetic. To all appearances, on such meagre evidence as does exist, a certain degree of antipathy had for some time been verily the position between himself and Margaret Farquhar. Writing even from his death-bed, poor Farquhar could no less write with feeling, with expostulation, if he had been bored, soured, beaten down by domestic wrangling. But how was he to write dialogue about divorce, this quite new thing in Restoration comedy? It must sound convincing, and he had no experience of it. He had been reading both the prose and the poetry of John Milton; his head was full of him.

And so 'Farquhar, in 1707, a man who if he had not already left his wife evidently wanted to, distilled [his] dialogue' from the 'promulgations written in 1643, by a man whose wife had left him'.[7] Connely may of course be right in supposing that Farquhar's desire for at least a vicarious divorce prompted his choice of subject. Perhaps Connely might even have been able to argue, had he chosen to, that the villain in the play has been made the husband so that Farquhar could disguise its biographi-cal relevance, or psychologically atone for his wish to get rid of poor Margaret. Perhaps too Connely might have been able to argue that Shadwell's *Epsom Wells* (1673) ends in a separation because Mrs. Shadwell nagged Thomas, or that one of the bachelor William Burnaby's female friends was such a virago as to impel him to end his *Ladies Visiting-Day* (1701) with Sir Testy Dolt's declaration: 'Well, I'll go to *Doctors Commons* [registry court] immediately, and be the first Citizen that ever had the honour of a Divorce.'[8] No evidence supports any of these contentions; and, more damagingly, they not only add little to understanding the plays, but also tend to usurp the place of artistic analysis with their rather facile biographical guesses.

Farquhar's use of Milton has a purpose similar to that of his allusions to *The Relapse*. In other words, he has moral and aesthetic ends to forward, not subconscious urges to express and exorcise. Nor do I think that he is proselytizing for Milton's ideas, surely not primarily. The tone of the play is much too light to shock the audience with the miseries of enforced marriage; and, as for introducing the ideas to a wide audience, that was probably unneeded, for they were, one would suppose, familiar to the well-read citizen. Such standard works as Pierre Bayle's *Dictionary* or Baron Pufendorf's *Law of Nature and Nations*, a compendious encyclopaedia of natural law, discussed Milton's thesis. Since interest in divorce was increasing, his ideas presumably became progressively better known and, if not accepted, respectable.[9]

What Farquhar is doing is trying to justify, aided by Milton's mind and metaphors, the dubious proceedings of Mrs. Sullen and Sir Charles Freeman at the end of the play. This was in part made necessary because the eighteenth-century wife was very much her husband's subordinate:

Women in *England*, with all their Moveable Goods so soon as they are married, are wholly *in potestate Viri*, at the Will and Disposition of the Husband.

If any Goods or Chattels be given to . . . a married Woman, they all immediately become her Husband's: She can't Let, Set [deposit as security], Sell, Give away, or Alienate any thing without her Husband's Consent.

Her very necessary Apparel, by the Law, is not hers in Property. If she hath any Tenure at all, . . . she holds it of, and by her Husband. . . .

So the Law makes it as high a Crime, and allots the same Punishment to a Woman that shall kill her Husband, as to a Woman that shall kill her Father or Master; and that is Petit-Treason, to be burnt alive.[10]

Under these circumstances, one can see that an eighteenth-century audience might well react with hostility to Farquhar's denouement if that denouement were not prepared for. Farquhar uses Milton's ideas as his enabling clause to ratify the final action of Sir Charles and his sister.

Understanding Farquhar's use of Milton clarifies what may be yet another allusion to Vanbrugh. Stonehill tells us that 'it is highly probable that the domestic infelicity between Sullen and his wife was suggested to Farquhar by Vanbrugh's *The Provok'd Wife*' (117). In that play, as in *The Relapse*, Vanbrugh handles the resolution of the plot carelessly. Lady Brute, the mistreated wife, acts with Constant very much as Mrs. Sullen acts with Archer, but the end of the play leaves their intrigue still uncertain, so that Sir John Brute can only remark: 'after all, 'tis a Moot Point, whether I am a Cuckold or not' (v v). Vanbrugh himself says, as Farquhar would not, 'I own there is no mighty Plot in the whole matter', and leaves his play, as Farquhar would not, moral only by negative example: 'the ill Consequence of [Sir John Brute's] Brutality appears in the Miscarriage of his Wife: for tho' his ill usage of her does not justify her Intrigue, her intriguing upon his ill usage, may be a Caution for some'.[11] I have pointed out above how Farquhar bests Vanbrugh aesthetically, at least in terms of plausible and pleasing structure. He bests Vanbrugh morally not only by presenting morally justifiable characters, as we have seen, but also by bracing his structurally apt conclusion with Milton's argument from natural law.

Before going further, 'natural law' ought to be defined. We may begin with an exposition given by John Locke, unpublished during Farquhar's life, but responsive to English thought of the time. Natural law, Locke wrote, is 'a law which each can detect merely by the light planted in us by nature', that is, by reason and sense-experience. It is 'the decree of the divine will . . . indicating what is and what is not in conformity with rational nature, and for this very reason commanding or prohibiting'. Such a law conforms with 'the natural constitution of the universe, and, particularly, with the nature of man' and therefore achieves universality 'like the laws attaching to natural phenomena but unlike those of different [political] states'.[12]

Of course, these laws were subject to disputation, since the 'nature of man' is an ambiguous proposition to reason from. Some of the conclusions, as Pufendorf's *Elements of Jurisprudence* confesses, 'can be deduced from the principles more clearly, some more obscurely, some are nearer and others further from the principles' 'the truth and necessity of which results immediately from the very circumstances of human nature'.[13] Nevertheless, jurists, theologians, and laymen all helped extend the province of natural law so that civil law, civil relations (buyer – seller, host – guest, etc.), and personal relations were all discussed as deductions or special cases of the universal law. *The Beaux' Stratagem* uses it to govern the latter two categories. For our purposes, we may note that natural law (*a*) replaces moral dogma, at least in theory, with argument based on reason and observation, (*b*) deals with a system of relationships instead of a code of individual behavior, (*c*) supplies a universal law applicable to people, or characters, of every social class or position, in a tremendous number of varied social circumstances. Farquhar accepts these tenets, and develops them theoretically and imaginatively.

The most overt statement comes from Mrs. Sullen. 'Nature', she says, 'is the first Lawgiver', and she proceeds to equate 'Nature' (in this context) with 'heaven':

> Wedlock we own ordain'd by Heaven's Decree,
> But such as Heaven ordain'd it first to be,
> Concurring Tempers in the Man and Wife
> As mutual Helps to draw the Load of Life.
> View all the Works of Providence above,
> The Stars with Harmony and Concord move;
> View all the Works of Providence below,
> The Fire, the Water, Earth, and Air, we know
> All in one Plant agree to make it grow.
> Must Man the chiefest Work of Art Divine,
> Be doom'd in endless Discord to repine?
> No, we shou'd injure Heaven by that surmise,
> Omnipotence is just, were Man but wise. (III iii 160)

Like the argument of Farquhar's 'Discourse', Mrs. Sullen reasons from final causes, rebelling against the marital version of the 'rules', and insisting upon pragmatic definition in terms of effect upon personal lives and divine order. This insistence, shared by Milton, on the rational deduction of law from the nature of things places the discussion of divorce in *The Beaux' Stratagem* within the context of arguments from natural law. But for that context to be morally operative in the play, Farquhar must establish it. In fact, he does better. He uses its regulatory power to establish the bases of judgment in all the plots of the play, and converts the connotations of 'Nature' into a central metaphor through which judgment can be embodied in aesthetically forceful terms.

All the events in the play focus on the house of Lady Bountiful. At first it is difficult to see why, for Lady Bountiful herself seems to be an extraneous character. She unravels no tanglings of the plot. She is not in general funny. The part could hardly have been inserted to please the actress who played it, Mrs. Powell, or her fans, if she had any – it is not enough of a plum for that, and not enough of a plum to be an eager exploitation of her individual talents. And Farquhar does not need Lady Bountiful's house, since the Sullens might just as well have lived together with Dorinda in their own. One can only presume that her thematic function must be of great importance. On inspection, she seems to have taken over much of the intellectual significance of Justice Balance in *The Recruiting Officer*. She is not, of course, his direct descendant, because the 'problem' of *The Beaux' Stratagem* is so different from that of its predecessor. For the renewal of society that the Shrewsbury marriages portend, the justice symbolized by Balance and the army must be extended creatively and naturally through Silva's imposture. In Lichfield, on the other hand, we begin with openhandedness and nature, and infuse it with justice. Both plays thus end by wedding justice and nature, but each play begins with a different half of the pair. Balance, who interprets nature as taking vengeance for past malfeasances (II ii 56), and who judges prospective sons-in-law by worldly prudence, suggests a good but limited justice. (In his niece Melinda, this sort of near-sighted justice becomes the vindictiveness that tries to block two desired marriages.) Lady Bountiful, on the other hand, stands for a limited but benevolent nature.

Her great house, as Mrs. Sullen's complaints testify, lies in a bucolic countryside, which suits the theme of nature. Here Lady Bountiful practices the art of natural healing, unjustly scorned by her daughter-in-law as 'spreading of Plaisters' brewing of Diet-drinks, and stilling Rosemary-Water' (II i 134). According to the more objective Boniface, this conversion of raw nature into healing or harmonious natural artifice is highly successful:

My Lady *Bountyful* is one of the best of Women: Her last Husband Sir *Charles Bountyful* left her worth a Thousand Pound a Year; and I believe she lays out one half on't in charitable Uses for the Good of her Neighbours; she cures Rheumatisms, Ruptures, and broken Shins in Men, Green Sickness, Obstructions, and Fits of the Mother in Women; — the Kings-Evil, Chin-Cough, and Chilblains in Children; in short, she has cured more People in and about *Litchfield* within Ten Years than the Doctors have kill'd in Twenty; and that's a bold World. (I i 127)

Her naïvete, however, which is so sparklingly plain in her

treatment of the 'sick' Aimwell (IV i 162 – 65), confines her to
superficial judgments of people, and deprives her of justice. It is
no accident that in her house the swords of justice 'won't draw' (V
iii 182), leaving the beaux to give the burglars their due.
'Foolishly fond of her Son *Sullen*', unable therefore to be just
about his faults, she must be excluded from the dialectic of the
play.

Lady Bountiful is a constant cornucopia: she gives freely and
unaffectedly whatever she has. The beaux, who do participate in
the 'dialectic', begin the play as skilled hunters (Aimwell,
Archer), completely self-interested predators out to shoot and
devour beauty and bounty. Their gifts are counterfeit, as
Farquhar indicates by having Archer take the name 'Martin',
probably a reference to the expression 'St. Martin's ware' ('sham
finery') and an obvious undercutting of his real Christian name,
Frank. We learn from their first dialogue that their allegiance is
to the values of the town, where Fortune protects '*Jack
Handycraft*, a handsom, well dress'd, mannerly, sharping Rogue'
and leaves 'poor *Jack Generous*' walking alone in 'his Autumnal
Perriwig, shading his melancholly Face, his Coat older than
anything but its Fashion, with one Hand idle in his Pocket, and
with the other picking his useless Teeth' (Ii 128). The beaux are
keen-sighted enough to recognize the inequity, but remain
totally committed to the society that promotes it: 'so much
Pleasure for so much Money, we have had our Penyworths, and
had I Millions, I wou'd go to the same Market again. O *London,
London!*' The tone is light, the gentlemen witty, the hedonism
popular, so that as yet Farquhar levies no moral tax upon
Aimwell and Archer. He merely sketches in their thematic
opposition to Lady Bountiful, whose normative character has
been the first real subject of conversation in the play.

As the play moves on, however, he so to speak squeezes them
away from their self-serving hedonism through making that
position morally unpleasant. To do this, Farquhar employs his
technique of surrogate characters, developed to fineness in *The
Recruiting Officer*. He lets the beaux' activities go on, but does not
continue stressing their motives; thereby he creates a vacuum of
intention into which he places surrogate characters. These
surrogates, whose motives are stressed, can receive moral blame

as proxies for the beaux. At the same time they induce a new moral consciousness that blocks the beaux from sinning with impunity.

Perhaps this process may begin to be seen more clearly in a specific instance of its use, the career of the innkeeper Boniface. His name is a token of his duplicity, since beside its etymology of do-good (Latin, *bonum facere*) float its English connotations of 'bonny face', the handsome *appearance* of virtue.[14] Boniface seems to be the stereotyped country innkeeper, who has 'liv'd in *Litchfield* Man and Boy above Eight and fifty Years', feeding 'purely upon [Lichfield] Ale; I have eat my Ale, drank my Ale, and I always sleep upon Ale' (I i 126). He serves sedulously and quaintly, and relays the country gossip. Without falsifying this first picture, Farquhar enriches it and qualifies it. Boniface turns out to be a highwayman, greedy and unnatural, who would 'betray his Guest, and debauch his Daughter into the bargain' (I i 132). He violates the natural, social, familial, and personal relationships with equanimity. His inn is appropriate for the beaux, then, for he, like them, is a hypocritical user of beauty and bounty for his own ends.

Like them, too, he is a purely sensual man. At first, Farquhar introduces Boniface's bulk merely as joke: plumpness was as funny then as it is now, and it fitted the popular idea of the lazy and untroubled country burgher. By the end of the play, however, Sir Charles Freeman can moralize the belly: 'You and your Wife, Mr. Guts, may be one Flesh, because ye are nothing else – but rational Creatures have minds that must be united' (V i 176). Alien to the rule of justice or nature, Boniface serves not only as a comment on the beaux but also as an antithesis to Lady Bountiful – scenically as well as thematically, because his inn is the only other setting used besides her house. Farquhar has made the polarity clear.

The principles exemplified by the inn and innkeeper must confront those exemplified by the healing manorhouse. Farquhar effects the confrontation through four variations on the theme of intrusion. Politically, the French officer Count Bellair and the chaplain 'Foigard' are interlopers in Lichfield, enemies of England, abusers of hospitality, and foreign plotters against the honor of Mrs. Sullen. Archer and Aimwell, particularly Archer, are parallel to these interlopers; and Scrub's notion that the beaux are Jesuits (III i 144), with the twin implication of zealous subversion and witty deceit, is at least morally just. So is Boniface's notion that the beaux, the second group of intruders, are highwaymen and therefore like his own gang, who are the third group of intruders.[15] In my discussion of Farquhar's allusions to *The Relapse*, I touched upon the thematic significance of the thieves' breaking into the house 'with Fire and Sword' while Archer, fired with lust and sexually armed, makes his violent attempt upon Mrs. Sullen. At this moment of juxtaposition, Scrub takes Archer, quite properly, for one of the thieves, while one of the thieves, Gibbet, unintentionally parodies Aimwell's only justification for acting as he has: 'alack a day, Madam, I'm only a younger Brother, Madam; and so, Madam, if you make a Noise, I'll shoot you thro' the Head; but don't be afraid, Madam' (v ii 180). Obviously, all these parallels are exculpatory as well as incriminatory: one can see that the beaux' actions differ from those of the French and the thieves, the external and internal foes of England. In other words, Farquhar's moral position uses, rather than merely expresses, its norms of nature and justice. Furthermore, the light tone prohibits us from taking the whole thing very earnestly. None the less, the parallels have moral as well as structural significance.

These three groups of interlopers are all vagrants, and in the plot oppose the fourth intruder, Mr. Sullen himself, whose beauty (Mrs. Sullen) or bounty (his strongbox) beckons them on. Sullen is not a Bountiful, as his name makes clear, but a son of Lady Bountiful's first marriage, and therefore only a half-brother to the elegant Dorinda. In a sense, then, he is a cuckoo in the Bountiful nest; thematically, he represents the selfish abuse of beauty and bounty, which excite in him only feelings of jealousy and greed. It is no wonder that he prefers Boniface's inn to the Bountiful house.

Phlegmatic melancholy makes him sullen in fact, emotionally and morally unnatural. This disease, 'the spleen' or 'vapours', was much fancied in the eighteenth century, as a proof of refined nervous sensibility – Cherry and Archer both unnaturally affect it (II ii 138; III iii 153) – but Farquhar casts these pretensions aside to treat 'spleen' medically and morally as a bondage of the spirit to the body. Presumably Lady Bountiful could cure it if she were not so blind to her son's disorders, for the mental disease proceeded from a physical. One eighteenth-century physician prescribed a regimen of '*total Abstinence* from Animal Foods of all Kinds, and all Sorts of strong and fermented Liquors, keeping only to Milk, with Seeds or Grains, and the different Kinds of Vegetable Food', as well as '*Bodily Exercise* and Action . . . towards the Evening, to prepare [the patients] for their Night's quiet Rest'. Sullen drinks, loafs, and stays out late: it is no wonder that his first and last lines in the play are 'My Head akes consumedly'. As our physician says, medical good sense can never help '*the* Voluptuous *and* Unthinking': 'neither of these will ever bear or can receive any Conviction or Reasoning from such *Principles* as I lay down. But the *Laws of Nature*, and the immutable *Relations of Things*, are too stubborn to bend to such Gentlemen.'[16]

These themes of disorder, or disease, infect all Sullen's actions and make them, too, unnatural. In the house of healing, he has intruded his surfeited body, his spoiled mind, and his distempered marriage. His violation of health and nature even cripples his wife, who protects her integrity by acting unnaturally herself. She intrigues with Archer and pretends to intrigue with Count Bellair; and in the bitter afterwash of her failure to make Sullen responsive, she can make 'merry with the Misfortunes of other People' (IV i 161). Her malicious counsel to the country woman, to cure a husband's sore leg by chopping it open, stuffing it with spices, and roasting it, plays on the supposition that husbands are beasts valuable only for the flesh. Mr. Sullen, an extension of Boniface into the Bountiful mansion, has never given his wife reason to believe otherwise.

Act IV ends with matters at their most complicated; their proper resolution seems distant and difficult, as Gibbet elevates discord into a universal principle: 'it is a Maxim that Man and Wife shou'd never have it in their Power to hang one another, for if they should, the Lord have Mercy upon 'um both'. Act V begins with the sudden bold arrival of Sir Charles Freeman, and the doubtful resolutions become clear. Farquhar's importing a knightly savior at the last minute does not stand as his most subtle or dexterous piece of dramatic management. The most that one can say for him is that Sir Charles functions more as a *raisonneur* and bringer of news than as an active figure. He is a narrative and thematic agent who precipitates a resolution that he has never effected. Thus he enters to enlighten Sullen about the letter and spirit of the law (v i 175–6) and to suggest the final divorce. As a fleshly man, Justice of the Peace Sullen knows only the letter of the law, such as the physical act of 'ly[ing] with my Wife' so as not to seem 'an Atheist or a Rake' – in fact, he is a version of both, as an offender against divine and social order. By analogy, he takes metaphor (like 'Sea of Truth') literally. It is no wonder that the card game he wants to play is named 'All-fours'. Sir Charles, not an 'all fours' player, asserts spirit as well as letter. He points out that justice must proceed from nature, that is, he insists upon the procedure of natural law.

The reclamations of the last act spring from the embodiment of these newly stated principles. I have already outlined how the freeing of Mrs. Sullen depends upon natural law. Aimwell's is the next simplest and, I think, the least well conceived. The virtue of Dorinda makes him confess his artifice, and marry only when natural affection and justice are joined. In doing this, he echoes Sir Charles, whose image of proper hierarchy has compared the precedence of the mind over the body to that of the master over the servant (v i 176): Aimwell tells Dorinda (v iv 195) that 'the Beauties of your Mind and Person have so won me from my self, that like a trusty Servant, I prefer the Interest of my Mistress to my own'. The letter of love is worthless without the spirit, and therefore his pretense must be dropped. Aimwell must stop aiming and start giving, if his liberality is to make him a fit member of the Bountiful family. When he does confess, nature and justice coincide and merit is rewarded through his acceding to his viscountcy. As a minor but harmonious note we may recall that Aimwell's brother had been introduced as an undiscriminating Londoner, interested in fashion and possessions. When Aimwell confesses, the brother is dead symbolically as well as literally.

While this resolution is intellectually justifiable, Farquhar's abandoning natural probability at this point damages the less superficial logic of the play. At a moment when he is about to invoke natural law to part his mismatched couple, he asks his audience to suspend their sense of natural movement in the drama and to accept an imposed conclusion. So eager was Farquhar to make his thematic point that he mistakenly gave Aimwell the same Christian name as Sir Charles Freeman, forgetting that Archer had been calling his friend 'Tom' (II ii 138; III ii 145; V iv 185).

Archer's character admits of less reform; and even after his exploits in thief-catching, his 'Adventures' are compared to those of the 'House-breakers' from whom he literally, as well as morally, has received an 'ugly Gash'. Yet he has captured the thieves, and, even more than his besting Bellair in the competition for Mrs. Sullen, the capture certifies him as a man of merit, for he acts as an agent of order in his society. To the extent that the thieves are Archer's likenesses, he has symbolically downed and bound his own passions in them. His success, unlike Aimwell's, remains on the material level, however: he ends up with money, not a girl. On this level, Archer deals with the material world on behalf of the romantic figures. His recovery of Mrs. Sullen's fortune, for instance, depends on his ability to extend the burglary – only the stealing of the strongbox makes its proper restitution possible – but to convert its purpose to that of justice. Complacent in his new riches, he can afford to renounce Mrs. Sullen's, and to restore the honor that he would have destroyed. This action itself represents an extension and conversion of that in the boudoir scene, where Archer's burglarious lust brings Mrs. Sullen back to the honor that she might have squandered. In the same way, his unmasking of Foigard, that false protector of the faith, now is repeated and varied in his unmasking of the venal Gipsey. As with the defeat of Bellair and the testing of Mrs. Sullen, the moral order that emerged because of the Foigard episode was, as far as Archer was concerned, accidental; as with the defeat of the thieves and restoring of the fortune, the moral order that results from the Gipsey episode is intentional. Gipsey, whose name connotes the roguery that also characterizes the old Archer, gives way to Cherry, whose name suggests the fruitful nature of which the new Archer seems to be at least a fitful devotee. Even Boniface, through Archer's and Cherry's intervention, is aligned with justice, resolving the disorders of the town.

If one accepts this reading of the play, and specifically of Archer's mildly spotty reform, one can see that it is impossible for Archer to go off with Mrs. Sullen. In saying this, I must dispute the opinion of Gellert Alleman, who accepts as accurate Mrs. Oldfield's protest that Farquhar 'had dealt too freely with the character of Mrs. *Sullen*, in giving her to *Archer* without a proper Divorce, which was not a Security for her Honour'; Alleman remarks that 'the little anecdote is helpful because it shows the only literal interpretation of Farquhar's fifth act: the heroine goes off into justifiable adultery'.[17] Given the text of the play as we now have it, however, this interpretation appears questionable. In the first place, Archer has accepted £10,000 from Aimwell, Dorinda's marriage portion, and has made the gesture of handing Mrs. Sullen's back to her: the stage picture does not encourage us to believe that they are going to live together. In the second place, the emphasis of Archer's curtain speech falls on the separation of the Sullens, not the promise of anything for the future; and even if just before this speech we have had a dance in which Archer and Mrs. Sullen are partners, the dance music, Archer's 'Song of a Trifle', has made it clear how fleeting any of his affairs must be.[18] In the third place, Mrs. Sullen has been cognizant of her honor during the play, and we are not led to believe that she will change. She refers Archer to Sir Charles to 'thank you for your Services, he has it in his Power' (v iii 184), implying that it is not in hers. Nor does Sir Charles seem to be a man who would forward a sister's adultery. For these dramatic reasons as well as for the thematic reasons that have been discussed, 'justifiable adultery' must be rejected as a sequel to the action of the play.

The Beaux' Stratagem stands as the culmination of Farquhar's brief career. I say this not only because of what Hopkins called (in a different context, of course) 'the achieve of, the mastery of the thing', but also because the problems that had faced him in the earlier plays are here so beautifully developed and resolved. The adjustment of moral values could be executed on a firm and flexible basis which accommodated the wide social range within which Farquhar could most ably work. The complexities of dramatic parody, of surrogate characters, of imposture were cultivated with as much intelligence and even more daring than in *The Recruiting Officer*. And, as with *The Recruiting Officer*, the play was immensely entertaining. Farquhar's tools were in his hands, and his apprenticeship emphatically ended. Before he could use the tools or the craftsmanship, he died.

SOURCE: *George Farquhar* (New York, 1967) pp. 142–59.

NOTES

1.   Stonehill (xxvi) quotes an obituary for Bond appearing in *The Grand Magazine* at the time of Bond's death in late December, 1758; this may be the source for the *Gentleman's Magazine* obituary that I have quoted here. Harwood's *History and Antiquities* was published in Gloucester, in 1806; the references to Farquhar occur on p. 501.

2.   Paul Mueschke and Jeanette Fleisher, 'A Re-evaluation of Vanbrugh', *P.M.L.A.*, XLIX (Sept 1934) 848–89, call attention to Vanbrugh's interest in 'a new code of social values'. They dwell – rather too much, I think – on Vanbrugh's social conscience, and make little distinction between his attitudes and those of Farquhar. As I have pointed out in discussing *The Twin-Rivals*, and point out again in this chapter, Farquhar was conscious of differences between himself and Vanbrugh; I have not emphasized, as Mueschke and Fleisher undoubtedly would, that the very forms of Farquhar's parodying Vanbrugh suggest a kinship between them. Etherege and Wycherley are so removed from Farquhar that he could not make his dramatic points precisely by parodying them.

3.   [The Stonehill edition is used throughout this essay – Ed.]

4.   My references to Vanbrugh come from *The Complete Works of Sir John Vanbrugh*, the plays edited by Bonamy Dobrée, 4 vols. (London, 1927). The seduction scene is IV iii (Vol. I, pp. 68–69). The speech by Berinthia quoted below, beginning 'Like Man and Wife, asunder' comes from II i 45.

5.   Vanbrugh, I 209.

6.   This discovery and my examples are due to the researches of Martin A. Larson, 'The Influence of Milton's Divorce Tracts on Farquhar's *Beaux' Stratagem*', *P.M.L.A.*, XXXIX (1924) 174–78.

7.   Connely biography, pp. 283–4.

8.   William Burnaby, *The Ladies Visiting-Day* (1701) in *The Dramatic Works of William Burnaby* (London, 1931) p. 270.

9.   Gellert Alleman, *Matrimonial Law and the Materials of Restoration Comedy* (Philadelphia, 1942) p. 112.

10. John Chamberlayne, *Magnae Britanniae Notitia*: *Or, the Present State of Great Britain* (London, 1718), part I, book iii, pp. 176–77. This standard handbook – the edition that I cite is the twenty-fifth after 1669 – presents what most Englishmen would have thought the salient points about women's legal rights. For a more detailed discussion, see Baron and Feme, *A Treatise of the Common Law Concerning Husbands and Wives* (London, 1700).

11. Vanburgh, I, 207; Sir John's "'tis a Moot Point', I, 181.

12. John Locke, *Essays on the Law of Nature*, ed. and trans. W. von Leyden (corr. ed.: London, 1958), p. 111; pp. 49–50. The former reference is to Locke's text in von Leyden's translation; the latter to von Leyden's introduction.

13. Samuel Pufendorf, *Elementorum Jurisprudentiae Universalis Libri II*(Cambridge, 1672) p. 183.

14. Perhaps the association of 'Boniface' with the Popes might have acted to denigrate the name with the Protestant English, and also to link the innkeeper with the Catholic Bellair and 'Foigard'.

15. It is significant that Gibbet (IV i 174) speaks of the robbery in terms of an inverted patriotism, calling the thieves' depredations 'a *Vigo* Business' in reference to Rooke's great naval victory of 1702. His earlier imposture as a captain is parodic in the same way.

16. George Cheyne, M.D., *The English Malady* (London, 1733), pp. 163, 180–81, xii.

17. Alleman, pp. 106–7.

18. Furthermore, as late as the end of the last scene (187), Archer is still referring to Cherry as 'my Wench', in Mrs. Sullen's and Sir Charles's presence.

Kenneth Muir

A NEW FORM OF THE COMEDY OF MANNERS (1970)

The Recruiting Officer and *The Beaux' Stratagem* are Farquhar's most original plays and greatly superior to anything he had written before. They both have excellent plots, amusing characters, and lively dialogue; and they both kept their popularity on the boards during the whole of the eighteenth century and after. Indeed, two of the most notable revivals in the present century were that of *The Beaux' Stratagem* by Nigel Playfair at Hammersmith, with Edith Evans as Mrs Sullen (1927), and the National Theatre production of *The Recruiting Officer* in 1963.

The Recruiting Officer was first performed on 8 April 1706 and it was an immediate success. It had been written so hastily that there are several inconsistencies.[1] Lucy forges Melinda's name and yet, later, steals her signature. Silvia calls herself Jack Wilfull and Captain Pinch in different scenes without anyone commenting on the discrepancy. In III ii Plume quotes two couplets previously used by Brazen though Plume had not overheard him. But it is unlikely that these points would be noticed during a performance of the play.

The scenes which give the play its title are concerned with recruiting, and the rivalry to obtain recruits between Plume and Brazen. This ends with Plume disposing of his recruits to Brazen when he himself is to 'raise recruits the matrimonial way'. The second plot is concerned with Silvia's disguising herself as a man for love of Plume; and in the end she wins his hand. The third plot concerns Worthy's love for the heiress Melinda and his jealousy of Brazen because of Lucy's tricks. The three plots are linked together in various ways. Melinda's quarrel with Silvia leads her to write the letter which makes Balance forbid his daughter to think of Plume for a husband, and this makes Silvia disguise

herself. Both Brazen and Plume attempt to enlist her; and Brazen
is Plume's rival as a recruiting officer and Worthy's rival in love.
Melinda and Lucy, as well as potential recruits, visit Kite when
he sets up as a fortune-teller. Balance as Justice of the Peace
decides which men shall be recruited.

Plume, the nominal hero of the play, is an amiable rake, who
will presumably turn over a new leaf when he is married to Silvia.
This, at least, is the implication of Balance's speech to Worthy
(III i) :

I was just such another Fellow at his Age. I never set my Heart upon any
Woman so much as to make my self uneasie at the Disappointment. But
what was very surprizing both to myself and Friends, I chang'd o' th'
sudden from the most fickle Lover to be the most constant Husband in
the World.[2]

There is, of course, an element of sentimentality in this attitude;
and elsewhere Farquhar feels it necessary to explain that, despite
his bastards, Plume is not as bad as his reputation. He tells the
disguised Silvia :

No, Faith, I'm not that Rake that the World imagines; I have got an Air
of Freedom, which People mistake for Lewdness in me, as they mistake
Formality in others for Religion – The World is all a Cheat; only I take
mine, which undesign'd, to be more excusable than theirs, which is
hypocritical. I hurt no body but my self, and they abuse all Mankind –
Will you lye with me?

The last five words of this speech are presumably not intended by
Plume in a sexual sense; but as he has already kissed 'Jack Wilfull'
and admitted 'his' charm, the spectator is bound to regard the
words as equivocal.

Melinda tells Silvia that if she had been a man she would have
'been the greatest Rake in *Christendom*'; and Silvia confesses: 'I
should have endeavour'd to know the World, which a Man can
never do thoroughly without half a hundred Friendships, and as
many Amours.'
In accordance with this view, she agrees to be godfather to
Plume's bastard, and she arranges to sleep with Rose, to protect
her from Plume, rather than out of jealousy. In her masculine

attire, she apes the manners and language of rakes, so that
through her Farquhar is able to satirise what he partly admires.

More interesting than either hero or heroine are the comic
rogues, Sergeant Kite and Captain Brazen. Some of Kite's illegal
methods of recruiting are reminiscent of those used by Falstaff in
Henry IV. But, in addition, he gets some of his recruits by
disguising himself as a fortune-teller; he goes through a form of
marriage with Plume's cast-off mistresses; and, despite his
roguery, he endears himself to the audience by his ingenuity and
by the effrontery of his autobiography:

You must know, Sir, I was born a Gypsie, and bred among that Crew
till I was ten Year old; there I learn'd Canting and Lying. I was brought
from my Mother, *Cleopatra*, by a certain Nobleman for three Pistols,
who, liking my Beauty, made me his Page; there I learned Impudence
and Pimping; I was turn'd off for wearing my Lord's Linen, and
drinking my Lady's Brandy, and then turn'd Bailiff's Follower. There I
learn'd Bullying and Swearing. I at last got into the Army, and there I
learn'd Whoring and Drinking – So that if you Worship pleases to cast
up the whole Sum, *viz.*, Canting, Lying, Impudence, Pimping,
Bullying, Swearing, Whoring, Drinking and a Halbard, you will find
the Sum Total will amount to a Recruiting Sergeant.

Brazen is an equally effective stage character – and a favourite
rôle of actors – but his lies and affectations and the exaggeration
with which Farquhar depicts them make him a figure of farce.
Rose and the recruits are nicely sketched in and the only
unsatisfactory characters in the play are Worthy and Melinda.
Worthy is dull and acts only as a foil to Plume; Melinda is
likewise a foil to Silvia and her actions are determined by the
necessities of the plot.

There is very little wit in the dialogue – perhaps Farquhar felt
that the comedy of wit had reached its apotheosis in Congreve –
but there is plenty of humour, which British audiences have
always found more to their taste. When, for example, Kite
translates 'Carolus' on a coin as Queen Anne; or when the
Constable introduces the three Justices and himself as 'four very
honest gentlemen'; or when the Justices enlist a man because his
wife has a child each year and the wife says, 'Look'e Mr Captain,
the parish shall get nothing by sending him away; for I won't lose

my teeming time if there be a man left in the parish'; or when Rose, disappointed with her bedfellow, complains to Silvia, 'I wonder you could have the conscience to ruin a poor girl for nothing' – such remarks reveal Farquhar as an admirable writer of comedy, but of a comedy far removed from that of the fashionable drawing-room. *The Recruiting Officer* is completely free from the sentimentality of the previous plays. This may be due to the fact that Farquhar knew more about recruiting than he did about fashionable society.

The laughter which the play provokes as M. Hammard says[3] is 'based on tolerance and the joyous acceptance of the world as it is – good in the eyes of the rational, sensible man'. Wit combats would be out of place in such a comedy.

The last of Farquhar's plays, written when he was dying, is also his best. *The Beaux' Stratagem* (1707) has a more original plot, a wittier dialogue, and a livelier group of characters than any of his previous plays. Some critics have complained that the comic Irish Jesuit, Foigard, is a comparative failure and that Count Bellair could be cut without great loss. As to Foigard, we may well agree; and the Bellair episode is a clumsy way of trying to arouse Sullen's jealousy. Another complaint which many critics have levelled against Farquhar is that the 'divorce' by mutual consent at the end of the play is too fantastic and farcical. To which one could argue that it is not intended to be realistic. The pretty ceremony is clearly Utopian. Farquhar had been studying Milton's plea for divorce on grounds other than adultery and he echoes several phrases from *The Doctrine and Discipline of Divorce*.[4] When Sullen tells his wife that they are 'two Carcasses join'd unnaturally together' and she retorts 'Or rather a living Soul coupled to a dead Body'; or when she asks if a bench can 'give Judgement upon Antipathies' and tells Dorinda that 'casual Violation is a transient Injury, and may possibly be repair'd' and that when there is a natural antipathy, 'not all the golden Links of Wedlock nor Iron Manacles of Law can keep 'em fast', Farquhar is paraphrasing or literally quoting from Milton's treatise. And when Mrs Sullen concludes Act III with some rhymed couplets –

> Must Man, the chiefest Work of Art Divine,
> Be doom'd in endless Discord to Repine?

we may be sure that the last word was suggested by Milton's account of the disappointed husband who 'sits repining'. It is reasonable to assume that the divorce scene, far from being farcical, was the thing with which Farquhar was deeply concerned. Mrs Sullen's predicament is pathetic and it could have been treated tragically. Married to a drunken boor, she has no escape under the actual laws at the beginning of the eighteenth century, and she is unwilling to adopt the usual recourse of ill-treated wives. She is allowed a number of complaints about the conduct of her husband, and in one or two places – for example, the end of Act III or the beginning of Act IV – the comic muse is put to flight. But, in general, Farquhar makes her use her misfortunes as a subject for her wit, as in her splendid account of the pleasures of matrimony:

O Sister, Sister! if ever you marry, beware of a sullen, silent Sot, one that's always musing, but never thinks: – There's some Diversion in a talking Blockhead; and since a Woman must wear Chains; I wou'd have the Pleasure of hearing 'em rattle a little. Now you shall see; but take this by the way: – He came home this morning at his usual Hour of Four, waken'd me out of a sweet Dream of something else, by tumbling over the Tea-table, which he broke all to pieces; after his Man and he had rowl'd about the Room, like sick Passengers in a Storm, he comes flounce into Bed, dead as a Salmon into a Fishmonger's basket; his Feet cold as Ice, his Breath hot as a Furnace, and his Hands and his Face as greasy as his Flannel Night-cap. – Oh Matrimony! He tosses up the Clothes with a barbarous swing over his Shoulders, disorders the whole Œconomy of my Bed, leaves me half naked, and my whole Night's Comfort is the tuneable Serenade of that wakeful Nightingale, his Nose! O, the Pleasure of counting the melancholly Clock by a snoring Husband!

Even if Squire Sullen had been a more amicable husband, it is doubtful whether his wife would have been happy, for she shares the opinions of most heroines of the comedy of manners about the superiority of London life to that of the country. When Dorinda tells her she shares in all the pleasures that the country affords, she retorts:

Country Pleasures! Racks and Torments! Dost think, Child, that my

Limbs were made for leaping of Ditches, and clambring over Stiles? or that my Parents, wisely foreseeing my future Happiness in Country Pleasures, had early instructed me in the rural Accomplishments of drinking fat Ale, playing at Whisk, and smoaking Tobacco with my Husband?

Dorinda, Sullen's sister, is a rather colourless foil to his wife, and she obtains as a husband the less interesting of the two adventurers. Aimwell's conversion has been condemned as the intrusion of sentimentality; but it is not so much the conversion as the language in which it is expressed that is at fault: 'Such goodness who cou'd injure! I find myself unequal to the Task of Villain; she has gain'd my Soul, and made it honest like her own: I cannot, cannot hurt her.'

His confession that he is not Viscount Aimwell hardly deserves Dorinda's exclamation: 'Matchless honesty!'

Archer, despite his unscrupulousness, is a gay and attractive figure, whether he is making love to Cherry, making friends with Scrub, trying to seduce Mrs Sullen, or fighting the robbers. Because he is posing as Aimwell's servant, he is able to move up and down the social scale and, being on the verge of penury, his conduct is treated by the author with leniency: for Farquhar himself, as he was writing the play, was dying in a garret.

A number of the minor characters are equally successful. Boniface, with his catch-phrase 'as the saying is', became the generic term for a country inn-keeper throughout the eighteenth century; Cherry, his daughter, has always been a favourite with audiences; Scrub, is a nice mixture of clown and simple-minded country servant; and Gibbet is an amusing rogue.

The dialogue of all these characters is sprightly and humorous. When Gibbet is asked to say a prayer before he is killed, he retorts: 'the government has provided a chaplain to say prayers for us on these occasions'. When Cherry says she is young and doesn't understand wheedling, Boniface exclaims: 'Young! why you Jade, as the saying is, can any Woman wheedle that is not young? Your Mother was useless at five and twenty. Not wheedle! would you make your Mother a Whore, and me a Cuckold, as the saying is?'

Occasionally the play drops into farce as in the scene where

Mrs Sullen, pretending to be her mother-in-law, advises a countrywoman how to cure her husband's sore leg:

Well, good Woman, I'll tell you what you must do. You must lay your Husband's Leg upon a table, and with a Chopping-knife you must lay it open as broad as you can; then you must take out the Bone and beat the Flesh soundly with a rowling-pin; then take Salt, Pepper, Cloves, Mace and Ginger, some sweet Herbs, and season it very well; then rowl it up like Brawn, and put it into the Oven for two Hours.

This is justified by its success. But, when Aimwell awakens from his bogus fit to declaim fustian, audiences tend to be embarrassed:

> Where am I?
> Sure I pass'd the Gulph of silent Death,
> And now I land on the *Elisian* Shore —
> Behold the Goddess of those happy Plains,
> Fair *Proserpine* — Let me adore thy bright Divinity.

In some respects the play looks forward to the novels of Fielding and Smollett; and in other respects it leads on to the comedies of Goldsmith. Farquhar is sometimes blamed for adulterating the comedy of manners; but he was writing for a different audience than the one which had witnessed *The Country Wife* a generation earlier. The old form of comedy was in decline and Farquhar was right to seek for a new form as well as a different subject-matter.

But Farquhar's most staunch admirer, William Archer, praises him for largely irrelevant reasons; that he has a 'sweeter, cleaner, healthier mind' than Congreve or Wycherley; that his characters are less repulsive; that he is more humane than his contemporaries; that his dialogue is more natural because he is not, like Congreve, always striving to be witty; that he gets on with the plot and does not engage in irrelevant discussions; and that he admitted a moral standard. [See extract in Part One, above.]

To all this one may retort that, from the moral point of view, Aimwell's desire to marry a wealthy heiress by pretending to be a lord is worse than any action of Valentine or Mirabell; and the actions of Aimwell and Archer are not rendered more moral by the former's repentance or the latter's failure. Some of Farquhar's dialogue is natural enough; but in many passages he is guilty of pseudo-poetic rant, much further from natural speech than anything in Congreve. Dialogue should not be a mere reproduction of everyday speech and, of course, characters in a play should not be assessed by their virtuousness or wickedness, or we should be in danger of supposing that Falstaff and Volpone were inferior to the Good-Natured Man.

SOURCE: *The Comedy of Manners* (London, 1970) pp. 147–53.

NOTES

1. Cf. Robert L. Hough's articles in *Notes and Queries*, CXCVIII (Aug 1953) and CXCIX (Nov 1954).
2. [The Stonehill edition is used throughout this essay – Ed.]
3. J. Hamard, *Le Ruse des Galants* (Paris, 1965) p. 91.
4. Cf. M. A. Larson's article, *P.M.L.A.*, XXXIX (1924).

Alan Roper

THE BEAUX' STRATAGEM: IMAGE AND ACTION (1971)[1]

To complete the patterns of literary history, it sometimes seems that if Farquhar had not existed, it would be necessary to invent him. In the customary division of neoclassic comedy into forty years of wit and sex and some eighty years of sentiment and love, Farquhar is that necessary thing, a transitional writer. He began his dramatic career in 1698, at a time that was 'in many profound respects a period of transition'.[2] By the laws of sociological determinism it is, then, not surprising to find that his heroes are 'too sincerely eloquent and passionate lovers to be the rakes of Restoration comedy, and are too joyously abandoned to dissipation to be the exculpated prodigals of sentimental comedy'.[3] Farquhar, we learn, is 'the connecting link between the older generation of the Restoration and the rising tide of Cibbers and Steeles'[4] (both of whom, incidentally, were older than Farquhar). Therein lies his sorrow. 'As the child of a transition, he was caught between two sets of antagonistic values; he necessarily formulated no harmonious values of his own.'[5] Poor Farquhar! It was a cross fate that visited upon such a child of his age the combined sins of Rochester and Jeremy Collier.

These formulas of literary history depend customarily upon what may be called a principle of moral extrapolation. Values and attitudes that are, at least potentially, contributions to a total structure of words are detached from that structure, scrutinized in themselves, and allocated a position in a pattern composed of similarly detached pieces from other plays. These pieces may be scenes, statements about the nature of fool, rake, or gentleman, or something to be ranged beneath the awful banner of themes. Such an activity is not especially perverse when it confines itself to descriptive classification, but it rarely does confine itself thus.

Moral values are intoxicating things to critics, and soon lead to the loud confrontation of ethical preferences. We are all familiar with the cries in this ethicocritical war: cynical, immoral, maudlin, mature, immature, responsible, frivolous, aware, myopic.

Critical reaction to one scene may serve to illustrate the possible consequences of such combat. In the fifth act of *The Beaux' Stratagem*, Archer, the unregenerate beau, gains entry into the bedchamber of Mrs. Sullen, a provoked wife of developed sensuality and enfeebled virtue. Archer woos Mrs. Sullen in a mixture of mock-heroic rant, impatient exhortation to hurry on to the right, true end of love, and a nervous reminder to Mrs. Sullen to keep her voice down. He kneels before her in randy excitement, and she, weak, womanly vessel that she is, knows the imminent capitulation of her virtue. 'Rise', she explains, 'rise thou prostrate Ingineer, not all thy undermining Skill shall reach my Heart'.[6] Rarely has the trope of chastity's besieged fortress been put to more pointed comic use. Archer's erotic tunneling is not, after all, directed to her heart. Abandoning the soft sell of persuasion by mythological tropes, Archer lays hold of Mrs. Sullen. 'Thieves, Thieves, Murther', she cries. Enter Scrub, the butler, calling 'Thieves, Thieves, Murther, Popery', and bringing news that a band of robbers has broken in. With seduction interrupted, Archer's attention is given to apprehending the burglars. To one critic, Archer's 'violent wooing' of Mrs. Sullen 'provides a very emotional scene', one of the 'slight sentimental touches in the love-affair' between them. But, fortunately for comedy, this sentimental moment is 'interrupted by a farcical burglary'.[7] To another critic, the scene exemplifies Farquhar's consistent failure to be either artistic or realistic, because his heroes, torn between 'license and honor',

will not commit themselves to either one. Occasionally an Archer steps completely into the comic picture, but then by his side there is always an Aimwell to spout high morality or a Gibbet [the chief burglar] to interfere with the impulses of nature. Archer is the last effort of the Comedy of Manners to maintain its position in the teeth of Jeremy Collier and eighteenth-century propriety.[8]

To the first critic the wooing is sentimental and the interruption a welcome return to the business of comedy, even if at the level of farce. To the second critic the wooing is comic apparently because it exhibits 'the impulses of nature', and the intrusive Gibbet is the rather startling avatar of Jeremy Collier.[9] Their disagreement partly results, I suspect, from an examination of the scene in itself and a measuring of it against some external standard of the comic. But what is important is the demonstrable fact that the scene is a necessary contribution to the total statement of the play, the sum of its doings and sayings. And the fact is important, critically important, just because it is demonstrable.

It was William Archer who pointed somewhere in the direction we should look. He drew a distinction between the dramatist as dramatist and the dramatist as social essayist. In the plays of Wycherley, Congreve, and Vanbrugh he found that the action frequently stands still 'while the characters expatiate in reflection, generalisation, description, and criticism of other characters; in short, in essays or leading articles broken up into dialogue'. Farquhar, by a contrast all in his favor, 'confines his characters within the action, and keeps the action moving. . . . He is much less given to the elaborate portrayal of a Jonsonian "humour" for its own sake.'[10] For William Archer, *The Country Wife* and *The Way of the World* were *The Spectator* struggling to come into being. Archer certainly underestimated both the dramatic effectiveness and the significance of the conversational mode in the best Restoration comedies. But he was right to distinguish it at least from Farquhar's final dramatic mode, in which the means of social definition are a combination of saying and doing, of significant action as a source of verbal analogy.

Such a dramatic mode differs from what we find in a play like *The Old Bachelor* where, instead of action as a source of verbal analogy, we have speech, proper and improper, as the effective action. Congreve's first play exhibits various acceptable and unacceptable life styles, styles that reveal themselves in the way characters use language. These uses of language require for their proper exposition an analysis more detailed than the limits of the present essay permit. But part of the use of language is the use of metaphor, and the use of metaphor in *The Old Bachelor* is not only interesting in itself; it also provides us with some of the terms with which to define, if disjunctively, the use of metaphor in *The Beaux' Stratagem*.

With *The Old Bachelor* before us, it is tempting to say that the wit of the best Restoration comedy is radically metaphorical. Certainly, *The Old Bachelor* displays a life style that uses language, especially metaphor, with a due sense of its signification and implication. This style also reveals itself negatively by indicating the reliance of those evidencing an improper life style upon cliché and a complacent display of rhetoric for its own sake – those false or would-be wits who have caught a trick of speaking without grasping the reason for so speaking. Such propositions will surprise few readers of Restoration comedy, and they may therefore be demonstrated briefly by reference, first, to an exchange between Belinda and Bellmour in *The Old Bachelor* (II ii):

BELINDA   Prithee hold thy Tongue – Lard, he has so pester'd me with Flames and Stuff – I think I shan't endure the sight of a Fire this Twelvemonth.

BELLMOUR   Yet all can't melt that cruel frozen Heart.

BELINDA   O Gad I hate your hideous Fancy – You said that once before – If you must talk impertinently, for Heav'ns sake let it be with variety; don't come always, like the Devil, wrapt in Flames – I'll not hear a Sentence more, that begins with an, I burn – Or an, I beseech you, Madam.[11]

Let us say, then, that proper speaking as an expression of a proper life style requires most conspicuously, in the use of image, an awareness of the concrete significance of vehicles and the necessity to hold to the tenor.

One way in which such proper speaking manifests itself is through the pursuit of a (generally cliché) metaphor or simile, showing the required mental agility by elaborating upon the vehicle in a manner consonant with the tenor. A second way is by drawing attention to another person's foolish or desperate use of cliché, especially the clichés of overstatement. Sometimes one character will ridicule the clichés of another, as in the 'fiery' exchange between Belinda and Bellmour. Sometimes a character, already established as witty, will use ranting tropes he knows or believes acceptable to another in order to gull him:

BELLMOUR   Well, I promise. – A promise is so cold. – Give me leave to swear – by those Eyes, those killing Eyes; by those healing lips. – Oh! press the soft Charm close to mine, – and seal 'em up for ever.   *He kisses her.*
LAETITIA   Upon that Condition.
BELLMOUR   Eternity was in that Moment. – One more, upon any Condition.
LAETITIA   Nay, now. – *(aside)* I never saw any thing so agreeably Impudent.   (IV ii)

And so to bed. A variation on this principle is operative in Archer's unsuccessful use of mythological tropes to seduce Mrs. Sullen. In exchanges of this kind the audience must respond, without explicit direction from a character, to the deliberate 'abuse' of language in the interests of deceiving one presumed incapable of seeing the abuse: the application of the clichés of adoration to a persuasion to merely physical indulgence.

A similar perception by the audience is required when a Heartwell engages in such rant as the following:

Is not this *Silvia's* House, the Cave of that Enchantress and which consequently I ought to shun as I would infection? To enter here, is to put on the envenom'd Shirt, to run into the Embraces of a Fever, and in some raving fit, be led to plunge my self into that more Consuming Fire, a Womans Arms. Ha! well recollected, I will recover my reason and be gone.   (III i)

The ludicrous inappropriateness of this rant to the situation is pointed for us when we recall Antony's tragically apt exclamation on his seeming betrayal by Cleopatra: 'The shirt of Nessus is upon me; teach me,/Alcides, thou mine ancestor, thy rage.' An incongruity or inappropriateness located in a single word or phrase is evident in Bluffe's thrasonical huff: 'I'll call a Council of War within to consider of my Revenge to come' (III i).

This has something of the wit of Terence's *hui! universum triduum!* whose elegance Dryden commended in his essay *Of Dramatick Poesie.*[12]

The practice of the proper life style, revealing itself in an intelligent awareness of language, both permits one to be a social predator, ridiculing, patronizing, and fooling others, and offers a defense against the sallies of other social predators. The aristocrat of intellect must not be outfaced by being caught in an unexamined use of language or by taking himself and others seriously, especially in matters of love. Above all, he must not be laughed at. To put oneself in a position to be laughed at by one's social peers is at least to smirch one's intellectual honor, and perhaps to lose title to the aristocracy or to be revealed as possessing a false title. It is, in fact, to make oneself the butt of a Hobbist laughter, those 'grimaces' prompted by the 'passion' of 'sudden glory', a laughter that is provoked by the folly and misfortune of others because the spectacle of their folly or misfortune ministers to our sense of superiority to others.[13] Such laughter accompanies the application of La Rochefoucauld's maxim, used by Swift in his verses on his death, that there is always something in the misfortune of our friends which does not displease us. Dorimant anticipates the application of this maxim when, outfaced by Mrs. Loveit with Sir Fopling in the Mall, he turns in supplication to Medley: ' 'Twere unreasonable to desire you not to laugh at me; but pray do not expose me to the town this day or two.'[14] Heartwell also anticipates his social disgrace as a result of pursuing Silvia, that 'Delicious, Damn'd, Dear, destructive Woman! S'death how the young Fellows will hoot me! I shall be the Jest of the Town' (III i). And so it proves, after Heartwell's supposed marriage to Silvia:

BELINDA   I swear, at the Month's End, you shall hardly find a Married-man, that will do a civil thing to his Wife, or say a civil thing to any body else. *Jesus!* how he looks already. Ha, ha, ha.
BELLMOUR   Ha, ha, ha.
HEARTWELL   Death, Am I made your Laughing-stock?(V ii)

If the poised, skeptically intelligent wit must not be caught out in seriousness or earnestness, then it is easy to see why the subject of love must be approached cautiously. The life style as fully practiced scarcely allows for the intimacy of love, in which one is, at least to some extent, at the mercy of another. Sex and adultery may be approached flippantly, but flippancy is easily if not necessarily destructive of love. Hence the difficulty of 'sententious Mirabell' in being serious with Millamant until, in their proviso scene, they achieve an extension of the life style of independence into the mutuality of love, the affection and sentiment fully understood, leaving the mind and tongue free to continue the game. More often, the poised flippancy of courtship requires a conversational style radically different from that needed for serious love and serious marriage. This disjunction is phrased most clearly by Belinda in *The Old Bachelor*, retorting to a sentimental sketch of marital bliss. 'Courtship', she says, is 'to Marriage, as a very witty Prologue to a very dull Play' (v i). Fortunately, the conventions of comedy permit a large emphasis upon the vicissitudes of courtship, with the prospect of a marriage of love sketched in the last scene with a few vows, prognostications, and, perhaps, a festive dance. The very economy with which the prospect is sketched disguises the actual disjunction between the style of living and speaking appropriate to courtship and the sex hunt and the style appropriate to marriage and a marriage of love, a disjunction between independence and mutuality.

Comedy, it is true, had customarily concerned itself in various ways with an abdication of responsibility, or a reluctance to enter upon responsibility, or an aberration from a pattern of behavior explicitly or implicitly endorsed within the play. The movement of such plays, and it is at least partly a narrative movement, is toward a final acceptance or reconciliation from which only the completely incorrigible are excluded, driven from court with Shylock or locked up as a madman and then laughed out of the house with Malvolio. The commonest preoccupation of such comedies is with permutations upon the motives that bring together the sexes – appetite, prudence, sentiment – often in order to endorse the wisdom of Tennyson's 'Northern Farmer, New Style': 'Doänt thou marry for munny, but goä wheer munny is!' Such a preoccupation permits a clearly marked movement through the competition of motives to an acceptable reconciliation of them. If this movement is most obviously ideological, it also has evident possibilities for illustration in character and plot.

Plays like *The Old Bachelor* and *The Man of Mode*, however, are notable less for a movement toward acceptance or reconciliation than for their display of a life style and various aberrations from it. Elements superficially contributory to narrative, principally the details of intrigues, are present not so much to forward a plot or to anatomize motives as to provide matter for discourse and the consequent display of proper and improper life and conversational styles. Despite the evident concern with bed, or clothes, or money, it is an intensely cerebral life.

And it demands an answering intelligence in the playwright who ventures to record it. To employ the distinction favored by Dryden in the preface to *Annus Mirabilis*, 'wit written' will not occur unless the author is capable of 'wit writing'.[15] The major fallacy of explanations of literary disparity in terms of historical shifts in taste and manners is that they unduly neglect the large contribution of the inequality of talents. Farquhar was simply less intelligent than Etherege or Wycherley, Vanbrugh or Congreve. The proposition can be illustrated by comparing the way in which a character in *The Old Bachelor* and a character in *The Beaux' Strategem* ridicule the reliance of another upon the clichés of précieuses exclamations. Here is Congreve:

VAINLOVE   Did I dream? Or do I dream? Shall I believe my Eyes, or Ears? The Vision is here still. – Your Passion, Madam, will admit of no farther reasoning. – But here is a silent Witness of your acquaintance. – *Takes out the Letter, and offers it: She snatches it, and throws it away.*

ARAMINTA   There's poison in every thing you touch. – Blisters will follow –

VAINLOVE   That Tongue which denies what the Hands have done.

ARAMINTA   Still mystically senceless and impudent. – I find I must leave the place.   (IV iii)

Nothing, indeed, can exceed the elegance of that 'mystically', superficially a mere intensifying adverb, amusing by its hyperbolic incongruity, but actually justifying itself by its pointed reference to Vainlove's 'visionary' exclamations and by the weight and appropriateness it gives to 'senceless'. The wit writing here, as so often in Congreve, produces in what is wit written an intelligent pressure on the words. Now Farquhar:

ARCHER   Well, but heark'ee, *Aimwell.*

AIMWELL   *Aimwel!* call me *Oroondates, Cesario, Amadis,* all that Romance can in a Lover paint, and then I'll answer. O *Archer,* I read her thousands in her Looks, she look'd like *Ceres* in her Harvest, Corn, Wine and Oil, Milk and Honey, Gardens, Groves and Purling Streams play'd on her plenteous Face.

ARCHER   Her Face! her Pocket, you mean; the Corn, Wine and Oil lies there. In short, she has ten thousand Pound, that's the English on't.   (III ii)

Archer is ridiculing less a lapse of style, a loss of poise, than what he takes to be a loss of candor, a self-deceiving cant. The jeering explicitness of 'Her Face! her Pocket, you mean' and 'that's the English on't' is remote from the sensibility responsible for Araminta's 'still mystically senceless and impudent'. It is very close to Rymer's brusque *Short View of* [and shortest way with] *Tragedy,* or Fielding's bluff English response to epic simile and heroic hyperbole in *Tom Jones,* or to Dr. Johnson, that *Jean Bull philosophe,* kicking the stone and thus refuting Berkeley. With such a passage as this between Archer and Aimwell before us, and with the memory of Araminta's snub of Vainlove, it is not hard to see how Pope, in his imitation of Horace's epistle to Augustus, came by his opinion of Farquhar's 'pert low Dialogue'.

If there were nothing more to say about this exchange between Archer and Aimwell, there would be no reason to see or read *The Beaux' Stratagem* with a greater expectation of pleasure than we might bring to Cibber's *The Careless Husband* or Susanna Centlivre's adaptation of *The Gamester.* But the exchange, whatever its inadequacy as humor, is also one of the many moments in *The Beaux' Stratagem* in which a concern with motive in matters of love finds expression in terms of metaphors drawn from the play's continuous movement, physical and ideological, between two places, the inn and the house. What Farquhar gives us in *The Beaux' Stratagem*, and to a lesser extent in *The Recruiting Officer*, is a play notable for a conspicuous (if at times forcibly imposed) integrity of action, character, dialogue, and setting. By making the moral world of his play commensurate with fully realized places he is closer, for all the lesser comprehensiveness and intensity of his imagination, to Shakespeare and Jonson than he is to Congreve and Etherege.

In Congreve and Etherege, the recurrence of related metaphors – epithets of the underworld, celestial tropes, images of fashionable materialism, mirrors, clothes, china – may encourage a search for patterns of metaphorical meaning. But the contribution of such patterns is obscured by the concentration on the local use of what were, after all, the cliché commonplaces of the age: Is the local cliché wittily renewed or complacently retailed? The relevant holism, what associates these local uses with one another, is the contribution of each part, each metaphor, not to the significant total meaning of the metaphors – a materialist society, say, desperately in search of a proper theology and a proper morality – but to the significant way in which metaphor is used to reveal proper and improper life styles founded on conversation. Farquhar, less intelligent than the best of his predecessors, produced, finally, a dramatic mode in which the smaller local pressure on the use of metaphors freed them to relate, manifestly, to one another and, by deriving from the action, to underline its meaning.

It was not so at the beginning of Farquhar's career. *Love and a Bottle*, his first play, offers an intrigue plot with a complex and farcical life of its own. As a vehicle for socially satiric conversations on love, friendship, soldiers, wine, seduction, foppery, snuff, dancing, poetry, theaters, fencing, Oxford, it is distracting in its robust complications. The protagonist is no self-aware honest man, but a randy Irishman just arrived in London, ready to chase off-stage with a priapic bellow in adolescent pursuit of a passing woman (IV iii). As the most lustful example of lusty *juventus*, he prompts not a set of analogies based upon clothes and cards, fruit and mirrors, but a series of quasi-theological references to paradise, forbidden fruit and forbidden knowledge, serpents, devils, flesh, and fall. Driven out of Ireland, that venomless paradise, by fleshly indulgence in forbidden fruit with

his whore, he comes to London to enter into sin (I i), to be a
rakehelly rascal (III i). He seeks in the back door to his mistress's
house 'the narrow Gate to the Lovers Paradice' (IV iv).
Reclaimed at the end by the love of a good woman, he pensions
off his whore, rejecting her as a stale iniquity, and is ready to
pronounce the moral: *'Paradice was lost by Woman's Fall; But
Vertuous Woman thus restores it all.'* The theology is, obviously,
confused by the indiscriminate use of paradise as a source both of
moral definition and double entendre. In addition, the physical
activity implied by the paradise references has only a tenuous
likeness to the physical activity of the intrigues. Paradise
organizes a set of quasi-theological glosses upon an action to
which it is only superficially analogous.

In subsequent plays Farquhar several times took up a favorite
topic of some of his predecessors: the social falsity of travel in
providing, not a broadening of a gentleman's understanding, but
matter for his folly or iniquity to feed upon. Both *The Constant
Couple* and *Sir Harry Wildair* are dominated by the past or future
travels of a number of the main characters. But the kind of
character definition the travels provide has, once again, little
reference to the details of what these busy characters actually do.
The drift of the plays is to the working out of relationships by a
reclamation from folly or incontinence or by the removal of
misapprehension over identity or personality. Travel certainly
contributes to misapprehension and redeemable incontinence,
and it is to some extent a unifying motif since so many of the
characters are affected by it. But there is no necessary connection,
no true analogy. Incontinence and misapprehension can originate elsewhere, as they do in *The Constant Couple* when the villain
revenges himself on the hero by persuading him that the heroine
is a whore, her mother a bawd, and their house a brothel.

It was in *The Recruiting Officer* and, less clearly, in *The Twin-
Rivals* that Farquhar found his way to uniting the busy activity of
his intrigue plots and the social definitions implied by the
occurrence of related metaphors in conversation. The very title of
The Recruiting Officer suggests those twin concerns with enlisting
soldiers and getting wives which serve not only as a means to
revitalize such aging literary preoccupations as love and honor
and the trope of the love battle; they also provide parallel actions

that are mutually revelatory because they are analogies for each other. Especially do they share a concern with financial trickery in the purchase of recruits or mistresses and the monetary disposition of daughters in marriage. The two activities are united by the heroine's disguising herself as a young man in order to be 'enlisted' by the hero so that she might test his love and worth and prove to her father the falsity of disposing of her only to a high bidder. The enlistment intrigues are both a source of metaphor for the love intrigues and the means by which the complications of the love plot are resolved. The chief weakness of *The Recruiting Officer* is that the important subplot of the civilian second lovers expresses its analogy with the main plot wholly in terms of the conventional tropes of the love battle, in contrast with the metaphorical density of the main plot itself – with its paralleling, often identification, of wenching and enlisting, fighting for money and marrying for money, false honor on the battlefield and false love at home. Consequently, the revitalized analogy emerges as true of a recruiting officer's situation, but lacking full relevance for more general social concerns as they affect sex relations and marriage. The Petrarchan tropes of the subplot insist upon an analogy with the main plot which exists only tenuously. If *The Recruiting Officer* is not completely satisfactory, however, it does point clearly to the grounds of success in Farquhar's last and best play, *The Beaux' Stratagem*.

The Beaux' Stratagem chiefly establishes its meanings by a fruitful juxtaposition of its two, alternating scenes of action, the inn of Boniface and the house of Lady Bountiful, and by an interrelation of hospitality and sexual emotion – love or appetite. In each place and activity it is chiefly the attitude toward money which distinguishes the right from the wrong way.[16] Such a movement and such attitudes are reminiscent of *The Merchant of Venice*, with its alternation between Venetian streets and the walks of Belmont.

Boniface's hospitality is, as his name promises, only superficially good. He bustles about, providing food and drink to distract from his chief concern with tricking guests out of their money. He overcharges the French prisoners of war, and when he thinks Aimwell and Archer are highwaymen, he plans to betray them and thus gain the £200 they deposit with him (I i). To prove his suspicions and gain the means for betrayal he is willing that his daughter Cherry be debauched by Archer, who is disguised as Aimwell's servant. He will harbor no rogues but his own Gibbet, Hounslow, and Bagshot, highwaymen and housebreakers based at his inn. But when they are caught he absconds with all the money he can lay hands on, leaving the highwaymen to swing (V iv). This false, financially motivated hospitality contrasts with the true hospitality of Lady Bountiful, who lays out half of her income 'in charitable Uses for the Good of her Neighbours' (I i). Lady Bountiful's care for the poor is given dramatic, if negative, realization in the scene between Mrs. Sullen and the country-woman with a sick husband (IV i). Mrs. Sullen's reaction to the countrywoman, her issuing of maliciously false advice, is so deliberately overstated as to effect a comic neutralization of any outrage at her careless cruelty. Her advice, reminiscent of Medea's instructions to the daughters of Pelias for the 're-juvenation' of their father, has something of the inventive hyperbole of Lady Wishfort's ritual commination of Foible in *The Way of the World*. Mrs. Sullen's response is, of course, that of the townee bored with the simple pieties of the country.

These contrasting attitudes to hospitality parallel in the main intrigue of courtship and marriage the distinction between those who approach marriage for love and those who approach it for money. Charity is the social counterpart of the private virtue of love. At the beginning of the play both Aimwell and Archer are fortune hunters, and marriage to them would be more tolerable than marriage to Squire Sullen, Lady Bountiful's son, with his similar financial motivation, only because they are more witty and agreeable. Sullen assures his wife's brother when he comes to take her away from an unhappy marriage that he has no quarrel with his wife's fortune, he only hates his wife (V i). In the final scene of separation by mutual consent, Sullen readily parts with his wife, but has to be forced to part with her portion by Archer's handing over the husband's papers to Mrs. Sullen's brother.[17] Aimwell is intent upon marrying the fortune of Dorinda, Lady Bountiful's daughter, although his final reclamation to selfless love is prepared for in the opening scene by Archer's characteri-zation of him as 'an amorous Puppy . . . [who] can't counterfeit the Passion without feeling it'. Archer can, and he demonstrates his sexual virtuosity by busying himself with minor speculations in sex and money with Cherry at the inn and an amour with the susceptible Mrs. Sullen at the house as incidental relief from intriguing on Aimwell's behalf. His appetite for Cherry is sharpened when she tells him she has £2,000, but he rejects her suggestion of marriage: 'what need you make me Master of your self and Money, when you may have the same Pleasure out of me, and still keep your Fortune in your Hands' (II ii).

In one of the early conflations of women and property, Archer remarks, 'I love a fine House, but let another keep it; and just so I love a fine Woman' (I i). Like the beaux, Mrs. Sullen, understandably embittered, thinks in terms of money. Her thoughts run on her dowry, and she observes shortly afterward that 'Women are like Pictures of no Value in the Hands of a Fool, till he hears Men of Sense bid high for the Purchase' (II i). Immediately, Mrs. Sullen is concerned with the property approach to women, but her simile prepares for the wooing of herself and Dorinda by the beaux in terms of the pictures in the house. When the women compare notes afterward, it emerges that Archer 'thought' Mrs. Sullen the original of a Venus, while Aimwell took Dorinda 'for *Venus* her self' (IV i). The mythological eroticism of the paintings recurs in the trope Archer indulges in when he first enters Mrs. Sullen's bedchamber (V ii), thus completing the circle of pictures, property, mythology and eroticism.

Even the innocent Dorinda has to lose her social and financial taint, her wish to marry a title. 'Why', she says to Mrs. Sullen, 'my Ten thousand Pounds may lie brooding here this seven Years, and hatch nothing at last but some ill natur'd Clown like yours: — Whereas, If I marry my Lord *Aimwell*, there will be Title, Place and Precedence, the Park, the Play, and the drawing-Room, Splendor, Equipage, Noise and Flambeaux' (IV i). When Aimwell's love for Dorinda has brought him to 'prefer the Interest of my Mistress to my own' and to confess that he has pretended to the title of his brother to trick her, she, in return, finds herself prouder that he is without title and fortune than she was when he apparently possessed them: 'Now I can shew my Love was justly levell'd, and had no Aim but Love' (V iv). Shortly

afterward, Sir Charles Freeman, who has come to take away his
sister Mrs. Sullen, gives the news of Lord Aimwell's death.
Although Freeman and his news are usually and with some
justice taken as a facile deus ex machina allowing virtue to live
happily ever after,[18] Lord Aimwell's death accomplishes two
things, one quasi-symbolic, the other morally realistic. When
Aimwell's conscience works on him and makes him declare to
Dorinda 'I'm all Counterfeit except my Passion' (v iv), he not
only echoes Archer's early marking of his inability to counterfeit
a passion without feeling it and the later discussion of imperfect
imitation in paintings, he has also, morally speaking, ceased to be
counterfeit at all. He is accordingly rewarded by becoming the
veritable Lord Aimwell. Dorinda and Aimwell do not need his
title and wealth, for they would still have £5,000, half her
portion, the other half going, in accordance with the beaux'
agreement, to Archer. They 'earn' the title and fortune as soon as
they renounce them. Aimwell's access of wealth also enables him
to propose a Solomonic test of motivation by offering Archer not
half of Dorinda's portion, but a choice between Dorinda and her
whole fortune. Archer takes the £10,000.

Love and hospitality are, then, paralleled in a manner richly
productive of incidental metaphor. The principal form of these
metaphors is to compare love with a dwelling or property, as in
Aimwell's rapture over Dorinda's cornucopian beauty and
Archer's jeering response to it. When Mrs. Sullen asks Archer
how he got into her bedchamber, he replies, 'I flew in at the
Window, Madam, your Cozen *Cupid* lent me his Wings, and your
Sister *Venus* open'd the Casement' (v ii). The visitation of Cupid
is also implied in Archer's catechism of Cherry: 'Where does
Love enter?' (ii ii), and it recurs in Mrs. Sullen's exclamation to
Dorinda, 'I own my self a Woman, full of my Sex, a gentle,
generous Soul, – easie and yielding to soft Desires; a spacious
Heart, where Love and all his Train might lodge. And must the
fair Apartment of my Breast be made a Stable for a Brute to lie
in?' (iv i). When, earlier, Dorinda endeavors to console Mrs.
Sullen with the recollection that her husband makes her an
allowance, she retorts, 'A Maintenance! do you take me,
Madam, for an hospital Child, that I must sit down, and bless my
Benefactors for Meat, Drink and Clothes?' And with such a low

view of charity, she naturally goes on to express contempt for Lady Bountiful's benevolence: 'spreading of Plaisters, brewing of Diet-drinks, and stilling Rosemary-Water with the good old Gentlewoman, my Mother-in Law' (II i).

In addition to producing incidental metaphors, the paralleling of love and hospitality is accompanied by a conventional discrimination of their values into selfishness and selflessness which is fully implicated into character, action, and setting. The schemes of the beaux involve Aimwell's pretending a fit calculated to play upon Lady Bountiful's hospitality and so bring them within the house. Because such an entry is devious and is designed to gain money, or sexual gratification, or both, it may properly be associated with the sexual and financial atmosphere of the inn. The beaux are intent upon carrying the values of the inn to the house. The infiltration, in fact, has already begun. Mrs. Sullen is involved in a liaison with Count Bellair, a captured French officer who lodges at the inn, by which she hopes to put a jealous edge on Sullen's dull appetite for her. But Sullen himself is also occupied in carrying the values of the inn to the house, for he spends long hours at the inn, returning to the house with an aching head to call for food and drink as if he were still at the inn, or, as Mrs. Sullen puts it, returning late at night to come 'flounce into Bed, dead as a Salmon into a Fishmonger's Basket; his Feet cold as Ice, his Breath hot as a Furnace, and his Hands and his Face as greasy as his Flanel Night-cap. – Oh Matrimony!' (II i). The nature of matrimony at the inn is further revealed in the exchange between Boniface and Sir Charles Freeman. Boniface asks, 'Are not Man and Wife one Flesh?' and Freeman replies, 'You and your Wife, Mr. Guts, may be one Flesh, because ye are nothing else – but rational Creatures have minds that must be united' (V i). The inn's values are flesh and money.

Lest there be any doubt about the nature of the values and social distinctions involved in character, action, and verbal analogy, there is in the activities of the highwaymen a superficially inconsequential subplot which is, in fact, integral with the total meaning and action of the play. The highwaymen, principally Gibbet, their leader and spokesman, are the most conspicuously predatory representatives of the inn at which they are based. Their attempted robbery of the house at the instigation of Boniface parallels the beaux' attempt to gain money from the house by pretended love. Just as the analogies in *The Recruiting Officer* depend in part upon the trope of the love battle, so the importance of Gibbet and his gang depends in part upon the convention that highwaymen are 'gentlemen of the road', a convention, of course, which Gay later put to good use in *The Beggar's Opera*. The parallel between the beaux' strategem and Gibbet's housebreaking is present in his insistence that 'there's a great deal of Address and good Manners in robbing a Lady, I am the most a Gentleman that way that ever travell'd the Road' (iv i). We should not forget that Aimwell and Archer are also gentlemen who travel the roads of England in search of a lady's fortune. When they first put up at Boniface's inn, he mistakes them for highwaymen because, like Gibbet, they have a box of money and keep their horses saddled. Gibbet laments that he is 'only a younger Brother' (v ii), a condition of notorious financial consequences which he shares with Archer (ii ii) and also with Aimwell, of course. The analogy between Archer's sexual housebreaking and Gibbet's monetary housebreaking is further prepared for by Bellair's remark that if Sullen 'but knew the Value of the Jewel he is Master of, he wou'd always wear it next his Heart, and sleep with it in his Arms' (iii iii). When Mrs. Sullen, her husband's neglected jewel, rallies her virtue to cry 'Thieves, Thieves, Murther' at Archer's offered familiarity, the echo of Scrub's 'Thieves, Thieves, Murther, Popery', inspired not by her plight but by the presence of robbers, serves to identify the activities of Archer and Gibbet. Lest the point should still prove elusive, Scrub proceeds to mistake Archer for one of the housebreakers, and Archer cheerfully admits that he too has come to rob Mrs. Sullen, but of a different jewel.

In addition to making even clearer the moral status of the beaux' stratagem, the highwaymen's adventure contributes largely to the comic resolution of the play. In the last act the inn and its values make a bodily assault upon the house and its values. Gibbet's housebreaking not only interrupts Archer at a crucial moment, it moves Cherry to rouse Aimwell to the rescue because Lady Bountiful is her godmother and she loves Dorinda. With the collapse of the burglary, Boniface absconds, robbing his own inn. It is, moreover, during the burglary that Sullen's papers are confiscated by Archer and handed over to Mrs. Sullen's brother to force the restitution of her portion. At the end of the play the forces of the inn are scattered, although none will be too severely punished, for even Gibbet has £200 in reserve to buy his life at the sessions. Gibbet and his gang may appear to operate, inconsequentially, within a buffo subplot, may be permitted a few rough jests from time to time, and may be ready, at authorial fiat, to dissolve sentiment into comedy or, perhaps, comedy into sentiment. But the presence of Gibbet, what he says and does, confirms the propriety of reading *The Beaux' Stratagem* as a play in which image and action are mutually enriching: what one character does provides others and himself with metaphors for conversation. I confess to a great fondness for Gibbet, and am reluctant to sacrifice him to those who would find him Jeremy Collier in disguise or the Comic Spirit made flesh. I think him an ineluctable highwayman, a gentleman of the road, and not the less interesting for that.

SOURCE: *Seventeenth-Century Imagery* (Berkeley, 1971) pp. 169–86.

NOTES

1. A shorter version of this essay was read at the 1966 meeting of the Modern Language Association.
2. Dale Underwood, *Etherege and the Seventeenth-Century Comedy of Manners* (New Haven, 1957) p. 72.
3. Ernest Bernbaum, *The Drama of Sensibility* (Boston and London, 1915) p. 84.
4. Henry Ten Eyck Perry, *The Comic Spirit in Restoration Drama* (New Haven, 1925) p. 108. Ronald Berman, 'The Comedy of Reason', *Texas Studies in Literature and Language*, VII(1965) 161–8 finds *The Beaux' Stratagem* to be 'a farewell to mores. . . . In the most general sense it marks a move from the world of Hobbes to that of Shaftesbury' (pp. 167–8). In their edition of *The Beaux' Stratagem* (Great Neck, N.Y., 1963), Vincent F. Hopper and Gerald B. Lahey say 'it would be heretical to approach Farquhar . . . without invoking the word *transitional*', but they find the word 'too ambiguous a label to affix to the diverse ingredients that make up *The Beaux' Stratagem*' (pp. 16–17). (This edition is cited hereafter as Hopper and Lahey.)

5. Louis Kronenberger, *The Thread of Laughter* (New York, 1952) p. 183.

6. Quotations from Farquhar follow the text of *The Complete Works of George Farquhar*, ed. Charles Stonehill (London, 1930).

7. Bernbaum, *Drama of Sensibility*, p. 102.

8. Perry, *Comic Spirit*, pp. 127−8.

9. Eric Rothstein, in his sensitive and informative *George Farquhar* (New York, 1967), is generally successful in keeping historical elucidation and critical evaluation separate, but he does occasionally simplify the complexity of historical elucidation. Like Hopper and Lahey, he contrasts the unconsummated seduction of Mrs. Sullen with the successful seduction of Berinthia in *The Relapse* as evidence that Farquhar was, in part, responding to a change in 'the subject matter of comedy' in 'the decade or so before *The Beaux' Stratagem*' (pp. 144−6). We ought to bear in mind not only *The Relapse* and Dorimant's way with Bellinda in *The Man of Mode*, but also such things as Fondlewife's fortuitous interruption of his wife and Bellmour in *The Old Bachelor* and the near misses in the third act of *Marriage A-la-Mode*.

10. William Archer (ed.), *George Farquhar* (New York, 1959) pp. 24−6.

11. Quotations from *The Old Bachelor* follow the text of *The Complete Plays of William Congreve*, ed. Herbert Davis (Chicago, 1967).

12. *Essays of John Dryden*, ed. W. P. Ker (New York, 1926) I, 51.

13. Hobbes, *Leviathan*, ed. Michael Oakeshott (Oxford, 1960) p. 36 (I, 6).

14. Etherege, *The Man of Mode* (III, iii), ed. W. B. Carnochan (Lincoln, Neb., 1966).

15. *Essays*, ed. Ker, I, 14.

16. If the scene changes whenever the stage is cleared of characters for a moment, then there are seventeen scenes, only eleven of which are marked in the text (II ii, and V i, comprise two scenes each, and Act IV, marked as one scene, contains five). There are two inn sets − the entrance hall and the beaux' chamber − and three or four house sets, principally the gallery and Mrs. Sullen's bed-chamber. The first act is set entirely in the inn, and the ethos thus established is recalled by brief inn scenes in each of the remaining acts, which are principally set in various apartments of the house. For a reconstruction of the probable method by which these sets were changed see George L. Hersey's note on staging in Hopper and Lahey's edition of the play (pp. 45−60).

17. Just why Archer's act should force the restitution of the portion constitutes a minor crux, as is noted by Hopper and Lahey (p. 36). The solution is probably to be found in Gellert Spencer Alleman's

Matrimonial Law and the Materials of Restoration Comedy (Wallingford, Pa., 1942), although Alleman's own explicit solution is unsatisfactory: he simply notes that by possessing Sullen's 'writings' Archer or Freeman would have Sullen at his mercy (p. 112). A fuller solution is implied by the data Alleman supplies on pages 107 – 8. Dorinda and Mrs. Sullen agree that there are no grounds for a 'Case of Separation' in the ecclesiastical courts (II i). The only possibility, then, is separation by mutual consent, the form the Sullens go through in the final scene. The law of the time provided for alimony for the wife in all cases of separation or divorce, even if she was an adulteress. The alimony consisted of her refunded portion and an allowance determined by her husband's income. Alleman describes a case in which a couple who separated by mutual consent disagreed, apparently over the terms of the settlement. Their case was heard by a civil court, which ordered the refund of the wife's portion and a small allowance. Since Sullen had gone through a separation by mutual consent before witnesses, he apparently hoped to keep his wife's portion by denying, if the dispute came to court, that she had brought him one. His 'writings', which included the articles of marriage, would prove the contrary. Moreover, if the case came to court, Sullen would also have to make his wife an allowance proportionate to his income. His 'writings' further contained the evidence on which that allowance would be based. He therefore compounds and refunds the portion. Farquhar's handling is certainly careless; one sentence from Archer or Freeman would have been sufficient to resolve the crux.

18. Berman, 'Comedy of Reason', p. 164; Hopper and Lahey, p. 21. Rothstein (*Farquhar*, pp. 156 – 7) discusses Freeman as 'a narrative and thematic agent who precipitates a resolution that he has never effected'.

Albert Wertheim

BERTOLT BRECHT
AND GEORGE FARQUHAR'S
THE RECRUITING OFFICER (1973)

What is most astonishing to any Anglo-German comparativist about Bertolt Brecht is not simply the impressive breadth of his reading in English literature but what English works seem to have caught his attention. When, for example, one considers Shakespeare's most powerful and probing dramas, *Coriolanus* is certainly not among the first that springs to mind. Likewise, *Edward II* has not, until recent years, been ranked with *Doctor Faustus* and *Tamburlaine* as a major Marlovian tragedy. There is, in fact, reason to believe that Brecht's 1924 version of *Edward II* has had not a little to do with the rather sudden new interest on the part of both producers and literary critics toward Christopher Marlowe's once nearly forgotten chronicle play. The relationship between Brecht's *Die Dreigroschenoper* [*The Threepenny Opera*] and John Gay's *The Beggar's Opera* presents a curiosity of another kind. To English audiences and to students of English literature, Gay's eighteenth-century ballad opera is no recondite work; for, despite the initial misgivings of as shrewd a producer as Colley Cibber, who turned down Gay's piece in favor of a first play by a new author named Henry Fielding, Gay and his producer John Rich soon found that they had an unprecedented hit on their hands. And indeed, *The Beggar's Opera* continues to hold its own on the English stage. Nonetheless, it comes as something of a shock that a member of the Scriblerian Club like Gay, whose ballad opera, like many works of his fellow club members, satirizes very specifically corruption in eighteenth-century London under the Walpole government, could have had a profound effect upon a twentieth-century writer like Brecht. Perhaps the most astounding case of Brecht's reliance upon English drama is one to which almost no attention has been paid: Brecht's 1955 adaptation of George Farquhar's

1706 comedy *The Recruiting Officer* under the title *Pauken und Trompeten* [translated as *Trumpets and Drums*]. Farquhar's comedy, though an excellent one and though occasionally revived by repertory and college companies, remains a play esteemed primarily by that *rara avis*, the eighteenth-century drama specialist. Nor can *The Recruiting Officer*, like perhaps Thomas Otway's *Venice Preserved*, boast any sort of underground reputation among the congnoscenti of dramaturgy. Moreover, unlike Brecht's other selections from English literature, it lacks the epic theatre potential that is patently present in *Edward II* and *Coriolanus*. In short, *The Recruiting Officer* is, at first glance, hardly the sort of play one would expect to have appeal for a modern German epic playwright. Placing Farquhar's comedy alongside Brecht's *Trumpets and Drums*, however, we soon realize what attracted Brecht to the 250 year-old play; and we can see, too, Brecht's version as a sensitive critical statement on Farquhar's play, finding in it, and enlarging upon, a social commentary that is there in latent, muted form.

The Brecht bibliographers label *Trumpets and Drums* an 'adaptation.'[1] This is something of a misnomer, for Brecht has changed the time of the play from the Wars of the Spanish Succession and the Battle of Blenheim to the American Revolution and Bunker Hill, he has expanded widely one of the play's plots, and he has added several new significant characters. It is more than a modern face-lifting for *The Recruiting Officer*; as the rubric 'adaptation' suggests, it is almost as much a new play from old materials as *The Threepenny Opera* is.

George Farquhar's *The Recruiting Officer* is a clever and witty comedy which evokes its humor and gentle satire largely from the analogous action of its two plots. In the one, the resourceful Captain Plume and his equally able sergeant, Kite, arrive in Shrewsbury to enlist young men for Her Majesty's army. In the other plot, two nubile young ladies, Silvia and Melinda, employ their own resourcefulness to lead Captain Plume and his gentleman friend Worthy to the marriage altar. The play is neatly structured around the comparison between the devices of the military high pressure salesmen to win recruits and the strategies of the determined females to recruit their men into the service of Hymen.

For the most part, Farquhar uses military idiom to vitalize metaphorically the classic 'battle of the sexes' that comprises the major action and interest of *The Recruiting Officer*. This is most apparent in Mr. Worthy's pursuit of Melinda. The rakish Worthy has had a near success in convincing Melinda, his economic inferior, to become his mistress. When the young lady suddenly comes into an unexpected legacy, Worthy is compelled to pursue her anew with the prospect of the marriage altar replacing that of the private boudoir. Worthy and Plume, characteristically and significantly, describe the situation in martial rhetoric:

WORTHY   What think you of Melinda?

PLUME   Melinda! Why she began to capitulate this time twelve-month, and offered to surrender upon honorable terms. And I advised you to propose a settlement of five hundred pound a year to her before I went last abroad.

WORTHY   I did, and she hearkened to't, desiring only one week to consider, when beyond her hopes the town was relieved and I forced to turn my siege into a blockade.

PLUME   Explain, explain.

WORTHY   My Lady Richly, her aunt in Flintshire, dies and leaves her at this critical time twenty thousand pound.

PLUME   Oh, the devil, what a delicate woman was there spoiled! But by the rules of war now, Worthy, your blockade was foolish. After such a convoy of provisions was entered the place, you could have no thought of reducing it by famine. You should have redoubled your attacks, taken the town by storm, or have died upon the breach.

WORTHY   I did make one general assault and pushed it with all my forces, but I was so vigorously repulsed that, despairing of ever gaining her for a mistress, I have altered my conduct, given my addresses the obsequious and distant turn, and court her now for a wife.

PLUME   So, as you grew obsequious, she grew haughty, and because you approached her as a goddess, she used you like a dog.[2]   (1 i 180−203)

Perhaps implicit here is the power of economics to transform Melinda from potential mistress to potential spouse and the application of supply-and-demand principles to both love and war. But these matters are only at best implicit and left largely unexplored by the playwright. Farquhar's emphasis is clearly and squarely upon the game of love, which is fruitfully compared to the gamesmanship of both war and recruiting.

The correlation between the recruiting of enlistees and the recruiting of husbands is largely carried out in the central plot involving Captain Plume and Silvia. Posing as a prospective enlistee, Silvia attaches herself to Plume and Kite in order to find the man beneath the reputation for promiscuity. Silvia finds what she is looking for when Plume declares:

No, faith, I am not that rake that the world imagines. I have got an air of freedom which people mistake for lewdness in me as they mistake formality in others for religion. The world is all a cheat, only I take mine which is undesigned to be more excusable than theirs, which is hypocritical. I hurt nobody but myself, but they abuse all mankind. Will you lie with me?   (IV i 153–9)

The irony here is that while Silvia pretends to be Jack Wilful to snare a husband, Plume pretends to chastity to impress Wilful favorably and enlist him into his regiment. Further, Plume's device for winning recruits is to entice his prospects with the derring-do and romance of military life. He recruits the Shropshire innocents, Costar Pearmain and Thomas Appletree, by telling them:

Come, my lads, one thing more I'll tell you. You're both young, tight fellows and the army is the place to make you men forever. Every man has his lot, and you have yours. What think you now of a purse full of French gold out of a monsieur's pocket, after you have dashed out his brains with the butt of your firelock, eh?   (II iii 151–6)

Likewise, Silvia's role playing to capture Plume is also a romantic device. And this is brought home to us both when her scheme is first taking shape and she is called a 'poor, romantic Quixote' (I ii 42), and at the conclusion of her adventures when her plot is called a romantic history (V vii 104). Clearly the love and recruiting plots, with the analogous romantic tricks that pervade each, are ripe for the satirist's pen, particularly when the seriousness of war and impressment is pitted against the triviality of courtship and its games. But if the satire is there at all in *The Recruiting Officer*, it is latent. Dominant is an interest in the comic possibility of dramatic irony, and Farquhar places much emphasis on the comedy that ensues when Silvia as Wilfull is sent to bed with the sexually free country girl, Rose, and when Justice Balance, Silvia's father, unwittingly impresses his daughter into Plume's regiment.

Throughout, Farquhar's emphasis is upon the ingenuity of his major characters and the effectiveness of the disguises of costume and language that they employ. The impressment of a mine-worker is, for example, countenanced by a panel of judges on the basis of a comic verbal trick and on the basis of the laughable revelation of the man's marital situation :

BALANCE   What are you friend?
MOB   A collier; I work in the coal pits.
SCRUPLE   Look'e, gentlemen, this fellow has a trade, and the Act of parliament here expresses that we are to impress no man that has any visible means of a livelihood.
KITE   May it please your worships, this man has no visible means of a livelihood, for he works underground.

*   *   *

SCRUPLE   Well, friend, what have you to say for yourself?
MOB   I'm married.
KITE   Lackaday, so am I.
MOB   Here's my wife, poor woman.
BALANCE   Are you married, good woman?
WOMAN   I'm married in conscience.
KITE   May it please your worship, she's with child in conscience.
SCALE   Who married you, mistress?
WOMAN   My husband. We agreed that I should call him

husband to avoid passing for a whore, and that he should call me wife to shun going for a soldier.

SCRUPLE   A very pretty couple. Pray, Captain, will you take 'em both.   (V v 83–9, 96–108)

All is carried off here in a tone of good humor shared by the characters, the playwright and the audience. The comic success of the moment is all that matters. The ethics of the impressment were clearly not an issue for Farquhar, who was himself in 1704 commissioned as a recruiting officer and who probably drew upon his firsthand experience to depict the laughable extremes to which the recruiting officer was frequently pressed in order successfully to fill the ranks of the British militia.

Only occasionally are there hints on Farquhar's part that the gaiety of the officers and their uniforms hide the grim realities of warfare. At the opening of the play, for example, Sgt. Kite harangues a crowd in the Shrewsbury marketplace and holds up his grenadier's cap saying, 'Pray, gentlemen, observe this cap. This is the cap of honor; it dubs a man a gentleman in the drawing of a tricker [trigger]; and he that has the good fortune to be born six foot high was born to be a great man' (1 i 12–15). When Kite encourages one of the men in the crowd to try on the cap for size, the man exclaims, 'It smells woundily of sweat and brimstone' (1 i 24). The smell of the cap, while hinting at the true nature of the soldier's profession, is not, however, a part of a structured satire levelled by the playwright against either war or recruiting. As elsewhere in *The Recruiting Officer* the possibilities for satire are surely there, but Farquhar clearly knew enough to realize that neither the patriotic English audience of good Queen Anne's day nor the theatrical license officers would have countenanced an attack upon the English army or its conduct. Indeed, Farquhar, himself a military man, would not have wished to turn the scourge of satire upon his own profession. As a recent commentator astutely puts it, 'The rhetoric and tone of good feeling, with which *The Recruiting Officer* keeps brimming over, soften the effect of Farquhar's candor in the particular scenes of recruiting and impressment.'[3]

The possibilities left open by Farquhar's comedy become the foci of Brecht's *Trumpets and Drums*. And in viewing seriously the

economic motives and grim realities that underlie the games and
frivolity of recruiting as Farquhar shows it, Brecht radically alters
the thrust and tone of *The Recruiting Officer*. The robust roast beef
and Yorkshire pudding guffaws characteristic of Farquhar's
Shrewsbury turn sour in Brecht's version. Reviewing a London
production of *Trumpets and Drums*, Kenneth Tynan catches in the
portrait of Capt. Plume this disparity between Farquhar and
Brecht: 'Captain Plume is the kind of role in which, formerly,
John Clements was wont to cut a charming dash. Dieter Knaup
plays him realistically, as a sallow and calculating seducer.'[4] In
making the play a vehicle for his social satire, Brecht retains
Farquhar's two plot interests – recruiting soldiers and recruiting
spouses – and, by turning the clock ahead 70 years, adds an
important third dimension: the nature of the war for which the
recruits are required. Moreover, in his three-headed analogy,
Brecht proceeds to discover for his audience that the romantic
schwärmerei of lovers, the patriotic rhetoric of recruiters, and
ethical idealism for which wars are fought are all, finally,
whitewashing for various forms of economic acquisitiveness.

   In one of his many new scenes, Brecht penetrates the idealism
of the American Declaration of Independence and the British
response to it. Here Justice Balance and his servant, Simpkins,
receive a copy of the radical American manifesto:

   BALANCE (*reading*)   'Draft of a Declaration of Independence.'
The gall! 'When in the course of human events it becomes
necessary for one people to dissolve the political bonds which
have connected them with another hitherto . . .' High treason!
   SIMPKINS   Scoundrels.
   BALANCE (*reading*)   'All men are created equal . . .' Where
does the Bible say that? – 'Liberty and the pursuit of happiness . . .' So here it is in black and white; these new ideas we've
heard so much about. It's base greed, that's what it is! Do these
rebels – these Franklins, Jeffersons, and Washingtons – really
think the English crown will stand for such ideas? . . . On the
pretext that it costs too much, they refuse to import our tea. More
than ten thousand cases of unsold tea are rotting in Liverpool
docks at this very moment. At the same time, these lawyers and
backwoods generals, reared in equality, want to sell their cotton,

which we need here, to God knows who, merely because they get better prices. Imagine a colony presuming to trade with the whole world. Whoever heard of such a thing![5] (258−9)

Balance goes on to suggest that English recruits, who will quell the American uprising, are to be obtained by chauvinistic harangue:

BALANCE   What's more, these 'new ideas' are contagious − they spread like the plague. The whole civilized world must join forces against these rebels. . . . Your presence will change all that, Plume. A bit of martial music in the square, a captured flag or two, a patriotic speech, not too high-flown for our good country folk, and, of course, you can always count on the ardent support of our fair sex. Shrewsbury will give you everything you need, captain, everything! (259)

The effect of Balance's remarks is, of course, calculated by the playwright to make the audience recognize the standard Brechtian view, which sees the disparity between the rhetorical idealism and the cash nexus reality of war. In this case on both the American and British sides. Against this backdrop, Brecht explores the romantic and recruiting plots involving the towns-people affected by the recruiting practices of Plume, Kite & Co.

In his brief remarks on *Trumpets and Drums*, Brecht comments on the class underpinnings of war: 'The ruling class find that patriotism and egotism coincide.'[6] Accordingly, he takes the figure of Worthy, who in Farquhar is simply a squire of independent means, and turns him into a manufacturer, a shoe manufacturer. He takes as well the figure of Justice Balance and stresses what is already there in Farquhar; namely, that officials like Balance often stood to make a handsome profit by releasing the prisoners under their jurisdiction to recruiting officers. We find, further, in *Trumpets and Drums* that Plume and Worthy are not, as they are in Farquhar, merely old acquaintances thrown together for the purpose of the romance plot, but that they are, together with Balance, business associates:

PLUME   Worthy, who serves the best wine? That's the place to discuss our business.

WORTHY   Yes, that's what I've come for. Where do you propose to buy boots for your grenadiers? From Worthy and Co., I trust?

PLUME   First I must find grenadiers for your boots, Worthy. I shall pay my respects to Mr. Balance at once. (254)

Recruiting is, finally, not a necessary evil to provide defenders of the national honor, but a commercial enterprise based on the complicity of military, business, and petty officialdom interests.

For his purposes, Brecht happily develops the character of Kite, giving him several brilliant recruiting speeches, including one in which, posing as a minister, he can use the jingoism so often a part of wartime pulpit oratory (294 – 5). Perhaps the most effective of Kite's speeches is the one that serves as prologue to Brecht's play and in which the audience is directly implicated, for it is to them that Kite's spiel is addressed:

> I'm Sergeant Barras Kite, now gathering a company
> To help our good King George. For across the sea
> In His Majesty's colony America
> There's rebellion such as no man ever saw.
> If anyone here should crave to join the forces –
> Veterans of previous wars, or heroes without horses
> Wild about living out of doors
> Or footloose, eager to see foreign shores
> Apprentices whose masters are too mean
> Sons of parents you have never seen
> A working man, who leads a hungry life
> A husband suffering from a nagging wife –
> Come to the Raven, apply to Sergeant Barras Kite
> An honest man who'll set you right.
> Now, gentlemen: Who among you, in exchange for a
>   handsome uniform and plenty of fodder
> Will defend our dear old England (to the exclusion, of
>   course, of his sister, his brother, his father and his
>   mother)? (249)

In the course of the play, however, one not only learns the
questionable economic bases, both local and national, of the war,
but also sees the disparity between the recruiter's rhetoric and the
actual wounds of war. In a brilliant comic scene, Brecht shows
Kite making his pitch to a stalwart broad-shouldered fellow:

KITE   Hey, boys. That's the soldier's life! Plenty of grub and
plenty of ale. We live, as the saying goes – we live – how can I
describe it? . . we live like lords. May I ask, sir, how you enjoyed
the king's ale, sir?
BROAD-SHOULDERED MAN   Couldn't be better, sir.
KITE   You'd enjoy the king's service even more, sir.

*   *   *

One moment, sir. You know the Severn, but do you know the
Mississippi?

As Kite begins his ritual recruiting patter, the apple of the
recruiter's eye arises and reveals a wooden leg:

KITE   Where's your leg?
BROAD-SHOULDERED MAN   Bunker Hill.
APPLETREE   He's lost a leg.
KITE   For the king, though. Hats off boys! – All right; he's lost
a leg. But so has some damned rebel over there.
BROAD-SHOULDERED MAN   For himself, though. (266 – 7)

The dramatic action of this comic sketch at one stroke captures
the underlying irony of the play. And at the same time it prepares
the way for a view of the American Revolution as a landmark in
the Marxist class struggle.

As a counterpoint to the main action of the play, Brecht creates
a set of townspeople largely absent in Farquhar. Among them is
Mike the tavernkeeper and Lucy, Melinda's maid, who is merely
a functional character in *The Recruiting Officer*. Particularly
through Mike and Lucy we can appreciate the pragmatic appeal
of the American Revolution to those classes traditionally re-
pressed by the classes of power:

LUCY   What's that?

MIKE (*Takes out a slip of paper*)   From the New World. It was given to me by a coachman who got it from a Liverpool sailor. Listen! . . . Down with the king. Down with the archbishop, down with the lords. We in the New World need no more kings and no more lords, who grew fat on our sweat. We in the State of America wish to be an English colony no longer. Signed: Franklin.

*   *   *

LUCY   It says something entirely different. . . . 'That all men are created equal, that they are endowed by their . . .' I can't make out that word . . . 'with certain . . . rights: Life, Liberty and the Pursuit of Happiness . . .' (293)

This scene obviously is meant for comparison with Justice Balance's monied-class reaction. For Mike and Lucy it is not a political but a social War of Independence, nonetheless not without its economic interest; but an economic interest that serves the people rather than the leisure class. The force of Kite's encounter with the wooden-legged soldier is once again brought home: the English soldier has lost his leg for the king, the American rebel loses it for himself!

Trumpets and Drums radically shifts the dramatic balance of *The Recruiting Officer*. In the eighteenth-century comedy, the romance plot overshadows the recruiting plot; in Brecht's version it is very much the contrary. Nonetheless, the romantic plot is used by Brecht to work together with his satire of war and, at the close of the play, to provide a trenchant and sardonic irony. In a direct analogy to the chauvinistic appeal and commercial reality of recruiting are placed, respectively, the romance of love and the realities of dowries. This is, to some extent, already there in Farquhar, but is exploited and enlarged by Brecht. In an excellent original scene, Brecht has the romantic Captain Brazen, who has been pursuing Melinda, quit his claims to the allegedly wealthy heiress when he is apprised, 'Tell him her entire fortune was invested in a cargo of tea, which the rebels have wantonly dumped into Boston harbor.' (313)

Trumpets and Drums ends with a grizzly scene of Brechtian dramatic genius. As in *The Recruiting Officer*, Plume relinquishes his commission to marry the affluent daughter of Justice Balance, Silvia, or as Brecht renames her, Victoria. Brecht's conclusion, however, is preceded by a much intensified and sharply pointed scene depicting the willful impressment of the lower classes. The drafting of the collier who works underground and therefore has no visible occupation is no longer laughable but shocking:

KITE   If it please the court, this man's means of support is not visible; he works underground.

MINER'S WIFE   It's work, though.

BALANCE   You can't be a miner any more, you shall be a grenadier. Thanks to you, other miners will be able to remain miners.

MINER   But I'm a married man.

BALANCE   Don't you know that we've lost Boston?

MINER   No, Your Worship. I don't know the gentleman.

BALANCE   You mean you don't even know what Boston is? Is that all the fate of England means to you? Into the army with you!

PLUME   Take him away.

MINER   Pack of Skunks!

MINER'S WIFE   You can't do this! Bob! I'm going to have a child!

UNEMPLOYED MAN'S WIFE   What's Boston got to do with him!

JENNY   The whole thing is illegal.

THE BROAD-SHOULDERED MAN   It's legal, but . . .

WIFE OF THE UNEMPLOYED MAN   They make the laws to suit themselves. (317)

As the miner and his fellows are ruthlessly pressed into war, Brecht pointedly interjects the resolution of the frivolous romance plot. And in a crescendo of moral outrage, the play counterpoints the reading of the articles of war to the impressed recruits with Plume's return to civilian life as the husband of the upper class and wealthy Victoria.

As the recruits leave the stage bound for battle in North America, the main characters – Justice Balance, Victoria and

Plume, Worthy the shoe manufacturer and his new bride the rich Melinda – remain with their servants sipping champagne and mechanically mouthing hollow patriotic toasts. When the marching songs of the exiting recruits are beyond earshot, the aristocracy returns to its normal pursuits, as Balance closes the play, asserting: 'and now: off to the pheasant shoot! . . . Simpkins! The coach and four!' (326). Clearly what Brecht saw in *The Recruiting Officer* was a comedy with tacit social and ethical assumptions shared by the playwright and his audience : love and recruiting are full of tricks; lower and serving classes are meant to perform the dirty work in both the loves and wars of the upper classes. By questioning Farquhar's comic assumptions, Brecht turns a basically robust eighteenth-century comedy into a probing twentieth-century satire.

SOURCE: *Comparative Drama*, VII (1973) 179–90

NOTES

1.   See for example Reinhold Grimm, *Bertolt Brecht* (Stuttgart, 1971) p. 87; John Willett, *The Theatre of Bertolt Brecht* (London, 1959) p. 60; and Martin Esslin, *Brecht: The Man and his Work* (Garden City, N.Y., 1961) p. 314.

2.   George Farquhar, *The Recruiting Officer*, ed. Michael Shugrue (Lincoln, Neb. 1965). All citations are from this edition. Parentheses following quotations indicate act, scene, and line numbers.

3.   Eric Rothstein, *George Farquhar* (New York, 1967) p. 133.

4.   Kenneth Tynan, *Curtains* (New York, 1961) p. 453.

5.   [German original of *Trumpets and Drums* is in Bertolt Brecht, *Gesammelte Werke*, VI (Frankfort-on-Main, 1967). Citations in this Casebook are from Bertolt Brecht, *Collected Plays*, ed. Ralph Manheim and John Willett (New York, 1972). Parentheses following quotations indicate page numbers. I am grateful to Professor Wertheim for his kind help in advising on the translation of German-language material in his original essay – Ed.]

PART THREE

Comment on Production

William L. Sharp

RESTORATION COMEDY: AN APPROACH TO MODERN PRODUCTION (1969)

Of all admittedly good drama in the English language I suppose none is harder to translate into modern production than Restoration and early eighteenth-century comedy. Sheridan and Goldsmith survive quite well. *She Stoops to Conquer* and *School for Scandal* are perennial favorites, but the works of Etherege, Wycherley, Congreve, Vanbrugh and even Farquhar are either consistently ignored for production or, from my own viewpoint, produced for the wrong reasons. . . .

. . . In our distance from the period, in our insistence on seeing the fops as long-dead types, as caricatures, and in our inability to recognize the flirtatious games played by Millamant and Mirabel as our own, we make of the plays museum pieces, period pieces that present for us a now extinct world to be laughed at like the dodo bird. We have even concocted a *style*, a manner of moving and talking, which has nothing to do with our own sense of reality but is our way of making the periwigs and the high heels the silly things they must have been. Who, after all, except the silliest kind of *poseur*, would ever dress like Witwoud, or Flutter, or even Mirabel? And so we have as astute a critic as Brooks Atkinson saying of Ritchard's Foppington in *The Relapse* of 1950, 'his stylized condescension and fripperies are all vastly entertaining, which is all that anyone should expect from a comedy'. That the play might be making a pertinent comment on the difficulties of constancy between the sexes, or even of its worth, apparently never entered his mind.

It seems to me that the only possibility of producing these plays successfully is to recognize that we are basically looking at a very realistic picture of the difficulties the sexes have in living with each other. Most often it concerns the webs woman spins to catch and marry a man, and man's attempts to avoid marriage and still have the woman. The result is usually a series of games, sometimes self-conscious and aware, sometimes more natural and aware, but still like games, a playing. It is obvious to say that these games are still in operation in our sexual concourse; and yet producers of Restoration Comedy seem to feel that the characters in the late seventeenth and early eighteenth centuries carried on in what we can today only call a quaint and outmoded manner of courtship which really has more to do with peacocks than humans, and hence may be ignored as any real kind of flirtation at all. As a result, the self-consciousness that exists in their games becomes the only thing demonstrated. The games become things in themselves put on for the audience's benefit, not for the benefit of each other. As a consequence, we usually see a series of poses with whatever funny business may help project them – which makes of the plays a quite meaningless series of conversations and situations which have as their *only* reason for being the entertainment of the audience, and no relation to either the entertainment or the needs of the characters on stage. It seems to me that if we recognize the relation of these conversations and situations as a pertinent comment on the way we act – that is, that we recognize we are looking at ourselves, not at peacocks – then we might see in the plays some semblance of situations that we ourselves have been involved in. If we admit such a connection, then the actor's job is not simply showing off glitteringly before an audience, dropping *bons mots* as he goes, but is involving himself, and thereby us, in a very real activity. Millamant is not displaying herself for the world, but to capture and hold on to Mirabel. It is to him, not us, that she plays her flirtatious games. We are permitted to watch. She may seem more self-conscious in her flirtation than we think ourselves, but that in no way makes her less a flirt or less anxious to get Mirabel. Her manner may not seem quite ours, but that is a matter of taste or even degree, not of kind. Laura in Strindberg's *The Father* has always seemed a bit overstated to me, but I never doubt that she has a good deal of every woman in her. . . .

. . . It is perfectly true that all of these playwrights do not play the game in the same way, or even with the same convictions about love and marriage.[1] Clearly Farquhar and Wycherley have very different views from Congreve about the value of marriage. And again, Farquhar's respect for human intercourse and its delights is very different from Wycherley's. They each have their view of the worth of connection between the sexes and one's enjoyment in it. That view, furthermore, is tempered not only by the personality of the playwright but by the period in which he is speaking and the audience to whom he speaks. Etherege, speaking as he does to a near-intimate five hundred friends, can be much tighter in his presentation of the way people flirt than can Vanbrugh or Farquhar. By tighter here I mean he can make private 'in' jokes, he can trust much more to an 'in' audience than can Vanbrugh and Farquhar, who must write to London at large, not to Charles II and his friends. One can write a school review which is a howling success to members of the school but a complete mystery to outsiders. And it is this that makes Vanbrugh and Farquhar a little easier to understand. The *double entendre* in *The Relapse* between Berenthia and Loveless (III ii) is hard to miss. My arguments for a somewhat similar reading in the proviso scene of *Way of the World* are much harder to support. It is partly for this reason that I would like to lay the burden of my case on an easier play to hear, but a play that is playing similar games – namely, *The Beaux' Stratagem*.

[Sharp here summarises the main plot – Ed.] . . . In such a brief summary I have overlooked two details of some importance. The first is Cherry, whose importance is her charm. She is the daughter of Boniface, the innkeeper, and one of the apples of Archer's eye. She is on the make for a husband with breeding and so fascinated by Archer. He finally refuses her offer of money for marriage, but not before the enacting of two charming courtship scenes which have a real connection with the theme of the play, if not its plot. The second detail is Farquhar's brief for easier divorce settlements. Sullen doesn't like his wife, nor Mrs Sullen her husband, but he refuses to divorce her unless he can keep her estate, a right he has according to law. Farquhar's solution, namely the thieves' theft of the contracts, is hardly a realistic one, but he does spend some time in the course of the play demonstrating the incompatibility of the man and his wife, and he pleads with some fervor for an easier means of divorce. In fact Archer, who is certainly the male character most to be admired in the play, ends up single still. And though Aimwell and Dorinda get married, I think it is demonstrable that they are married during the pink haze of love, and as a consequence their troth seems both naive and a little foolish.

The center of the play and the games that characters play to demonstrate it is the conviction on Farquhar's part that, given the energies of the human animal, it is hard, if not impossible, to chain them comfortably to an institution like marriage. For all the play's fun, it is a very tough-minded look at the difficulty, to say the least, in maintaining an intelligent and comfortable relation in marriage. It may be saying that this adjustment exists primarily in the young, for certainly the play abounds with youth. On the other hand, there is nowhere in the play a suggestion that age might handle the difficulty any better. There simply is not that age in the play except in Lady Bountiful, a widow, and Boniface, a widower. Certainly, what one is most struck by is the zest for life that abounds in all the characters, particularly the two lead couples, and the problem of containing that zest without killing it. Love generates it. 'You never talked so well in your life', says Mrs Sullen to the younger Dorinda. 'I was never in love before', she replies. But quite clearly marriage kills it. The only time Mrs Sullen and her husband have anything like a joyful conversation is when they play their little game of separation (v iv):

MRS SULLEN   In the first Place I can't drink Ale with him.
SULLEN   Nor can I drink Tea with her.
MRS SULLEN   I can't hunt with you.
SULLEN   Nor can I dance with you.
MRS SULLEN   I hate Cocking and Racing.
SULLEN   And I abhor Ombre and Piquet.
MRS SULLEN   Your Silence is intollerable.
SULLEN   Your Prating is worse.
MRS SULLEN   Have we not been a perpetual Offence to each other – A gnawing Vulture at the Heart.
SULLEN   A frightful Goblin to the Sight.
MRS SULLEN   A Porcupine to the Feeling.
SULLEN   Perpetual Wormwood to the Taste.

MRS SULLEN   Is there on Earth a thing we cou'd agree in?
SULLEN   Yes – To part.
MRS SULLEN   With all my Heart.
SULLEN   Your Hand.
MRS SULLEN   Here.
SULLEN   These Hands join'd us, these shall part us – away –
MRS SULLEN   North.
SULLEN   South.
MRS SULLEN   East.
SULLEN   West – far as the Poles asunder.

For the first time in the play we hear the Sullens engaged in a conversation with the same kind of delight that marks the rest of the characters throughout, unfettered as they are by permanent alliances.

The play is made up of witty, put-on conversations that smack either of one-upmanship (if played by members of the same sex) or flirtations, with all the flattery and game-playing and dishonesty that flirtation implies (if played by members of the opposite sex). Nowhere do the characters talk seriously – that is to say, as if the issue they discussed were serious – except as stated above when they speak of marriage or as an already married couple. This is what one expects from the genre, of course. The whole archetypal pattern is of two lovers working their way toward marriage, the 'gay couple' as they are often called. Since I believe that this progress is not only modern but, more important, available to modern actors and directors in production, I would like to look at some particular scenes and show how they outline playable and dramatic situations as well as point to a whole and consistent reading of the play. If the play is still available to us as producible drama, it must be made up of situations that have immediate parallels in an actor's experience, not made up of some imagined idea of preciosity that could be labeled seventeenth-century fop, or a carefully wrought piece of baroque artistry called Millamant. If the play is drama as we understand drama, then it should be acted as we act drama, as confrontations that have their roots in real experience and their place in the author's attempt to make sense of that experience. Plays, at least as we talk and write about them, seem to have something to say. If one talks of Jonson's *Volpone*, he speaks of the particular view of the human animal that Jonson presents to us — his stupidity, his greed, and his illusory sense (most clearly seen in Volpone and Mosca, but clearly true for the others as well) that he can rise above these limitations and control his destiny, be more than the limited fool Jonson insists he is. We do not say that any character in the play is 'vastly entertaining, which is all that anyone should expect from a comedy'. If *The Beaux' Stratagem* or any Restoration piece is good drama, one should be able to describe it in similar terms. As a step towards that end, I would like to look at a few particular scenes in some detail.

Here is a passage from Act IV, scene i, between Dorinda and Mrs Sullen:

MRS SULLEN   Well, Sister.

DORINDA   And well, Sister.

MRS SULLEN   What's become of my Lord?

DORINDA   What's become of his Servant?

MRS SULLEN   Servant! he's a prettier Fellow, and a finer Gentleman by fifty Degrees than his Master.

DORINDA   O'my Conscience, I fancy you cou'd beg that Fellow at the Gallows-foot.

MRS SULLEN   O'my Conscience, I wou'd, provided I cou'd put a Friend of yours in his Room.

DORINDA   You desir'd me, Sister to leave you, when you transgress'd the Bounds of Honour.

MRS SULLEN   Thou dear censorious Country-Girl — What dost mean? you can't think of the Man without the Bedfellow, I find.

DORINDA   I don't find any thing unnatural in that thought, while the Mind is conversant with Flesh and Blood, it must conform to the Humours of the Company.

MRS SULLEN   How a little Love and good Company improves a Woman; why, Child, you begin to live — you never spoke before.

DORINDA   Because I was never spoke to. — My Lord has told me that I have more Wit and Beauty than any of my Sex; and truly I begin to think the Man is sincere.

MRS SULLEN   You're in the right, *Dorinda*, Pride is the Life of a

Woman, and Flattery is our daily Bread; and she's a Fool that won't believe a Man there, as much as she that believes him in any thing else − . . .

This exchange between the two women takes place just after their first encounter with their young gentlemen: Aimwell, who would marry Dorinda, and Archer, who would seduce Mrs Sullen. Clearly, Mrs Sullen starts the attack with a sense of 'and what have you been up to?'; but when Dorinda counters it with the same attack it would appear she is one up on Mrs Sullen, or at least ready to counter the attack. However much their defenses may have been down as they entered the unrecognized arena, they are both up as the verbal exchange starts. They are able to cover in a hurry the dangerous condition of being vulnerable. The scene continues in what could be read as a serious fight but appears, given the stakes and the already established intimacy of the two, to be a game of one-upmanship. It is a game that Dorinda seems to win at first. Through the first four lines, certainly, it is she who mocks Mrs Sullen in the repetition of phrases, and it is Mrs Sullen who seems to retreat, in her 'Servant'! He's a prettier Fellow' etc., in some confusion. It even looks as though Dorinda has won as she moves in confidently, no longer repeating Mrs Sullen's accusations but beginning her own with her 'my Conscience' etc. It is only when we hear Mrs Sullen's return, now using Dorinda's repetition tactics, that we suspect the younger woman may have walked into a trap. The trap, of course, is to admit that you have lost control, and that is what Dorinda does when in some shock she says, 'you desir'd me, Sister, to leave you . . . ', apparently too shocked to continue, and hence defeated. Her exit is stopped by Mrs Sullen, who laughingly points out that she has lost − only to be finally topped by Dorinda's beautiful rejoinder that even Mrs Sullen must admit defeats her. The phrasing is delicious, and shows us something of this young lady's awakening to her own vitality. And though the comment, in its admission of her interest in men, is by that very fact a surrender, it is a surrender so nicely phrased that Mrs Sullen must applaud her with 'why, Child, you begin to live − you never spoke before'. It is a delicious speech because it is a retreat that says 'let's not play at being angry any more; let's admit we both like men and play the next game in the script, namely, which man is the better wooer'. The speech shows that Dorinda is perfectly willing to admit her feelings, but in the way she phrases those feelings she also shows us that she is not, at least as yet, mastered by them: '. . . while the Mind is conversant with Flesh and Blood, it must conform to the Humours of the Company'. This is no priggish statement of high-flown but unsupportable philosophizing; it is in fact a mocking of such a position. Certainly the vocabulary – the 'conversant with Flesh and Blood' – suggests a philosophical or moral sermon, but the conclusion makes a mock of any such preachment. We do not hear something like 'indulge in their necessities', which says much the same thing but completes the priggish attitude with which the speech began. One suspects Dorinda is almost as delighted and surprised at her ability to talk as is Mrs Sullen. She is coming of age; and though her connection to Aimwell at the end of the play is not yet a mature one (I think she is a little too much in love when she marries him to see straight), it does suggest the awakening involved in falling in love, if not the dangers.

There are many such games in the play. The Dorinda – Mrs Sullen scene is basically one-upmanship. There are others: Gibbet playing suave highwayman on his first entrance, where he demonstrates his brilliance at derring-do. Certainly one cannot take the following speech as a serious description of the occupation of thievery:

GIBBET   No matter, ask no Questions, all fair and honourable, here, my dear *Cherry* [*Gives her a Bag.*] Two hundred Sterling Pounds as good as any that ever hang'd or sav'd a Rogue; lay 'em by with the rest, and here – Three wedding or mourning Rings, 'tis much the same you know – Here, two Silver-hilted Swords; I took those from Fellows that never shew any part of their Swords but the Hilts: Here is a Diamond Necklace which the Lady hid in the privatest place in the Coach, but I found it out: This Gold Watch I took from a Pawn-broker's Wife; it was left in her Hands by a Person of Quality, there's the Arms upon the Case. (II ii)

The speech is a strut for Gibbet, a chance to show off. It is not just information he is presenting, but himself – and with a flourish.

He is not as committed to robbery as he is to the way of doing it. Throughout the play we are struck by people defending their activities with a kind of posture that always allows them a way out. They refuse to take themselves seriously.

Perhaps the most obvious games are those between Archer and Mrs Sullen, and Cherry and Archer. The Archer – Mrs Sullen scenes are fairly straightforward. He speaks and acts like some eighteenth-century Errol Flynn, and while she knows his compliments are for the fun of it, she finds him irresistible, not for love but for joy.

> MRS SULLEN   Pray, Sir, what Head is that in the Corner there?
> ARCHER   O, Madam, 'tis poor *Ovid* in his Exile.
> MRS SULLEN   What was he banish'd for?
> ARCHER   His ambitious Love, Madam. [*Bowing*] His Misfortune touches me.
> MRS SULLEN   Was he successful in his Amours?
> ARCHER   There he has left us in the dark. – He was too much a Gentleman to tell.
> MRS SULLEN   If he were secret, I pity him.
> ARCHER   And if he were successful, I envy him.
> MRS SULLEN   How d'ye like that *Venus* over the Chimney?
> ARCHER   *Venus!* I protest, Madam, I took it for your Picture; but now I look again, 'tis not handsome enough.
> MRS SULLEN   Oh, what a Charm is Flattery! . . . (IV i)

The delight that Mrs Sullen takes in leading Archer on – with her 'Was he successful in his Amours?' and again, 'If he were secret, I pity him', only to lead him off with her 'How d'ye like that *Venus* over the Chimney?' – suggests something far less intense than the blind rapture with which Dorinda and Aimwell are examining the picture.

Dorinda and Aimwell do not play games in their wooing. They take each other very seriously; it is, in fact, one of their limitations for Farquhar; and we are asked, I think, to recognize their pink haze and laugh at it. Love may be very moving, but it is also blind – and neither Mrs Sullen and Archer nor Cherry and Archer are ever blind or unaware of what they are doing. The conversations here are self-conscious, and the participants are perfectly aware of what they are doing and where it might lead – its delights and its dangers.

The picture scene is an excellent example of both the awareness of Mrs Sullen and Archer and the blindness of Dorinda and Aimwell. The latter do not even see the pictures. They try, but their eyes can obviously only see each other. The former couple are quite aware of the pictures and of whither a close scrutiny of them might lead. Archer is headed for the bedroom and Mrs Sullen knows it. She has the contradictory task of leading him away from the obvious and yet not away from her. As Gay says, 'by keeping men off, we keep them on'.

It is her self-awareness of how she has led Archer on that keeps the later near-rape scene (vii) from being unpleasant. Her pleas for help are less and less persuasive both to Archer and to herself. We just see, regardless of the words, her gradual melting into Archer's embrace. And I suspect her last 'Thieves, Thieves, Murther—' is about as loud as Berinthia's whispered 'Rape' in Vanbrugh's *The Relapse*. Certainly it is not her screams that have brought Scrub a-running, though Archer can first understand his appearance in no other way. The fact is, of course, that he has seen thieves and is in no way aware of what is going on in Mrs Sullen's bedroom. She is playing the age-old game of saying 'no' when she means 'yes', and Archer the age-old game of saying 'I love you' when he means 'I want you'. The important thing to recognize here is that both of them know it. There is no self-delusion about true love overcoming all, or this-is-too-big-for-both-of-us. Mrs Sullen may repent of what she is doing – indeed she does – but there is no cry of 'I have been betrayed', or 'You have taken advantage of me'. Her only criticism of him in the last scene of the play, just before the arrival of her brother, is that he is a little cold-blooded and bad-mannered about his proposition now. Unless he keeps up the appearance of wooing, even if he doesn't mean it, she cannot keep up the pretence of being a lady.

The Cherry – Archer scenes are much the same, but the game here is so obvious, so nearly danced, that there is a tendency in production to dance it, to make it an entertainment in its own right with no reference to the event it delineates. Their second scene (II ii) is the most formal, since it is in the form of a skit to be played by Cherry for Archer, starting with his 'Come, my Dear, have you con'd over the Catechism I taught you last Night?', and ending with 'Hold, hold, Mr *Martin*'. The sequence of the scene is much like the Archer – Mrs Sullen scene in the picture gallery. Archer, here disguised as Martin, would lead Cherry to the bedchamber; and Cherry is even more ready than Mrs Sullen to go – that is the reason she has learned 'Love's Catechism', and repeats it as charmingly as possible – and I might add, with the same touch of refusal that the lines suggest. Cherry, as she admits later in the scene, wants to marry a gentleman; and she thinks Archer is one. As a consequence she is using the catechism as a come-on, but coyly. The lover must 'desire much, and hope little'; 'He must adore the Person that disdains him'; and so on. In other words, the wooing game must be played, and Cherry knows it. I think that in doing the scene Cherry simply cannot play the putting-off with the lines alone. Perhaps she enters with an armful of sheets which she might make Archer help her fold as she recites, and behind which she could duck to avoid, or peep over to receive, any kisses that the script says she must deal with. Somehow the whole recital is too naked a compliance with Archer's request, and makes her too easy a conquest. The making him work for her gives her back just enough of her own to keep the game from being too one-sided.

Farquhar's world, at least in so far as it includes the relation of the sexes, is a game-playing world, made up of healthy animals of sound body and quick mind who, when they drop their conviction that any relation between them must be casual, careful, friendly and uncommitted, become a little silly (the falling in love of Dorinda and Aimwell) or a little vicious (the marriage of Sullen and Mrs Sullen). There is no delight in the relation between Sullen and his wife, and I think it demonstrable that Aimwell and Dorinda, though occasionally charming, are also to be laughed at. Aimwell is, in fact, continually chastised by Archer for his tendency to ruin things by falling in love, and is finally rather seriously attacked by his companion when it looks as though all is lost. Aimwell's weakness is his heart, his sentimental nature. Dorinda's weakness is slightly different. She is innocent: an innocent who is waking up, to be sure, but in the course of this play only waking up to the joys of love, not to its dangers. In her scene with Mrs Sullen in which she tries to duel verbally (IVi: from Mrs Sullen's 'But I'll lay you a Guinea, that I had finer things said to me than you had'), she comes close to losing continually, finally being saved only by her insistence that 'my Fellow' asked for her hand:

MRS SULLEN . . . But I'll lay you a Guinea, that I had finer things said to me than you had.

DORINDA   Done—What did your Fellow say to ye?

MRS SULLEN   My Fellow took the Picture of *Venus* for Mine.

DORINDA   But my Lover took me for *Venus* her self.

MRS SULLEN   Common Cant! had my Spark call'd me a *Venus* directly, I shou'd have believed him a Footman in good earnest.

DORINDA   But my Lover was upon his Knees to me.

MRS SULLEN   And mine was upon his Tiptoes to me.

DORINDA   Mine vow'd to die for me.

MRS SULLEN   Mine swore to die with me.

DORINDA   Mine spoke the softest moving things.

MRS SULLEN   Mine had his moving things too.

DORINDA   Mine kiss'd my Hand Ten thousand times.

MRS SULLEN   Mine has all that Pleasure to come.

DORINDA   Mine offer'd Marriage.

MRS. SULLEN   O Lard! D'ye call that a moving thing?

DORINDA   The sharpest Arrow in his Quiver, my dear Sister, — Why, my Ten thousand Pounds may lie brooding here this seven Years, and hatch nothing at last but some ill natur'd Clown like yours:—Whereas, If I marry my Lord *Aimwell*, there will be Title, Place and Precedence, the Park, the Play, and the drawing-Room, Splendor, Equipage, Noise and Flambeaux— Hey, my Lady *Aimwell's* Servants there—Lights, Lights to the Stairs—My Lady *Aimwell's* Coach put forward-Stand by, make room for her Ladyship—Are not these things moving? . . .

She is not up to Mrs Sullen's *double entendre*. I suspect that she can understand; but it is not the kind of compliment that charms her, since what she sees in marriage is herself as Lady Aimwell with all its attendant social pleasures. One cannot say with any certainty that she will never lose those pleasures, but one can imagine Mrs Sullen having seen the same world before she got married. There is a certain illusionary quality in Dorinda's vision of being Lady Aimwell and her assurance that she will have 'Title, Place, and

Precedence', especially when one remembers that the man she is talking about marrying is the younger brother, not Lord Aimwell at all. The sense of that blindness is also carried out in the relation between Aimwell and Dorinda. Not only is this apparent in their gazing at each other in the picture gallery scene, but also in the near-marriage scene in Act V, scene iv. It is here that Farquhar most obviously tips his hand, I think, and makes it clear that his sympathies are not entirely with Aimwell and Dorinda:

DORINDA   Well, well, my Lord, you have conquer'd; your late generous Action will, I hope, plead for my easie yielding, tho' I must own your Lordship had a Friend in the Fort before.

AIMWELL   The Sweete of *Hybla* dwell upon her Tongue. – Here, Doctor –

Enter FOIGARD *with a Book*

FOIGARD   Are you prepar'd boat?

DORINDA   I'm ready: But, first, my Lord one Word; – I have a frightful Example of a hasty Marriage in my own Family; when I reflect upon't, it shocks me. Pray, my Lord, consider a little –

AIMWELL   Consider! Do you doubt my Honour or my Love?

DORINDA   Neither: I do believe you equally Just as Brave. – And were your whole Sex drawn out for me to chuse, I shou'd not cast a look upon the Multitude if you were absent. – But my Lord, I'm a Woman; Colours, Concealments may hide a thousand Faults in me; – Therefore know me better first; I hardly dare affirm I know my self in any thing except my Love.

AIMWELL   [*Aside.*] Such Goodness who cou'd injure; I find my self unequal to the Task of Villain; she has gain'd my Soul, and made it honest like her own; – I cannot, cannot hurt her. (*To* FOIGARD.) Doctor, retire.

Exit FOIGARD.

Madam, behold your Lover and your Proselite, and judge of my Passion by my Conversion. – I'm all a Lie, nor dare I give Fiction to your Arms; I'm all Counterfeit except my Passion.

DORINDA   Forbid it Heaven! a Counterfeit!

AIMWELL   I am no Lord, but a poor needy Man, come with a mean, a scandalous Design to prey upon your Fortune: – But the Beauties of your Mind and Person have so won me from my self, that like a trusty Servant, I prefer the Interest of my Mistress to my own.

DORINDA   Sure I have had the Dream of some poor Mariner, a sleepy image of a welcome Port, and wake involv'd in Storms. – Pray, Sir, who are you?

AIMWELL   Brother to the Man whose Title I usurp'd, but Stranger to his Honour or his Fortune.

DORINDA   Matchless Honesty – Once I was proud, Sir, of your Wealth and Title, but now am prouder that you want it: Now I can shew my Love was justly levell'd, and had no Aim but Love. Doctor, come in.

Enter FOIGARD *at one* Door, GIPSEY *at another, who whispers* DORINDA.
Your Pardon, Sir, we shall not want you now, Sir you must excuse me, – I'll wait on you presently.

Exit with GIPSEY.

FOIGARD   Upon my Shoul, now, dis is foolish.

The most obvious thing in the scene, demonstrated most particularly in the way Foigard is handled, is that Farquhar is consciously laughing at the marriage. The continual interruptions to dismiss or recall the comic priest; his necessary comic confusions and suspicions as he wonders whether he is to marry the couple or not; and finally, a little later, Archer's command to him to 'Make hast, make hast, couple 'em any way' cannot help but suggest a lack of seriousness in the coupling. There is something silly about marriage based on such flimsy foundations as the clichéd kind of true love that we see here. One is persuaded not only by the farcical coming and going of the priest, but by such a line as Dorinda's 'Sure I have had the Dream of some poor Mariner, a sleepy image of a welcome Port, and wak'd involv'd in Storms. – Pray, Sir, who are you?'. No matter how seriously this is delivered, one is struck with the self-consciousness of the metaphor, which must take one a little away from a completely personal and heartfelt response on Dorinda's part. There is something precious here that is a comment on the situation. The language qualifies the emotion as surely as, in Moliere, Alceste's rhymed couplets qualify his anger. Such evidence by itself might simply be proof of bad writing, but – given the use of Foigard throughout the play, the comic Irishman with a brogue trying to be a Frenchman; Farquhar's general distrust of marriage throughout the play; and the *deus ex machina* arrival of Charles Freeman with his announcement of Aimwell's sudden inheritance of his brother's title – I think a pretty good case can be made to suggest Farquhar's awareness of the limitations of the kind of foundation upon which Dorinda and Aimwell are basing their happiness. Here is Sir Charles Freeman arriving with the news:

> SIR CHARLES   My dear Lord *Aimwell*, I wish you Joy.
> AIMWELL   Of what?
> SIR CHARLES   Of your Honour and Estate: Your Brother died the Day before I left *London*; and all your Friends have writ after you to *Brussels*; among the rest I did my self the Honour.
> ARCHER   Hark'ye, Sir Knight, don't you banter now?
> SIR CHARLES   Tis Truth upon my Honour.
> AIMWELL   Thanks to the pregnant Stars that form'd this Accident.
> ARCHER   Thanks to the Womb of Time that brought it forth; away with it.
> AIMWELL   Thanks to my Guardian Angel that led me to the Prize –
> > *Taking* DORINDA'S *Hand.*
> ARCHER   And double Thanks to the noble Sir *Charles Freeman.* My Lord, I wish you Joy. My Lady I wish you Joy. – I Gad, Sir *Freeman*, you're the honestest Fellow living. – S'death, I'm grown strange airy upon this matter –. . .   (IV iv)

The grammatical parallelism of their responses suggests a playful dance that winds up a theatrical entertainment, rather than a believable or convincing solution to the problem presented. Such accidents as Lord Aimwell's death are hardly worth assuming in making a marriage arrangement, and I don't think Farquhar is any more convinced than I am that true love has done any more than to help end the play. Farquhar is as aware of the contrivance as Shakespeare is in *Twelfth Night*, and uses it to much the same purpose. The accidents that end *Twelfth Night* suggest not the accident of successful marriage, which the play does not deal with, but the accident of falling in love. So here, the accident of

sudden wealth in no way saves what was previously unhealthy
without it. Until Dorinda and Aimwell get down to earth, one
cannot evaluate their future. Their present is in a pink haze, to
which money is a joyful addition. There is no suggestion that it is
a salvation.

I think the play is not only very well put together, but makes a
very real comment on the difficulty, if not the impossibility, of
committing oneself to one love, to one person. Such commitment
denies change, which would seem a necessary part of man's
interest in the other sex. It is feasible, it would seem, if one could
remain in that pink haze that so surrounds Aimwell and Dorinda,
but I do not think Farquahr has any great trust in the
continuance of such a state for very long. Certainly he chuckles at
it while it is going on. Throughout the play, however, the most
compelling interest in scene after scene is the ebullient and
effervescent life that comes from these young lovers: an ebul-
lience that seems to thrive on novelty, on a new conquest, on a
new man or a new woman. And what seems to feed this life is
man's refusal to commit himself to one view of the world, his need
to look continually elsewhere. Farquhar, of course, limits this
observation to the relation of the sexes and it would be foolish to
stretch it beyond that relation; but there is something particularly true about all of youth's interests that certainly is not
contradicted by what is said here. Perhaps age puts some blinkers
on, or perhaps it simply gets too tired to look. Certainly Lady
Bountiful is laughed at, though gently, for her one-track-minded
views of health and the cures that maintain it. Youth would never
be sure of itself. Even Boniface, Cherry's father, is a little too set in
his ways in his insistence that Aimwell is a highwayman. Cherry
tosses the observation off as a possibility, but that does not stop
her from observing his servant and coming to the rather different
conclusion that he is not the servant of a highwayman but of a
gentleman. If one lives with the continual admission that no
experience is final, and that new experience is an essential part of
life, marriage clearly is a rather impossible estate. If, on the other
hand, fettering such energies is the price of marriage, it would
seem to take away from the principals all of the charm, the life,
the interest one has in them. I think of Sullen and Mrs Sullen in
marriage's bonds. The play abounds in games we all play, and

the fun we have in playing them. It even goes the rather modern step further to suggest that it is very dangerous to commit oneself any further than to the playing of games. Permanent commitment is boring and stultifying. While one can recognize the dangers of espousing such a position, it seems to me that Farquhar is persuasive about the difficulties of committing oneself to more permanent attachments, however morally satisfying this may be. In this, *The Beaux' Stratagem* seems to me a very modern piece about our own youthful enthusiasms and the difficulties of finding a humanly defensible reason for giving them up. The 'games people play' is almost a modern aphorism. One of the delights of this comedy is the freshness with which it illustrates it.

SOURCE: extracts from essay in *Drama Survey*, VII (1968 – 9) 69 – 86.

NOTE

1. By 'game' here I mean that the characters say one thing but intend something more (or, occasionally, less) than what they say. For the game to work, both participants (it is usually a duo) must recognize that more than what is said is meant. The most obvious kind of fool in these plays is he or she who takes the words at their face value, not recognizing any meaning other than the surface meaning of the words.

William Gaskill

FINDING A STYLE FOR FARQUHAR
(1971)

Extracts from an interview with Mr Gaskill, who, as an Associate Director of the National Theatre, was responsible for its production of *The Recruiting Officer* in 1963 and of *The Beaux' Stratagem* in 1970.

Was 'The Recruiting Officer' your own choice of play or a communal selection?
Well, we arrived at a rough allocation of what we would do in the first season, and this included one Shaw, one Ibsen, one Chekhov, and one Restoration comedy. The Restoration comedy was left to me to choose. All the plays were to some extent dependent upon casting, but *The Recruiting Officer* was my first choice.

Why Farquhar rather than one of his earlier contemporaries?
I think he seems a very grown-up person. I don't feel that he's a bit sniggery, which I do about Congreve sometimes – that for all the brilliance, there's something a bit mean-spirited about him. And there's a kind of pornographic element in Dryden, I think – not real bawdy, but to do with that peculiar semi-poetic sort of metaphor, like using 'dying' for 'coming'. And always talking about Corydon.

Yet isn't there something more physical about the sensuality of Farquhar, just because it is less persistently on this level of verbal titillation?
Yes: one's total impression of Farquhar is of someone who is mature. I do think every director has a relationship with the personality of the playwright, even when he's been dead hundreds of years, and I certainly do have this strong affinity for Farquhar.

Why did you decide to do 'The Recruiting Officer' rather than 'The Beaux' Stratagem' in the first instance?

Well, I'd seen *The Beaux' Stratagem* in the production in 1949 at the Phoenix, with Kay Hammond as Mrs Sullen and John Clements as Archer. And this is also a favourite choice of amateur groups – it's a very easy play to perform *reasonably* successfully, and *The Recruiting Officer* was the less familiar play; it hadn't been done in London since Trevor Howard played Plume at the Arts in 1943. And I suppose it was also prompted by seeing Brecht's adaptation, *Trumpets and Drums*, in the Berliner Ensemble season at the Palace in 1956.

Would you say that the London performance of Brecht's play influenced your own approach to 'The Recruiting Officer'?
Not particularly. I thought *Trumpets and Drums* was very charming, but it was a bit camp – that swan that wiggled around a lot, for instance.

Yet there obviously was a new orientation to your production, in the sense that you did strip away the stylistic accretions that had grown up around the play – style for its own sake, as it were.
I think I wanted to do a Restoration comedy that was *about* something, and certainly in the recruiting episodes themselves the play offers a kind of socially-critical documentation which goes far beyond that of any other Restoration comedy. And, of course, Farquhar does deal with the problems of working-class people in a way that no other Restoration writer attempted. I think this is close to the core of the play.

Did you want to give it contemporary relevance?
I think it *is* relevant, but I didn't want to *make* it relevant. At one time I considered setting it in the First World War, but before that came to anything Joan Littlewood had done *Oh What a Lovely War*. You have to remember the kind of feeling (which has now disappeared almost completely in the theatre), that almost romantic social awareness of the early sixties. For me, it had some relationship to Unity Theatre, which was where I first saw *The Recruiting Officer*, as well as to Joan Littlewood's work. . . .

. . . Just before the National Theatre opened, I remember Kenneth

Tynan saying that one of the main tasks ought to be to rediscover a classical comic style – a style of playing in which the clothes didn't all look as though they were being worn for the first time. And one does think back on NT Restoration productions as more tatty-wigged and scruffy-trousered than the usual immaculately dressed Restoration sort.

You remember that Brecht was a big influence, and we hadn't ever really seen that sort of thing. The idea of what is called 'breaking down' of costumes to make them look worn and used became very commonly accepted. At the time I did *The Recruiting Officer* the thought of having mud on Plume's clothes was considered really revolutionary. I'm not sure now that it doesn't look a little phoney – it's something to do with defining the theatricality of those plays that is very important. But that's all post-Brecht; and René Allio, besides, is essentially a Brecht-influenced designer. . . .

What were you both looking for in the designs for 'The Recruiting Officer'?

Oh, I just took Allio to Amersham, which was the nearest Queen Anne main street that I knew, and said, That's what I think an eighteenth-century main street would look like. And he drew Amersham and put the main street on the stage.

It was important to get it right historically?

Well, Queen Anne was a period of building. There are whole towns which are predominantly of that period, so that it is a very clear image. Also, being French he'd never seen an English town of that period; he'd never seen that kind of brickwork. I said: There are three basic scenes in the play; how are we going to put the main street of Amersham on the stage? And he devised these very simple *periaktoi*, which gave us houses which would turn. This pleased me very much, because I wanted the street to be three-dimensional, and yet I wanted to be able to move quickly from scene to scene. The opening sequence – starting in that rather bleak courtroom set and then moving to the town – was entirely his idea.

So this was already beginning to define the style of the production. What other factors influenced the style – practical ones, or your own preconceptions – before rehearsal actually began?

Well, the choice of designer is one of the two main factors. The other, of course, is in the casting. What is called the style of the production will usually be the product of those two decisions, which once made are very difficult to go back on. . . .

. . . Did you set out to create a particular kind of style?
Not really. I don't know any directors in this country who work out the style of a production in advance.

And yet 'The Recruiting Officer', in particular, did achieve a quite distinctive style of its own. There was a certain roughening of the edges, a coarsening of the grain, as opposed to the usual 'mannered' approach: and yet at the same time there was a greater verbal clarity about the production than is customary in Restoration comedy. Wasn't this the intention from the outset?
Yes, but you see the process from the outside. You think that a director comes along and wishes to change something, that he has a kind of purpose and says, that's wrong, and what I will do instead is this. It's not usually like that. What I myself try to do is to get to the centre of a play – that always means working directly at the text and getting the maximum from it. I don't just mean in the speaking of it well, but in establishing character and situation and the clarity of what the line *means* before anything else. Now the intention of many directors isn't that, whatever they may say: they go after *style*. I think they have an idea of what style is, that you *do* certain things, behave in certain ways. But what you should actually work at in Restoration comedy is to make people say it as if it was them speaking, which is not easy. You've got to tell them, this is *you* saying it: it isn't Millamant, it's you. Now say the line as if you said it. It's not an easy thing to do, and it requires a lot of concentration on the part of the actors. . . .

At the same time as you're plotting loosely, are you beginning to give the actors some sense of the period – of its social relationships particularly?
I don't think anyone cares a——about whether they bow in the right manner or any of those 'quaint' period things. But there are two problems to solve. One is class attitudes, which have changed, and which actors often find difficult to identify: they use over-simplifications of working-class attitudes – and of attitudes towards the working class. For example, take the way the

servants are treated: they are always 'fellow', whereas one's equal
would be a 'gentleman'. Actors *always* get that wrong, saying
'fellow' in the modern colloquial sense, to describe an equal
rather than an inferior. The other problem is that there are
certain things which women do now which they couldn't do
then – though curiously enough this wasn't such a difficulty in
The Recruiting Officer because Silvia is such an outspoken and free
person. But even in that play there are certain things which are
just horrific to us now, like when Balance hears that his son has
died and says, 'I was pleased with the death of my father, because
he left me an estate, and now I'm punished with the loss of an heir
to inherit mine.' In all the writings of that period until the family
became a cult, there were no sentimental relationships between
sons and fathers. All that a father meant to a son was that he
inherited his property, and the sooner he died the better. This is a
very difficult attitude for actors to understand. I think it's
something Brecht said, that when money is the object it cannot be
the subject. When the object of people is to make money, they're
not going to write about making money: they'll write romantic
fantasies, which is how they make their money. So the idea of the
happy family around the Christmas fire is really post-Dickens,
and then you get a kind of dishonesty in art. I don't think there is
that kind of dishonesty in the Restoration.

*One always feels that there is a similar directness and honesty about the
treatment of sexual relationships in Farquhar, though this is not something
you find in his earlier contemporaries.*
Yes: so that the writing is not, in fact, particularly sensual, but
the characters *are* meant to be. It's a very difficult balance to get
nowadays because actors imagine that the sensuality should
somehow be expressed by what you say, whereas obviously
people in those days were extremely physically aware of each
other, so that in the plays the writing is often a kind of defence
between the individual and the open expression of this awareness.

*Is this fuller sensuality – as distinct from purely verbal
bawdiness – something that is lacking in the traditional Restoration style?*
I don't want to generalize, but there is a tendency among English
actresses not to be heavily sensual. That's not the quality they

most exhibit on stage, anyway: they exhibit quickness of wit, for instance, and a certain kind of amused aloofness, but they don't often convey deep sensuality. . . .

There must be moments during rehearsals when certain discoveries about character or situation change the direction of what's happening? Take the character of Sullen in 'The Beaux' Stratagem', who was presented, surely, as an unusually intelligent person, not the conventional clown.
Sullen is a difficult character: he does keep coming on and having a scene and going off again. He's very un-integrated into the action of the play, and his best scene is almost at the end, his long dialogue with Sir Charles. This has a lot of substance to it, but it's as if it's a set piece, there only to set up the divorce properly for the final scene.

You made him more an educated man, less a rustic buffoon, than usual, though.
There is no indication that he is a rustic. Anyway, one *knows* Sullen even today – this man who really prefers drinking with people of a different social class. But I don't think we really caught the image of him in the context of his *own* society, so that the audience could recognize him.

Gibbet, on the other hand, seemed slightly fantasticated, almost out of a different play?
I think you have to be careful about assuming that what is stylistic is not there in the part already. Gibbet *is* a very extravagant character. It's a marvellously written part: but the actor has to make clear that this is the character as written, not self-indulgence. This to some extent is true of Foigard as well: it's like an actor playing an actor on stage, the same problem.

Gipsey is another odd character: from all the tiny touches about her, it's almost as if she was meant at one time to be rather more important in the action.
Yes, the image of her, the things that are said *about* her make her marvellously vivid – dinging about the house like a fury, sitting in the closet devouring my lady's marmalade, and so on. It's a little gem of a part, but it needs an actress who can be type-cast into it.

You cut the sub-plot concerning Count Bellair: was this because it made the play too long, or because you feel it doesn't fit?
I think the reason it doesn't work is that it makes Mrs. Sullen look rather odd – after she's met Archer, then to have a scene with another lover in a sort of attempt to have a scene with her husband————

It does perhaps make Sullen that bit more integral . . .
It does. I thought about this a lot, but in the end decided it would weaken the relationship between Archer and Mrs. Sullen to keep it in.

Whilst you try to avoid the dangers of actors indulging in amateur psychoanalysis of their characters, in some way relationships between people – between one man and another, as well as between the sexes – do work themselves out. How?
A lot follows naturally from properly establishing the social relationships. It's sentimentalizing on our part, for instance, to suppose that the treatment of the working-class was wicked. It was unthinking, but not wicked: and that's much more difficult to catch, actually. It's much easier to give an actor a strong moral intention for good or bad. It's the thing one used to say about Brecht, you know, that one of the most difficult things to present in a theatre is what is habitual, what people do every day without thinking – the habits and social attitudes they've acquired by *custom*. There's no specific moment at which they have to be suddenly shown, they're just *there*, all the time. The upper-class characters mustn't just be rude to the servants in whispers, for example: they have to be told, you can say what you like about the servants aloud, in their presence, you're not worried if it hurts them. This crops up very often in the play: and you have to get it right, because you can't play a psychological relationship until the social relationship is right. Anyway, to me that's what a lot of plays are really about – just about how people live in a society together. Now the individual emotional relationships usually are so indicated by the flow of the action – simply by *what happens* – that you don't have to particularize very strongly. It's much less difficult to make it clear that two people have fallen in love than that they despise their servants without being wicked.

I can see that this could be clear enough in relationships that form in the course of the action. Yet between Archer and Aimwell, and even between Dorinda and Mrs. Sullen, there is an established modus vivendi *before the action has begun. How do you create the sense of their being confidantes — as a 'given' of the situation?*

That's one of the things you have to work towards, producing enough real sympathy between these actors. The danger is that they will play objectives which produce antagonisms: they feel, ah, we must play something strong. In fact there's nothing particularly strong to play. It's very common in rehearsal to find two actors who should be just talking easily, playing against one another. You say, no, really you rather like each other, which is a much more difficult emotion to realize. . . .

Part of the social complexity, I suppose, is that there are also middle and merchant class characters — tradesmen, like Boniface, the Landlord in ' The Beaux' Stratagem'.

And his daughter Cherry, who is socially hard to place. I mean, they all remark on how extraordinary she is.

Do you regard this as a separable part of the play in rehearsal, a sub-plot perhaps?

No, I don't think of it like that. Cherry in the first part seems all set to be a very important character, doesn't she? It's disappointing that Farquhar didn't find a way of writing a good scene for her in the last part of the play, though: she almost disappears, as does her father. I think they're both marvellous creations.

It's perhaps better sustained, this sense of rich social complexity, in ' The Recruiting Officer'.

That's right. There are very few writers who have been so well able to keep a whole cross section of society moving all the way through a play.

Probably this is one reason why ' The Beaux' Stratagem' is the easier play to do in a conventional Restoration manner.

Yes, I think so, We had endless trouble, for example, in that courtroom scene in *The Recruiting Officer* where all the villagers are present: it's late in the play, a central scene, and you need really good actors, realistic actors, in the smallest parts. . . .

The Royal Shakespeare Company's recent production of 'The Relapse' perhaps illustrated the kind of 'deeply romantic' approach to Restoration comedy one could describe as the opposite of your own.

They all wore black and silver, and huge wigs up to here, didn't they? I thought it was appalling: like a nightmare. It was a new kind of fantastication of design and presentation – to do everything in that colour scheme of black and silver and pink and silver. I don't think they had any feeling that social context was important, and I don't think that they would ever say it was. I think they are interested in theoretical, abstract concepts of what a play is.

This could never be of any value in approaching Farquhar?

Nor any Restoration comedy. All of them are plays about people at a certain time in society, about people's social behaviour. You can say Shakespeare's mythical if you like, but you can't say Farquhar has any mythical or allegorical elements. Not for one second.

Is this a positive defect, or just a limitation on the range of work they should attempt?

Well, I think it is a defect. I think when you stop remembering how people live and how they behave it's always a danger sign. You need to be pulled back.

You don't attempt to create any sort of abstract quality in your own productions? Not even, say, in occasionally placing actors to make pretty stage pictures?

Sometimes. It's really more like a painter trying to isolate a single moment through the relationship of one person with another.

Do you place actors so as to emphasize power relationships, the dominance of one person over another?

Yes, but in a realistic not a symbolic way, inasmuch as these things are expressed in life. Then the symbolism is inherent, it doesn't need to be stressed. I had great pleasure directing the recruiting scene in *The Recruiting Officer*. It was very difficult, but finally I thought it was one of the best scenes I've ever directed. I felt absolutely satisfied with the relationships of those four people – Plume, Kite, Pearmain, Appletree – on stage.

And you obviously relished directing that slightly set-piece scene at the beginning of 'The Beaux' Stratagem' – the arrival of the stage-coach.
Yes. We spent really too much time on that. To get it even half-way right was a nightmare. And to *keep* it right . . . ! The group scenes are of course always the most difficult to keep up to scratch.

Did you find you could keep a closer eye on the progress of 'The Recruiting Officer' in the repertory, as an associate director, then, of the National Theatre?
Well, yes, but also we had better assistant directors: we had people who were *only* assistants, not in the production as well. When you have assistants whose job is to monitor the production, it is easier to maintain standards. I think they've rather slipped on this at the National. We used to have a body of people actually watching the shows every night, and the assistants would also go back and give notes which I don't think they do now.

Do you think that the National Theatre has lost its sense of direction since the earlier days?
I think the invitation to Jacques Charon was the beginning of the end. The moment you pay homage to that kind of theatre, you are wide open to influences that are wrong for a British National Theatre. I think it is without an absolutely clear sense of purpose at the moment – not that a National Theatre should ever be too exclusive, but neither need it be too catholic. I've never felt that a National Theatre needed or ought to be an International Theatre.

SOURCE: extracts from 'Finding a style for Farquhar' (editorial interview), *Theatre Quarterly*, 11 (1971) 15–20.

SELECT BIBLIOGRAPHY

EDITIONS

Good introductions and texts are found in the following:
Michael Shugrue, *The Recruiting Officer* (Lincoln, Nebraska: Regents Restoration Drama Series, 1965).
A. Norman Jeffares, *The Beaux Stratagem* (Edinburgh: Fountainwell Drama Texts, 1972) and *The Recruiting Officer* (1973).
Kenneth Tynan, *The Recruiting Officer* (London, 1965) has the text of the National Theatre production with commentary and reviews.
Charles Stonehill, *The Complete Works of George Farquhar* (London, 1930; New York, 1967) is the standard edition.

BOOKS AND ARTICLES

Willard Connely, *Young George Farquhar* (London, 1949).
Garland J. Gravitt, 'A Primer of Pleasure: Neo-Epicureanism in Farquhar: *The Beaux' Stratagem*', *Toth*, XII (1972) 38 – 49.
George L. Hersey, 'The Staging', in Hopper and Lahey (eds) *The Beaux' Stratagem* (New York, 1963) pp. 45 – 60.
Eugene Nelson James, *The Development of George Farquhar as a Comic Dramatist* (Mouton, 1972).
Robert John Jordan, 'George Farquhar's Military Career', *The Huntington Library Quarterly*, XXXVII (1974) 251 – 64.
Peter Kavanagh, *The Irish Theatre* (Tralee, 1946)
Louis Kronenberger, *The Thread of Laughter* (New York, 1952).
Martin A. Larson, 'The Influence of Milton's Divorce Tracts on Farquhar's *Beaux' Stratagem*', *P.M.L.A.*, XXXIX (1924) 174 – 8.
Barry N. Olshen, '*The Beaux' Stratagem* on the Nineteenth-Century London Stage', *Theatre Notebook*, XXVIII (1974) 70 – 80.
Fitzroy Pyle, 'George Farquhar (1677 – 1707)', *Hermathena*, XCII (1958) 3 – 30.
Sybil Rosenfeld, 'Notes on *The Recruiting Officer*', *Theatre Notebook*, XVIII (1963 – 4) 47 – 8.

NOTES ON CONTRIBUTORS

WILLIAM ARCHER (1856 – 1924). Critic, editor, translator, and journalist, he published the first English translation of Ibsen's works.

RONALD BERMAN, Professor of English at the University of California, San Diego, is now Chairman of Humanities for the National Endowment for the Humanities. Among his works are *Henry King and the Seventeenth Century*, *America in the Sixties*, and *A Reader's Guide to Shakespeare*.

BONAMY DOBRÉE (1891 – 1974) was Professor of English at the University of Leeds. A general editor of the *Oxford History of English Literature*, he published in the series *The Early Eighteenth Century*. His many other works include *Modern Prose Style* and *Restoration Tragedy*.

ALBERT JOHN FARMER was Professor of English at the Sorbonne. Among his publications, in addition to many essays, is *Pater as a Critic of English Literature*.

WILLIAM GASKILL is a freelance director. He has been associated with the theatre as Artistic Director of the Royal Court Theatre, Associate Director at the National Theatre, and advisory editor for *Theatre Quarterly*.

VINCENT FOSTER HOPPER is Professor Emeritus at New York University. His works include, beside a number of editions, *Medieval Number Symbolism* and *Backgrounds of European Literature*.

GERALD B. LAHEY, Professor Emeritus at New York University, has written many critical introductions to plays.

KENNETH MUIR, formerly King Alfred Professor of English Literature and now Professor Emeritus at the University of Liverpool, is the editor of *Shakespeare Survey*. He has published numerous books and editions, particularly in the areas of Shakespeare, the sixteenth and the seventeenth centuries.

JOHN LESLIE PALMER (1885 – 1944). A drama critic and later

Permanent Secretariat of the League of Nations, he wrote a number of books including studies of Shakespeare, Jonson, Molière and the contemporary theatre.

ALAN ROPER is Professor of English at the University of California, Los Angeles. He is the author of *Arnold's Poetic Landscapes*, *Dryden's Poetic Kingdoms*, and various essays.

ERIC ROTHSTEIN is Professor of English at the University of Wisconsin. Co-editor of *Literary Monographs* and an editor of *The Augustan Milieu*, he has also published *Restoration Tragedy*.

WILLIAM L. SHARP is Professor and Chairman of Dramatic Arts at Emerson College. He is the author of *Language in Drama* and essays on drama.

LOUIS A. STRAUSS (1872 – 1938) was Professor of English at the University of Michigan.

ALBERT WERTHEIM is Associate Professor of English at Indiana University. His essays include studies of Restoration and eighteenth-century drama.

INDEX